ASSEMBLY LANGUAGE SUBROUTINES FOR MS-DOS® COMPUTERS

ASSEMBLY LANGUAGE
LANGUAGE
SUBROUTINES FOR
MS-DOS®
COMPUTERS

LEO J. SCANLON

TAB BOOKS Inc.

Blue Ridge Summit, PA 17214

FIRST EDITION
FIRST PRINTING

Copyright © 1986 by Leo J. Scanlon
Printed in the United States of America

Library of Congress Cataloging in Publication Data

Scanlon, Leo J.
Assembly language subroutines for MS-DOS computers.

Includes index.
1. Assembler language (Computer program language)
2. Subroutines (Computer programs)   3. MS-DOS
(Computer operating system) I. Title.
QA76.73.A8S284   1986   005.26   86-14491
ISBN 0-8306-0867-2
ISBN 0-8306-2767-7 (pbk.)

Contents

Read the Interrupt Vector (GETINTV) 312
Change the Interrupt Vector (SETINTV) 313
Check for a Math Coprocessor (MATHCHIP) 315

Preface

When writing an assembly language program, I often need a short sequence that does some common task, such as display a message or read a keyboard character. In the past, I had to dig into the IBM or Microsoft *Programmer's Reference* manual and find the DOS function call for that task, and then insert its numeric code into my program and continue. After a while, I knew some codes by heart, but I'd still find myself searching the *Programmer's Reference* to look up ones I didn't know.

Finally, after a day particularly filled with page-flipping, I decided to spend a few hours creating subroutines that do the jobs I use most often. With them, I could simply call a file from my main program and continue programming: no more trying to remember function call codes ("Let's see, is the character display call code 2 or 3?"); no more thumbing through the *Programmer's Reference*—not to mention trying to *find* the *Programmer's Reference* in the first place!

I started with five or six subroutines, and added more as time went by. I also developed a few non-function-call subroutines to do things such as convert numbers from binary to decimal or move a block in memory. Thus, eventually I had a library of subroutines to draw from.

One day I told a programmer friend about the subroutines and he asked for copies of them. He called a couple of weeks later to say that he found subroutines useful and suggested a few more. That gave me an idea: Why not add some more subroutines that people need often and publish them in a book? You are reading the result of that idea.

While you might not find a subroutine for everything you want to do, I believe the most useful ones are included. If you can suggest others or find an easier way to perform some of these tasks, I would appreciate hearing from you; please write to me in care of TAB BOOKS Inc. I'd also like to learn of any errors in the subroutines (or anywhere else in the book, for that matter); they've been thoroughly tested, but Murphy's Law is ever present. Finally, I assembled the subroutines using the IBM and Microsoft Macro Assemblers; if you have successfully assembled them using a different assembler, I'd appreciate knowing about it.

Introduction

This book contains source listings for over 100 assembly language subroutines that you can assemble with either the IBM or Microsoft Macro Assembler. Six of the subroutines are IBM PC-specific, but the rest will run on any MS-DOS or PC-DOS computer, regardless of whether it has an 8086, 8088, 80186, or 80286 microprocessor.

The book can, then, serve as a "cookbook" or "toolbox" from which programmers can draw subroutines as needed. It should save time for experienced programmers by freeing them from creating the subroutines from scratch. It should prove equally useful to beginners and occasional programmers because it not only gives them pretested and (hopefully) error-free code, but also illustrates a correct way to prepare programs.

This is not simply a cookbook, however; it is also a minitutorial on assembly language programming. Note the term *minitutorial*. I have not provided an all-you-need-to-know book about assembly language programming because there are many good ones already on the market. What I *have* done, though, is summarize the most important details about the microprocessors, the Macro Assembler, and the assembly language instruction set.

By providing tutorial material, I have attempted to put all the essential details in one place. This should save you from flipping between this book and whatever tutorial or manual you're using. It should also help fill any gaps in your main reference.

THE INTENDED AUDIENCE

The book assumes you have done some assembly language programming on an

MS-DOS computer. It also assumes you have read at least one tutorial on the subject (and generally understand it) or have read the manual that comes with your assembler.

WHAT YOU NEED WITH THIS BOOK

To use the subroutines in this book, you need a computer with MS-DOS (or PC-DOS) 2.0 or later. You also need an assembler. I have tested the subroutines with both the IBM and Microsoft Macro Assembler. They may work on other assemblers as well, but you may have to make some changes if your assembler's directives are different from IBM's and Microsoft's.

WHAT THIS BOOK CONTAINS

This book has 21 chapters. Chapter 1 describes the four different microprocessors that are used in current MS-DOS computers (the Intel 8086, 8088, 80186, and 80286), and discusses their internal registers and addressing modes.

Chapter 2 covers the Macro Assembler's commands (directives) and discusses the steps needed to develop assembly language programs. This includes everything from entering the program into the computer through producing the final, executable *run module*.

Chapter 3 describes the entire microprocessor instruction set in functional groups. By grouping the instructions by function, you not only get to understand what the instructions do, but you also appreciate how they fit together.

Chapter 4 presents two program models that you can use as starting points for creating programs of your own. These contain the *boilerplate* that the assembler requires each program to have.

Chapters 5 through 21 present the subroutines, grouped by function. Besides providing the source code listing for each subroutine, I describe how it operates and specify its entry values and results, and the command needed to link it to the calling program and any other subroutines it calls. In many cases, I also provide an example of the subroutine's use.

Chapter 5 provides subroutines that perform memory operations. These include filling a block with a value, moving and comparing blocks, searching for a specific value, and taking the average of consecutive locations.

Chapters 6, 7, and 8 include subroutines that extend the microprocessor instructions to perform multiprecision operations. These include 32-bit binary arithmetic, 16-bit decimal arithmetic, and 32-bit shifts and rotates.

Chapter 9 offers a variety of code conversion subroutines. Chapter 10 deals with string manipulation. It includes subroutines that insert one string in another or append a string to another, and subroutines that find, delete, copy, or move a substring. In essence, this chapter provides word processor-like functions.

The next three chapters deal with lists. Chapter 11 provides subroutines that manipulate unordered lists; Chapter 12 includes sorting subroutines; and Chapter 13's subroutines manipulate ordered (i.e., sorted) lists.

For the most part, the subroutines in the remaining chapters use the resources of DOS, rather than those of the microprocessor, to perform their tasks. The subroutines in Chapter 14 provide general-purpose input and output operations, such as reading and displaying characters and strings.

Chapter 15 covers time and date operations, while Chapter 16 includes subroutines that access the ROM in the IBM PC to perform some useful tasks (e.g., moving the cursor and clearing the screen) that DOS doesn't provide.

The subroutines in Chapters 17, 18, and 19 perform DOS-like operations on disk drives, subdirectories, and disk files. Chapter 19 also includes subroutines that let you hide and unhide files, and write-protect and unprotect them.

Chapter 20's subroutines let you work with the internals of disk files, to create them, open and close them, read data from them, and write data to them.

The final chapter, 21, contains four subroutines that don't fit in any other category. The first reports which version of DOS you are using, the second and third let you read or change the contents of an interrupt vector, and the last reports whether the computer has an 8087 or 80287 math coprocessor chip.

At the end of the book are three appendices. Appendix A has tables that help convert hexadecimal numbers to decimal, or vice versa. Appendix B summarizes the ASCII character set—the characters you can read from the keyboard and display on the screen. Appendix C summarizes the microprocessor instruction set in alphabetical order. It lists the allowable assembler formats for each instruction and shows which status flag it affects.

SUPPLEMENTARY MATERIAL

When you start DOS, it loads several interrupt routines into memory. For programmers, the most important DOS interrupt is 21H, which provides a large number of options, or *function calls*, and I have incorporated the most useful function calls in subroutines. For full details on DOS in general and the function calls in particular, get a copy of IBM's *DOS Technical Reference* manual or Microsoft's *MS-DOS Programmer's Reference* manual. These books are similar, probably because Microsoft Corp. prepared both of them.

For details on your computer's microprocessor and its instruction set, get a copy of the *iAPX 86/88, 186/188 User's Manual — Programmer's Reference* or the *iAPX 286 Programmer's Reference Manual*. These books are available from Intel Literature Distribution, SC6-714; 3065 Bowers Ave.; Santa Clara, CA 95051.

Chapter 1

Overview of
the Microprocessors

This book contains programs that will run on any MS-DOS computer, regardless of whether it has an Intel 8086, 8088, 80186, or 80286 microprocessor. Since assembly language programming requires a working knowledge of the microprocessor, it is worthwhile starting with an overview of all four models and pointing out their differences.

THE MICROPROCESSORS FROM A PROGRAMMER'S VIEWPOINT

The Intel Corporation manuals and most chip-specific books on the market describe the microprocessor architecture in detail. They discuss how it generates addresses, how it treats memory in terms of function-specific segments (code, data, extra, and stack), how interrupts operate, and so on. Since I assume that you own one of these books (and have *read* it and more or less *understand* it), I have chosen to omit most of the technical details. Instead, I simply summarize the microprocessors from a programmer's viewpoint. That is, I briefly discuss the details programmers, rather than hardware designers, need to know.

Programmers can view the 8086 and 8088 as being the same. They have the same instruction sets, the same internal registers, the same status flags, and so forth. Both can address up to *one megabyte* (1024K bytes) of memory. The main difference between them is that the 8086 has a 16-bit data bus, while the 8088 has an 8-bit data bus. Of course, that's really a hardware feature, but it means that if the two chips are running at the same speed, the 8086 transfers 16-bit words twice as fast as the 8088 does.

The 80186 is essentially an 8086 with a few new instructions, and improved performance (Intel claims twice the performance). It also includes the circuitry of 15 other

1

chips, making it a "computer on a chip."

The 80286 marks a significant advance in that it can operate in two modes, called the *real address* mode and the *protected virtual address* mode (or *protected mode,* for short). In the real address mode, the 80286 operates like the 80186. In the protected mode, it provides some sophisticated features for data protection and memory management. The most significant aspect of the protected mode is that it allows the 80286 to access huge amounts of memory using a technique called *virtual addressing.*

With virtual addressing, the 80286 maintains two kinds of memory: a *physical address space* and a *virtual address space*. The physical address space is the memory that the 286 can work with directly, while the virtual address space is the amount that is available to it. The physical address space can be up to 16 megabytes long; the virtual address space can be up to one billion bytes, or one *gigabyte*, long. All of this is just for your information. Until software that provides virtual addressing is available, most programmers should ignore the protected mode.

INTERNAL REGISTERS

All four microprocessors provide the registers shown in Fig. 1-1. Note that the registers at the top of the figure are divided into three functional groups: data, pointer and index, and segment.

Data Registers

You may treat the data registers as either four 16-bit registers or eight 8-bit registers, depending on whether you are operating on 16-bit words or 8-bit bytes. The 16-bit registers are named AX, BX, CX, and DX. Within these "X" registers are 8-bit registers named AL, AH, BL, BH, CL, CH, DL, and DH.

AX, the *accumulator*, is used in word-size multiplication, division, and I/O operations, and in some string operations. Its low byte, AL, is used in the byte-size counterparts of these operations and in translate and decimal arithmetic operations. The AH register is also used in byte-size multiplications and divisions.

BX, the *base register*, is often used to address data in memory. CX, the *count register*, acts as the repetition counter for loop operations and as an element counter for string operations. The CL register holds the shift count for multiple-bit shift and rotate operations.

DX, the *data register*, is used in word-size multiplication and division operations. It can also provide the port number in I/O operations.

Pointer and Index Registers

SP, the *stack pointer*, keeps track of data and addresses on the microprocessor's stack in memory. Generally, you never refer to it directly in programs. The other registers, BP, SI, and DI, are used to address operands in memory. SI and DI are also used in string instructions as *source* and *destination* pointers, respectively.

Segment Registers

Segment registers are used in EXE-type programs. In this book, you work exclusively with COM-type programs, which have only one segment.

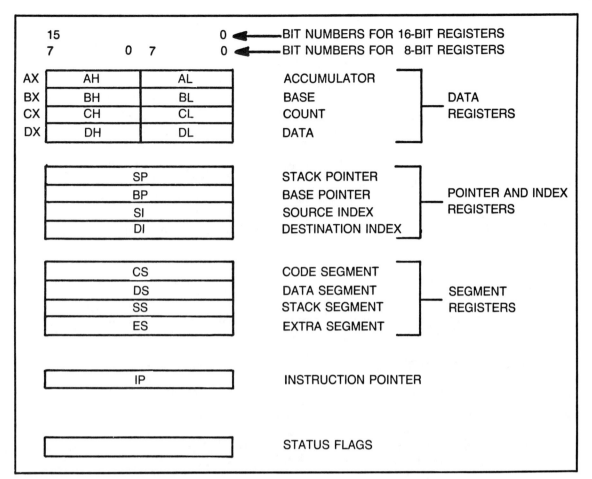

Fig. 1-1. Internal registers.

The Instruction Pointer

The instruction pointer is an internal register that points to the instruction the processor will execute next. You never refer to IP in a program.

Flags

The 16-bit *flags register* reports various status conditions that help your programs make decisions, as shown in Fig. 1-2. Six bits hold status flags, and three let you control the microprocessor from within a program. The 80286 flags register uses three additional bits, 12 through 14, when operating in its protected mode.

Here is a quick summary of the flags:

1. The *Carry Flag (CF)* is 1 if an addition produces a carry or a subtraction produces a borrow. CF also holds the value of a bit that has been shifted or rotated out of an operand, and acts as a result indicator for multiplications.

3

2. The *Parity Flag (PF)* is 1 if the result of an operation has an even number of 1 bits. It is used primarily in data communications.
3. The *Auxiliary Carry Flag (AF)* reflects a carry or borrow out of bit 3. AF is useful for operating on packed decimal numbers.
4. The *Zero Flag (ZF)* is 1 if the result of an operation is zero.
5. The *Sign Flag (SF)* is only meaningful during operations on signed numbers. It is 1 if the most-significant bit of a result is 1, which indicates a negative number.
6. The *Trap Flag (TF)* makes the processor "single-step" through a program, for debugging purposes.
7. The *Interrupt Enable Flag (IF)* is 1 if the processor is to recognize interrupt requests and 0 if it is to ignore them.
8. The *Direction Flag (DF)* determines the direction the processor proceeds through strings; 1 makes it go forward, 0 makes it go backward.
9. The *Overflow Flag (OF)* is primarily an error indicator during operations on signed numbers.

ADDRESSING MODES

All four processors provide the same addressing modes. There are seven of them, as follows:

1. *Register Operand Mode:* The operand is located in an 8- or 16-bit register. Example: INC BX.

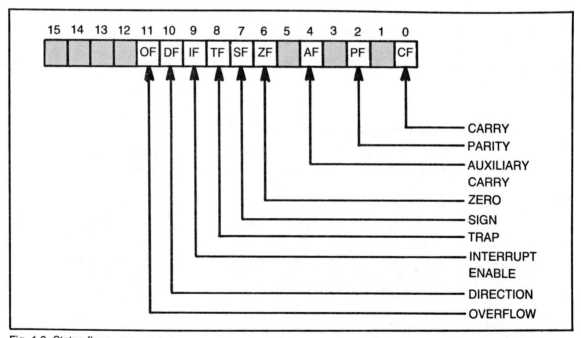

Fig. 1-2. Status flags.

4

2. *Immediate Operand Mode:* The operand is included in the instruction. Example: MOV CL,5.
3. *Direct Mode:* The operand's offset is included in the instruction as an 8- or 16-bit offset. Example: MOV BX,TABLE.
4. *Register Indirect Mode:* The operand's offset is in SI, DI, BX, or BP. The Macro Assembler requires you to enclose the register in brackets. Example: MOV [BX],AX.
5. *Base Relative Mode:* The operand's offset is the sum of an 8- or 16-bit displacement and the contents of BX or BP. Example: MOV AX,[BX]+4.
6. *Indexed Mode:* The operand's offset is the sum of an 8- or 16-bit displacement and the contents of SI or DI. Example: MOV AX,[SI]+4.
7. *Base Indexed Mode:* The operand's offset is the sum of the contents of a base register (BX or BP), an index register (SI or DI), and, optionally, an 8- or 16-bit displacement. Example: MOV AX,[BX][SI]+2.

Chapter 2

Using the Assembler

When programming in assembly language, you write instructions as English-like abbreviations and then run an *assembler* program to convert the abbreviations to their numeric equivalents. The program written using abbreviations is called the *source* program, and the numeric, microprocessor-compatible form of it is the *object* program. Thus, the assembler's job is to convert source programs into object programs.

ASSEMBLY LANGUAGE INSTRUCTIONS

Each assembly language instruction in a source program can have up to four fields, as follows:

> [*Label:*] *Mnemonic* [*Operand*] [; *Comment*]

Of these, only the mnemonic field is always required. The label and comment fields are always optional—that's what the brackets indicate. You may enter these fields anywhere on a line, but you must separate them with at least one space (or tab).

The Label Field

The label field assigns a name to an assembly language instruction. Labels in assembly language programs serve the same purpose as line numbers in BASIC programs.

An instruction label can be up to 31 characters long and must end with a colon (:). It may consist of the letters A through Z or *a* through *z*, (the assembler isn't particular), the digits 0 through 9, or these special characters: ? . @ _ $. You can begin a label with any character except a digit, but if you use a period, it must be the first character.

The Mnemonic Field

The mnemonic field contains the two- to seven-letter acronym for the instruction. The assembler uses an internal table to translate each mnemonic into its numeric equivalent.

The Operand Field

The operand field tells the processor where to find the data it is to operate on. Not all instructions require operands, but those that do take either 1 or 2 operands, separated from the mnemonic by at least 1 space or tab. If 2 operands are required, you must put a comma between them.

In two-operand instructions, the first operand is the *destination* and the second is the *source*. The source operand specifies the value that the microprocessor should add to, subtract from, compare to, or copy into the destination operand. For example, this Move instruction

```
MOV   CX,DX
```

tells the microprocessor to copy the word in the source operand DX into the destination operand CX.

The Comment Field

Like a REM in BASIC, this optional field lets you describe statements in a source program, to make the program easier to understand. You must precede a comment with a semicolon (;). You should also put at least one space or tab between a comment and the preceding field, although you don't have to.

ASSEMBLER DIRECTIVES

Directives (called *"pseudo-ops"* in IBM literature) are commands to the assembler, rather than to the microprocessor. They can be used to set up segments and procedures (i.e., subroutines), define symbols, reserve memory locations for temporary storage, and provide a variety of other important housekeeping tasks.

Assembler directives can have up to four fields:

[*Name*] *Directive* [*Operand*] [; *Comment*]

As the brackets indicate, only the directive field is always required.

The IBM and Microsoft Macro Assemblers provide about 60 directives. Table 2-1 lists the most commonly used directives, and divides them into two groups: data and mode.

Data Directives

The data directives can be divided into five functional groups, as shown in Table 2-2.

Table 2-1. Common Assembler Directives.

Type	Directives			
Data	ASSUME DB DW DD	END ENDP ENDS EQU	= (equal sign) EXTRN INCLUDE ORG	PROC PUBLIC SEGMENT
Mode	.186	.286C	.286P	.8086

Table 2-2. Data Directives.

Directive	Function
Symbol Definition **EQU**	*Format:* name EQU text or name EQU numeric-experssion Assigns *text* or value of *numeric-expression* to *name*, permanently.
=	*Format:* name = numeric-expression Assigns value of *numeric-expression* to *name*, but can be reassigned.
Data Definition **DB**	*Format:* [name] DB expression[,. . .] Defines a variable or initializes storage. DB allocates one or bytes.
DW	*Format:* [name] DW wzpewaaion{, . . .] Similar to DB, but allocates two-byte words.
DD	*Format:*[name] DD exprension[,. . .] Allocates four-byte double words.
External Reference **PUBLIC**	*Format:* PUBLIC symbol[, . . .] Makes the specified *symbol(s)* available for use by other object modules that will be linked to this module.
EXTRN	*Format:*EXTRN name:type[, . . .] Specifies symbols defined in another assembly module.
INCLUDE	*Format:* INCLUDE filespec Reads the contents of the specified source file into the current source file.
Segment/Procedure Specification **SEGMENT**	*Format:* seg-name SEGMENT [align-type] [conbine - type] ['class'] .. .. seg-name ENDS Defines the boundaries of a segment. Each SEGMENT definition must end with an ENDS statement.
ASSUME	*Format:* ASSUME seg-reg:seg-name[, . . .] Tells the assembler which segment register (CS, DS, ES, or SS) a segment belongs to.

Directive	Function
PROC	*Format:* name PROC [NEAR] or name PROC FAR .. .. name ENDP Assigns a *name* to a sequence of assembler statements. Every PROC definition must end with an ENDP statement.
Assembly Control **END**	*Format:* END [entry-point label] Marks the end of a source program.
ORG	*Format:* ORG expression Sets location counter to the value of *expression*. Assembler stores subsequent object code starting at that address.

The *symbol definition* directives assign a symbolic name to an expression. The expression may be a 16-bit constant, an address reference, another symbolic name, a segment identifier (prefix) and operand, or an instruction label. After assigning the name, you can use it anywhere you would normally use the expression.

The EQU (Equate) and = directives are similar, but you can redefine symbols defined with = , while symbols defined with EQU are permanent. Furthermore, = can only be used for numeric expressions, while EQU can be used for text expressions as well as numeric ones.

The *data definition* directives DB *(Define Byte)*, DW *(Define Word)*, and DD *(Define Doubleword)* allocate space for variables. When defining a variable, you can either give it a specific value or simply reserve the space and insert the value later. For example, MYVAR DB 1 sets the byte variable MYVAR to 1, whereas MYVAR DB ? simply reserves space for it.

The DB directive can also accept a text string as an expression. This lets you store menus, messages, prompts, and other text in memory, as in this example:

```
PROMPT   DB   'Press any key to continue.'
```

Note that text strings must be enclosed with single or double quotation marks.

The *segment/procedure specification* directives SEGMENT and END divide the source program into segments. A program may have up to four segments: data, code, extra, and stack. COM programs, which I am dealing with in this book, must have only a code segment. It is defined with statements of the form

```
CSEG   SEGMENT   PARA PUBLIC 'CODE'
. .               (Instructions)
. .
CSEG   ENDS
```

The words SEGMENT and ENDS simply mark the beginning and end of a segment; they don't tell the assembler which *kind* of segment you are defining. A separate directive, ASSUME, does that. In a COM program, you must make all four segment registers point to the code segment. To do this, you enter a statement of the form

```
ASSUME   CS:CSEG,DS:CSEG,ES:CSEG,SS:CSEG
```

The PROC and ENDP directives mark the beginning and end of a procedure, or subroutine. A procedure always has one of two distance attributes: NEAR or FAR. Procedures in COM programs must be NEAR, so you define them with a statement of the form

```
MYPROC   PROC
```

The missing operand makes the assembler assign NEAR.

The *external reference* directives allow you to share information between modules that you will eventually link to form a program. The PUBLIC directive makes one or more symbols available to other modules. It tells the linker, "Here is a list of items I have. If anyone needs one of them, you can tell them to get it from me." A PUBLIC directive can list variable names, labels (including PROC labels), and symbols defined by an EQU or = directive.

EXTRN tells the linker to obtain an item from another, unspecified, module. EXTRN has the general form

EXTRN *name*:*type*[, . . .]

where *name* is a symbol defined (and declared PUBLIC) in some other module and *type* can be any of the following:

- If *name* is a variable, then *type* can be BYTE, WORD, or DWORD.
- If *name* is a procedure label or subroutine label, the *type* can be NEAR or FAR (always NEAR in COM programs).
- If *name* is a constant defined by an EQU or = directive, then *type* must be ABS.

PUBLIC and EXTRN are generally used to share subroutines. For example, to run a subroutine called SORT from a main program, the module that contains SORT must include PUBLIC SORT and the main program must contain EXTRN SORT: NEAR.

The INCLUDE directive reads a specified source file into the current source file at assembly time. You can also use INCLUDE to read macros into a program.

The assembler recognizes several *assembly control* directives, but only END and ORG are frequently used. END marks the end of a program module. Therefore, you *must* include END in every source program. End's general form is

END [*entry-point label*]

where *entry-point label* identifies the place where DOS starts executing the program. For example,

```
END   MYPROG
```

marks the end of the program MYPROG.

If your program consists of several modules, you must label the END in the main module, but omit it from the ENDs in secondary modules. For example, if your main program calls subroutines that are in separate modules (as the ones in this book are), each subroutine module's END directive must be unlabeled.

The ORG (Origin) directive alters the location counter, to make the assembler store data or instructions some place other than where it would store them otherwise. ORG is used in COM programs, where you give the form

```
ORG   100H
```

to make the assembler store the program 256 bytes past the current location, thus reserving space for an information area called the *Program Segment Prefix* (PSP).

Mode Directives

The IBM Macro Assembler is designed to work with the Intel 8086, 8088, and 80286 microprocessors. The Microsoft Macro Assembler also supports the 80186. Each assembler assumes you have an 8086 or 8088, but you can enter a *mode* directive to tell it otherwise.

To assemble programs that have instructions unique to the 80186, you must enter a .186 directive at the beginning of the program, immediately after your listing directives (if any). Similarly, to make the assembler accept 80286 unprotected instructions, enter .286c; to make it accept 80286 protected instructions, enter .286p. Finally, to disable assembly of 80186 and 80286 instructions, enter .8086.

Other Directives

Most people will need only the directives I have just described. There are, however, quite a few others, and you may need one or more of them from time to time. Table 2-3 lists these ''advanced'' directives and groups them by function. See your Macro Assembler manual for details.

Table 2-3. Advanced Assembler Directives.

Type	Directives			
Data	COMMENT	EVEN	GROUP	LABEL

Conditional	ELSE
	ENDIF
	IF
		IFDEF
		IFNDEF
		IFDIF
			IFE
			IFIDN
			IF1
				IF2

Listing	.CREF .LFCOND .LIST	%OUT .SFCOND .XREF	.XLIST PAGE SUBTTL	TITLE

OPERATORS

An operator is a modifier used in the operand field of an assembly language instruction. The most commonly used operators fall into three categories: arithmetic, value-returning, and attribute. Table 2-4 summarizes them.

Table 2-4. Common Operators.

Operator	Function
Arithmetic	
+	*Format:* value1 + value2
	Adds *value1* and *value2*.
−	*Format:* value1 − value 2
	Subtracts *value2* from *value1*.
*	*Format:* value1 * value2
	Multiplies *value* by *value1*.
/	*Format:* value 1 / value 2
	Divides *value1* by *value2*, and returns the quotient.
MOD	*Format:* value1 MOD value2
	Divides *value1* by *value2*, and returns the remainder.
Value-Returning	
$	*Format:* $
	Returns the current value of the location counter.
SEG	*Format:* SEG variable
	or
	SEG label
	Returns the segment value of *variable* or *label*.
OFFSET	*Format:* OFFSET variable
	or
	OFFSET label
	Returns the offset value of *variable* or *label*.
Attribute	
PTR	*Format:* type PTR expression
	Overrides the type (BYTE or WORD) or distance (NEAR or FAR) of a memory address operand. Here, *type* is the new attribute and *expression* is the identifier whose attribute is to be over-written.
CS:	*Format:* seg-reg:addr-expr
DS:	or
ES:	seg-reg:label
SS:	or
	seg-reg:variable
	Overrides the segment attribute of a label, variable, or address expression.

Arithmetic Operators

The arithmetic operators combine numeric operands and produce a numeric result. The assembler provides operators that add (+), subtract (−), multiply (*), and divide (/). It also provides an MOD operator that returns the remainder of a divide operation.

Value-Returning Operators

Operators in this group provide information about variables or labels in a program. The $ returns the value of the location counter; that is, it returns the offset of the current statement.

This operator is handy for making the assembler calculate the length of a text string. For example, the following calculates the number of characters in the MESSAGE string and assigns this count to MESSAGEL:

```
MESSAGE     DB    'Press any key to continue.'
MESSAGEL    EQU   $-MESSAGE
```

When you want to display the message, you would use the value MESSAGEL to tell the program how many characters to send to the screen.

SEG and OFFSET return the segment number and offset of a variable or label. For example, the following statements load the segment and offset values of TABLE into AX and BX, respectively:

```
MOV   AX,SEG TABLE
MOV   BX,OFFSET TABLE
```

Attribute Operators

The PTR (Pointer) operator overrides the type (BYTE or WORD) or distance (NEAR or FAR) attribute of an operand. PTR is often used to specify what size data you're operating on. For example, the statement

```
MOV   [BX],1
```

will produce an error message, because the assembler doesn't know whether BX is pointing to a byte or word location. If it's pointing to a byte location, the correct form is

```
MOV   BYTE PTR [BX],1
```

The *segment override* operators (CS:, DS:, ES:, and SS:) are used in EXE-type programs to override the microprocessor's assumption about which segment holds a specific data item.

Other Operators

Table 2-5 lists other operators you can use in your programs. See your Macro Assembler manual for details.

TYPES OF ASSEMBLY LANGUAGE PROGRAMS

MS-DOS can work with two different types of assembly language program files; one type is called an EXE (Execution) file, the other a COM (Command) file. You must use the EXE format for programs that are longer than 64K bytes; you can use the COM

Table 2-5. Advanced Operators.

Type	Operators			
Arithmetic	SHL	SHR		
Logical	AND	OR	XOR	NOT
Relational	EQ	LT	LE	
	NE	GT	GE	
Value-Returning	LENGTH	SIZE	TYPE	
Attribute	THIS	HIGH	LOW	

format for shorter programs.

The subroutines in this book are all COM files. I chose the COM format here not only because the subroutines are small, but because COM format programs are somewhat easier to write than EXE programs. Moreover, COM files load faster than their EXE counterparts.

COM programs have a format that is quite different from that of EXE programs, but I won't go into the details here. Instead, in Chapter 4, I provide two program models (one for calling programs, the other for subroutines) that follow all of the COM rules. The models allow you to produce valid COM programs by simply inserting the instructions for your particular program.

DEVELOPING ASSEMBLY LANGUAGE PROGRAMS

While assembly language programs look quite different from BASIC and Pascal programs, you follow the same procedures to develop them. In assembly language, however, the *mechanics* are more involved. There are seven steps in developing a COM-type assembly language program (the kind I deal with in this book). They are:

1. Define the task and design the program. This often requires drawing a *flowchart*, a blueprint of how the program should operate.
2. Type the instructions into the computer using an *editor* or any word processor that can produce pure ASCII text (most can); then save the program on disk.
3. Assemble the program using an *assembler*. If the assembler reports errors, correct them with the editor and reassemble.
4. Convert the assembler output to an executable "run module" using the linker.
5. Convert the run module to COM format using the DOS EXE2BIN command.
6. Run the program.
7. Check the results. If they differ from what you expected, you must find and correct the errors, or "bugs"; that is, you must *debug* the program.

I will now list the commands for each of these steps. In each case, I assume the program is on the disk in drive B, the Macro Assembler is on the disk in drive A, and the B> prompt is on the screen.

Editing with EDLIN

Step 2 above refers to an *editor*. If you don't have an editor or a word processor that can produce ASCII text files, you can use the EDLIN line editor program that comes with DOS. To create a new source (.ASM) file or edit an existing one, start ED-LIN using a command of the form

B > a:edlin *progname*.asm

Although EDLIN is a simple line editor, and not a word processor, it has commands that let you do most things you want on program files. Table 2-6 summarizes the most useful ones.

Table 2-6. Common EDLIN Commands.

Edit Lines
Format: [*line*]
Action: Displays a line for editing.
Comment: Pressing Return selects the next line.

C—Copy Lines
Format: [*start-line*],[*end-line*],*target-line* C
Action: Copies the specified line(s) to just ahead of *target-line*.
Comment: See also the Move Lines command.

D—Delete Lines
Format: [*start-line*][,*end-line*] D
Action: Deletes the specified line(s).
Comment: EDLIN automatically renumbers all lines that follow the deletion.

E—End Edit
Format: E
Action: Saves the program on disk and then returns to DOS.
Comment: To exit EDLIN without saving changes, use the Quit command.

I—Insert Lines
Format: [*line*] I
Action: Inserts lines from the keyboard ahead of the specified line. To leave the insert mode, press Ctrl-Break.

L—List Lines
Format: [*start-line*][,*end-line*] L
Action: Displays the selected range of lines.

M—Move Lines
Format: [*start-line*],[*end-line*],target-line M
Action: Moves the specified line(s) just ahead of *target-line*.
Comment: See also the Copy Lines command.

R—Replace Text
Format: [*start-line*][,*end-line*] R*old-string*[< F6 >*new-string*]
Action: Replaces *old-string* with *new-string* throughout the specified range.
Example: 1,40 RFINISH < F6 >END changes FINISH to END in lines 1 through 40.

S—Search for Text
Format: [*start-line*][,*end-line*] S *string*
Action: Searches for string. If EDLIN locates it, you may press S and Return to find the next occurrence.

Assembling

To assemble a program, you generally enter a command of the form

B>a:masm *progname*,,,;

This tells the assembler to use the specified source file (*progname*.ASM) to create an object file with the same name (*progname*.OBJ) and a source listing file (*progname*.LST).

The listing file contains the program instructions and their numeric codes and locations. This is a convenient, printable file that shows how the assembler interpreted your program. The fact that it lists locations also comes in handy for executing to a certain point (or *tracing*). To display the listing file, enter a DOS **type** command.

Linking

DOS can store an object program at any convenient place in memory. To use this facility, you must create a *relocatable* run file. The program that creates relocatable run files is called the *linker*, because it can link several object files to form one large run file. If your program has only one object module, run the linker by entering

B>a:link *progname*;

When you link a COM-type program (as you will do for programs in this book), the linker always produces the message

Warning: No STACK segment.

Don't panic—this is just a warning, not an error message. COM programs have no separate stack segment, so this message is to be expected.

If the program consists of several object modules (say, a calling program and one or more subroutine modules), assemble the modules separately, and then link them by listing their names separated with + symbols. For example, the following command links object modules MAINPROG.OBJ, SUBR1.OBJ, and SUBR2.OBJ to produce a run file called MAINPROG.EXE:

B>a:link mainprog + subr1 + subr2;

Admittedly, having to remember the names of all the modules a program needs is annoying, and it's time-consuming to enter them in the link command. An easy solution is to store your object modules in an *object library*, and let the linker extract the ones it needs. With an object library, your link command takes the simple form

B>a:link *progname*,,nul,*libname*

The optional disk contains a library called OBJECT.LIB that includes object files for every subroutine in the book. To link it with a program, substitute **object** for *libname* in the preceding command.

Creating a COM file

The next step is to convert your relocatable run file to COM format (provided, of course, it's a COM program), using a command of the form

B>a:exe2bin *progname progname*.com

Once you have the COM file, you can delete the EXE run file.

Running the Program

To run a completed program, you can either enter its name from DOS or run it under control of the Macro Assembler's debugger program. If you have the IBM Macro Assembler, you can use the *DEBUG* program that comes with DOS; if you have the Microsoft Macro Assembler, you can use the *SYMDEB* (for Symbolic Debugger) program that comes on the assembler disk.

You should run a program under DOS only when you're sure it's error-free or produces some kind of visible or audible result; until then, run it under DEBUG or SYMDEB. Starting SYMDEB can be different than starting DEBUG, depending on what kind of computer you have. To start DEBUG with a program, enter a command of the form

B>a:debug *progname* .com

To start SYMDEB on an IBM-compatible computer (but not an IBM PC), enter

B>a:symdeb /ibm *progname*.com

To start SYMDEB on an IBM PC or a computer that is not IBM-compatible, enter

B>a:symdeb *progname*.com

The screen shows the debugger's hyphen (-) prompt, which means the computer is waiting for a command. Table 2-7 shows the most common DEBUG and SYMDEB commands.

Table 2-7. Common DEBUG and SYMDEB Commands.

Note: Shaded commands are available with SYMDEB, but not DEBUG.

Execution Commands

G—Go

Format:	G [*offset*][,*offset*]
Action:	Executes a program starting at the current location. Offset values are temporary breakpoints. Upon encountering a breakpoint instruction (or a "sticky" breakpoint set by the Breakpoint Set command), the processor stops and displays registers and flags.
Example:	*G 4B* executes to the instruction at offset 4BH.
Comment:	The T and P commands let you step through a program one or more instructions at a time.

T—Trace

Format:	T [*instruction-count*]
Action:	Executes one or more instructions and displays registers and flag values for each of them.
Example:	*T 5* executes the next five instructions.

P—PTrace

Format:	P [*instruction-count*]
Action:	Same as Trace, but treats subroutine calls, interrupts, loop instructions, and repeat string instructions as single instructions.

Quit Command

Q—Quit

Format:	Q
Action:	Exits DEBUG or SYMDEB and returns to DOS.

Help Command

?—Help

Format:	?
Action:	Displays a summary list of SYMDEB commands.

Display/Change Commands

D—Dump

Format:	D *seg:offset* [*offset*]
	D *seg:offset* L *byte-count*
Action:	Displays the numeric contents of memory locations and their ASCII equivalents (if any).
Example:	*D DS:0* displays locations starting at the beginning of the data segment.

18

E—Enter Memory Values
Format: E *seg:offset* [*byte-list*]
Action: Enters one or more byte values into memory, starting at a specified address.
Example: *E DS:100 2B 10* changes the contents of locations 100H and 101H in the data segment to 2BH and 10H, respectively.
Comment: Omitting the list causes DEBUG or SYMDEB to display the current value and wait for you to enter a new one.

R—Register
Format: R [*register-name* [*value*]]
Action: Displays contents of one or all 16-bit registers.
Example: *R AX* displays the contents of the AX register and prompts for a new value. (Press Return to keep the current value.)

U—Unassemble
Format: U [*seg:offset* [*offset*]]
             U [*seg:offset*] L *instruction-count*
Action: Translates (unassembles) memory contents into instructions.

Breakpoint Commands

BP—Breakpoint Set
Format: BP[*n*] *offset*
Action: Sets a "sticky" breakpoint at the specified offset in the code segment. Upon encountering a sticky breakpoint, the processor stops and displays registers and flags. You may set up to ten sticky breakpoints, by giving *n* a number between 0 and 9.
Example: *BP 2A* sets a sticky breakpoint at offset 2AH.

BC—Breakpoint Clear
Format: BC *list*
             BC *
Action: Removes one or more sticky breakpoints from a program.
Example: *BC 0 5 7* removes breakpoints 0, 5, and 7.
Comment: To turn breakpoints off but leave them intact, use the Breakpoint Disable command.

BD—Breakpoint Disable
Format: BD *list*
             BD *
Action: Disables one or more sticky breakpoints temporarily.

Command Summary

Following is a summary of the commands you need to construct programs. Included are the commands to start EDLIN, the Macro Assembler, the linker, EXE2BIN, and DEBUG or SYMDEB.

B>a:edlin *progname*.asm

B>a:masm *progname*,,;

B>a:link *progname* ;	(One object module)
B>a:link *progname* + *mod1*[+...] ;	(More than one module)
B>a:link *progname*,,nul,*libname*	(With library)

B>a:exe2bin *progname progname*.com

B>a:debug *progname*.com	
B>a:symdeb /ibm *progname*.com	(IBM-compatible)
B>a:symdeb *progname* .com	(Others)

Batch Files for Assembling

Entering the assemble-link-EXE2BIN sequence for every new program is pure drudgery. And if you're fumble-fingered, like me, you often end up with the added nuisance of retyping commands. Fortunately, you can automate the process by using a batch file to perform the assembly sequence.

Figure 2-1 shows batch file commands for assembling on a computer that has two floppy disk drives. This file, FIN.BAT (short for "finish"), assembles and links up to five source modules. Then it converts the resulting run file (%1.EXE) to COM format and erases the EXE file. Note that the commas in the command *a:masm %1,,,;* make FIN.BAT produce a list file (%1.LST) as well as the object and COM files.

FIN.BAT assumes that the assembler disk is in drive A, the program modules are in B, and the B> prompt is on the screen. To run it, enter a command of the form

B>a:fin *callprog* [*mod*] [*mod*] [*mod*] [*mod*]

```
a:masm %1,,;
if not exist %2.asm goto dolink
a:masm %2;
if not exist %3.asm goto dolink
a:masm %3;
if not exist %4.asm goto dolink
a:masm %4;
if not exist %5.asm goto dolink
a:masm %5;
:dolink
a:link %1+%2+%3+%4+%5;
a:exe2bin %1 %1.com
erase %1.exe
```

Fig. 2-1. Assembly batch file for a floppy disk system (FIN.BAT).

For example, to assemble, link, and debug a calling program named CALLER.ASM that calls subroutines in SUB1.ASM and SUB2.ASM, enter

B>a:fin caller sub1 sub2

FINH.BAT, shown in Figure 2-2, is the same as FIN.BAT, but it is used on a disk (generally a hard disk) that contains the assembler files, program files, and FINH.BAT itself. If these files are in different directories, you must tell DOS by using the PATH command.

```
masm %1,,;
if not exist %2.asm goto dolink
masm %2;
if not exist %3.asm goto dolink
masm %3;
if not exist %4.asm goto dolink
masm %4;
if not exist %5.asm goto dolink
masm %5;
:dolink
link %1+%2+%3+%4+%5;
exe2bin %1 %1.com
erase %1.exe
```

Fig. 2-2. Assembly batch file for a hard disk system (FINH.BAT).

OBJECT LIBRARIES

The IBM and Microsoft Macro Assemblers let you create *object libraries*. An object library is simply a file that you can use to store your object modules. With it, you can enter a link command of the form

> B>a:link *callprog*,,nul, *objlib-name*

and the linker will go into the library (*objlib-name*) and extract any modules that *call-prog* calls; you don't have to specify them.

The Macro Assembler has a library manager utility called LIB that lets you create object libraries and operate on the entries in them. To use LIB, type a command of the form

> B>a:lib *libname* [*command(s)*],*list-file*;

where the *command(s)* are one or more module names preceded by an operator and *list-file* is a file that contains the names of the modules in the library.

The operators tell LIB to add a module to the library (+), delete a module from it (−), or update the library by replacing a module with a new version (− +). It also has a copy operator (*) that copies a module to an object file of the same name and a move operator (− *) that not only copies the module, but also removes it from the library.

For example, to add a module called MYMOD.OBJ to an object library called OB-JECT.LIB (or to create OBJECT.LIB and make MYMOD.OBJ its first entry), enter

> B>a:lib object + mymod,object.dir;

Here, OBJECT.DIR is the list file. To display its contents, enter **type object.dir**. To replace the APPEND$.OBJ module in OBJECT.LIB with a newly assembled version, enter

> B>a:lib object −+ append$,object.dir;

```
a:masm %1,,;
a:link %1,,nul,%2
a:exe2bin %1 %1.com
erase %1.exe
```

Fig. 2-3. Assembly batch file using an object library, floppy disk system (FINLIB.BAT).

```
masm %1,,;
link %1,,nul,%2
exe2bin %1 %1.com
erase %1.exe
```

Fig. 2-4. Assembly batch file using an object library, hard disk system (FINHLIB.BAT).

OBJECT LIBRARY BATCH FILES

Having an object library allows you assemble programs by running the FINLIB.BAT (with floppy disks) or FINLIBBAT.BAT (with a hard disk) batch file listed in Fig. 2-3 and 2-4, respectively. To run either, you must only specify the names of the calling program and library. For example, to assemble a calling program named CALLER.ASM and link it with one or more object modules in OBJECT.LIB, enter

B>a:finlib caller object

Chapter 3

Microprocessor Instruction Sets

The 8086 and 8088 microprocessors have 92 instruction types, while the 80186 has 99 and the 80286 has 115 (the 80186 instructions plus 16 "protected mode" instructions). Table 3-1 shows the assembler mnemonic for each instruction and tells what the mnemonic stands for. Shaded instructions are new with the 80186 and 80286; they are not available with the 8086 or 8088. (I have omitted the 80286's protected mode instructions because only system programmers ever use them.)

In this chapter, I provide an overview of the instructions and have divided the instruction set into eight functional groups:

1. *Data transfer instructions* move data between registers and memory locations or I/O ports.
2. *Arithmetic instructions* perform add, subtract, multiply, and divide operations on binary or binary-coded-decimal (BCD) numbers.
3. *Bit manipulation instructions* perform shift, rotate, and logical operations on memory locations or registers.
4. *Control transfer instructions* can change the sequence in which a program executes. They include procedure calls and jumps, both conditional and unconditional.
5. *String instructions* operate on blocks of consecutive bytes or words in memory.
6. *Interrupt instructions* interrupt the microprocessor to make it service a specific condition.
7. *Processor control instructions* manipulate status flags and change the microprocessor's execution state.

24

Table 3-1. Instruction Set.

Assembler Mnemonic	Description
AAA	ASCII Adjust for Addition
AAD	ASCII Adjust for Division
AAM	ASCII Adjust for Multiplication
AAS	ASCII Adjust for Subtraction
ADC	Add with Carry
ADD	Add (without Carry)
AND	Logical AND
BOUND	Check Array Index Against Bounds
CALL	Call a Procedure
CBW	Convert (Extend) Byte to Word
CLC	Clear Carry Flag
CLD	Clear Direction Flag
CLI	Clear Interrupt Flag
CMC	Complement Carry Flag
CMP	Compare Destination to Source
CMPS, CMPSB, or CMPSW	Compare Byte or Word Strings
CWD	Convert (Extend) Word to Double Word
DAA	Decimal Adjust for Addition
DAS	Decimal Adjust for Subtraction
DEC	Decrement Destination by One
DIV	Divide, Unsigned
ENTER	Make Stack Frame for High-Level Procedure
ESC	Escape
HLT	Halt the Processor
IDIV	Integer Divide, Signed
IMUL	Integer Multiply, Signed
IN	Input Byte or Word
INC	Increment Destination by One
INS, INSB, or INSW	Input String
INT	Interrupt
INTO	Interrupt If Zero
IRET	Interrupt Return
JA or JNBE	Jump If Above/If Not Below nor Equal
JAE, JNB, or JNC	Jump If Above or Equal/If Not Below/ If No Carry
JB, JNAE, or JC	Jump If Below/If Not Above nor Equal/ If Carry

Assembler Mnemonic	Description
JBE or JNA	Jump If Below or Equal/If Not Above
JCXZ	Jump If CX is Zero
JE or JZ	Jump If Equal/If Zero
JG or JNLE	Jump If Greater/If Not Less nor Equal
JGE or JNL	Jump If Greater or Equal/If Not Less
JL or JNGE	Jump If Less/If Not Greater nor Equal
JLE or JNG	Jump If Less or Equal/If Not Greater
JMP	Jump Unconditionally
JNE or JNZ	Jump If Not Equal/If Not Zero
JNO	Jump If No Overflow
JNS	Jump If No Sign (If Positive)
JO	Jump On Overflow
JP or JPE	Jump On Parity/If Parity Even
JS	Jump On Sign (If Negative)
LAHF	Load AH from Flags
LDS	Load Pointer Using DS
LEA	Load Effective Address
LEAVE	Exit High-Level Procedure
LES	Load Pointer Using ES
LOCK	Lock the Bus
LODS, LODSB, or LODSW	Load Byte or Word String
LOOP	Loop Until Count is Zero
LOOPE or LOOPZ	Loop While Equal/While Zero
LOOPNE or LOOPNZ	Loop While Not Equal/While Not Zero
MOV	Move
MOVS, MOVSB, or MOVSW	Move Byte or Word String
MUL	Multiply, Unsigned
NEG	Negate (Two's-Complement)
NOP	No Operation
NOT	Logical NOT
OR	Logical Inclusive-OR
OUT	Output Byte or Word
OUTS, OUTSB, or OUTSW	Output String
POP	Pop Word Off Stack
POPA	Pop All General Registers
POPF	Pop Flags Off Stack
PUSH	Push Word onto Stack
PUSHA	Push All General Registers
PUSHF	Push Flags onto Stack
RCL	Rotate Left through Carry
RCR	Rotate Right through Carry
REP, REPE, or REPZ	Repeat String Operation/While Equal/ While Zero

Assembler Mnemonic	Description
REPNE or REPNZ	Repeat String Operation While Not Equal/ While Not Zero
RET	Return from Procedure
ROL	Rotate Left
ROR	Rotate Right
SAHF	Store (Copy) AH into Flags
SAL or SHL	Shift Arithmetic Left/Logical Left
SAR	Shift Arithmetic Right
SBB	Subtract with Borrow
SCAS, SCASB, or SCASW	Scan Byte or Word String
SHR	Shift Logical Right
STC	Set Carry Flag
STD	Set Direction Flag
STI	Set Interrupt Enable Flag
STOS, STOSB, or STOSW	Store Byte or Word String
SUB	Subtract (without Borrow)
TEST	Test (Logically Compare Operands)
WAIT	Wait
XCHG	Exchange Two Operands
XLAT	Translate
XOR	Logical Exclusive-OR

8. *High-level instructions* let you communicate with programs that are written in Pascal or other block-oriented languages.

In the sections that follow, I briefly describe the instructions within each group and provide a table that lists the valid assembler formats and shows how the status flags are affected. (Appendix C summarizes the entire instruction set.) For each table, the abbreviations in the operand field of the Assembler Format column have the following meanings:

count:	the bit count for a shift or rotate instruction.
dest$:	the destination string in a string instruction.
immed:	an immediate byte or word value.
immed8:	an immediate byte value (0-255).
immed16:	an immediate word value (0-65535).
label:	a label in the same code segment as this instruction.
mem:	a memory location. Any memory addressing mode may be used.
mem8:	a byte operand in memory. Any memory addressing mode may be used.
mem16:	a word operand in memory. Any memory addressing mode may be used.

mem32:	a double-word operand in memory. Any memory addressing mode may be used.	
memptr:	a word or double-word pointer operand in memory. Any memory addressing mode may be used.	
reg:	one of the byte registers AL, AH, BL, BH, CL, CH, DL, or DH, or one of the word registers AX, BX, CX, DX, SP, BP, SI, or DI.	
reg8:	one of the byte registers AL, AH, BL, BH, CL, CH, DL, or DH.	
reg16:	one of the word registers AX, BX, CX, DX, SP, BP, SI, or DI.	
regptr16:	a memory offset in a word register.	
segreg:	one of the segment registers CS, DS, ES, or SS.	
short-label:	a label in the range from 128 bytes before the end of this instruction to 128 bytes after the end of this instruction.	
source$:	the source string in a string instruction.	

In the Flags columns, - means *unchanged*, * means *may have changed*, and ? means *undefined*.

DATA TRANSFER INSTRUCTIONS

Data transfer instructions move data and addresses between registers and memory locations or I/O ports. Table 3-2 lists these instructions in four groups: general-purpose, input/output, address transfer, and flag transfer.

Table 3-2. Data Transfer Instructions.

	Flags								
Assembler Format	**OF**	**DF**	**IF**	**TF**	**SF**	**ZF**	**AF**	**PF**	**CF**
General-Purpose									
MOV reg,reg	-	-	-	-	-	-	-	-	-
MOV reg,mem	-	-	-	-	-	-	-	-	-
MOV mem,reg	-	-	-	-	-	-	-	-	-
MOV reg,segreg	-	-	-	-	-	-	-	-	-
MOV segreg,reg	-	-	-	-	-	-	-	-	-
MOV segreg,mem	-	-	-	-	-	-	-	-	-
MOV mem,segreg	-	-	-	-	-	-	-	-	-
MOV reg,immed	-	-	-	-	-	-	-	-	-
MOV mem,immed	-	-	-	-	-	-	-	-	-
PUSH reg16	-	-	-	-	-	-	-	-	-
PUSH segreg	-	-	-	-	-	-	-	-	-
PUSH mem16	-	-	-	-	-	-	-	-	-
PUSH immed16	-	-	-	-	-	-	-	-	-
PUSHA	-	-	-	-	-	-	-	-	-
POP reg16	-	-	-	-	-	-	-	-	-
POP DS	-	-	-	-	-	-	-	-	-

Instruction									
POP ES	-	-	-	-	-	-	-	-	-
POP SS	-	-	-	-	-	-	-	-	-
POP mem16	-	-	-	-	-	-	-	-	-
POPA	-	-	-	-	-	-	-	-	-
XCHG mem,reg	-	-	-	-	-	-	-	-	-
XCHG reg,reg	-	-	-	-	-	-	-	-	-
XLAT mem8	-	-	-	-	-	-	-	-	-

Input/Output

Instruction									
IN AL,immed8	-	-	-	-	-	-	-	-	-
IN AX,immed8	-	-	-	-	-	-	-	-	-
IN AL,DX	-	-	-	-	-	-	-	-	-
IN AX,DX	-	-	-	-	-	-	-	-	-
OUT immed8,AL	-	-	-	-	-	-	-	-	-
OUT immed8,AX	-	-	-	-	-	-	-	-	-
OUT DX,AL	-	-	-	-	-	-	-	-	-
OUT DX,AX	-	-	-	-	-	-	-	-	-

Address Transfer

Instruction									
LEA reg16,mem16	-	-	-	-	-	-	-	-	-
LDS reg16,mem32	-	-	-	-	-	-	-	-	-
LES reg16,mem32	-	-	-	-	-	-	-	-	-

Flag Transfer

Instruction									
LAHF	-	-	-	-	-	-	-	-	-
SAHF	-	-	-	-	*	*	*	*	*
PUSHF	-	-	-	-	-	-	-	-	-
POPF	*	*	*	*	*	*	*	*	*

General-Purpose

The most common general-purpose instruction, *Move (MOV)*, can transfer a byte or word between two registers or between a register and a memory location. MOV has the general form

MOV *destination,source*

There are a few things you cannot do with a MOV instruction:

1. You cannot move data between two memory locations directly. Instead, you must

move the source data into a general-purpose register and then move that register to the destination. For example, if POUNDS and WEIGHT are variables in memory, you can give them the same value with

```
MOV   AX,POUNDS
MOV   WEIGHT,AX
```

2. You cannot load a constant into a segment register directly. As with rule 1, you must pass it through a general-purpose register. For example, to load the number of the data segment DSEG into DS, use

```
MOV   AX,DSEG
MOV   DS,AX
```

3. You cannot copy data from one segment register directly. As before, you must transfer it through a general-purpose register.
4. You cannot use the CS register as the destination of a MOV instruction.

As I mentioned earlier, the stack holds return addresses while the microprocessor is executing a procedure. The *Call (CALL)* instruction places an address on the stack; a *Return (RET)* instruction retrieves it at the end of the procedure.

The stack is also a convenient place to deposit data temporarily. For example, you may want to save the contents of AX while you put this register to some other use. The two instructions that let you use the stack are *Push Word onto Stack (PUSH)* and *Pop Word Off Stack (POP)*. They have these general forms:

```
PUSH   source
POP    destination
```

The 80186 and 80286 also let you push a 16-bit constant onto the stack. The general form is:

```
PUSH   immediate
```

The 80186/286 instructions *Push All General Registers (PUSHA)* and *Pop All General Registers (POPA)* let you push or pop all of the general registers: AX, BX, CX, DX, SP, BP, SI, and DI.

Exchange (XCHG) swaps the contents of the source and destination operands, while *Translate (XLAT)* looks up a byte value in a table and loads it into AL. Before executing XLAT, you must load the table's offset into BX (use LEA BX,*table name*) and the index value of the desired byte into AL.

Input and Output

The input and output instructions communicate with the computer's peripherals. They have the general forms

IN *accumulator,port*
IN *accumulator,* DX
OUT *port,accumulator*
OUT DX,*accumulator*

Address Transfer

Load Effective Address (LEA) transfers the offset of a memory operand into any 16-bit general pointer, or index register. The *Load Pointer Using DS (LDS)* and *Load Pointer Using ES (LES)* instructions read the address of a 32-bit double word in memory and put the offset into a specified register and the segment number into either DS or ES.

Flag Transfer

The *Load AH from Flags (LAHF)* and *Store AH into Flags (SAHF)* instructions transfer the Flags register's CF, PF, AF, ZF, and SF bits to or from the AH register. Similarly, *Push Flags onto Stack (PUSHF)* and *Pop Flags Off Stack (POPF)* transfer the contents of the flags register to or from the stack.

ARITHMETIC INSTRUCTIONS

The microprocessor can perform arithmetic operations on binary numbers (signed or unsigned) and on decimal numbers (packed or unpacked). As Table 3-3 shows, there are instructions for the four standard arithmetic functions—addition, subtraction, multiplication, and division—as well as instructions that *sign-extend* operands. *Sign-extending* lets you combine data of different sizes; you can, for example, add a byte to a word.

Table 3-3. Arithmetic Instructions.

Assembler Format	Flags								
	OF	DF	IF	TF	SF	ZF	AF	PF	CF
Addition									
ADD reg,reg	*	-	-	-	*	*	*	*	*
ADD reg,mem	*	-	-	-	*	*	*	*	*
ADD mem,reg	*	-	-	-	*	*	*	*	*
ADD reg,immed	*	-	-	-	*	*	*	*	*
ADD mem,immed	*	-	-	-	*	*	*	*	*
ADC reg,reg	*	-	-	-	*	*	*	*	*
ADC reg,mem	*	-	-	-	*	*	*	*	*
ADC mem,reg	*	-	-	-	*	*	*	*	*
ADC reg,immed	*	-	-	-	*	*	*	*	*
ADC mem,immed	*	-	-	-	*	*	*	*	*
AAA	?	-	-	-	?	?	*	?	*
DAA	?	-	-	-	*	*	*	*	*

Flags

Assembler Format	OF	DF	IF	TF	SF	ZF	AF	PF	CF
Addition									
INC reg	*	-	-	-	*	*	*	*	-
INC mem	*	-	-	-	*	*	*	*	-
Subtraction									
SUB reg,reg	*	-	-	-	*	*	*	*	*
SUB reg,mem	*	-	-	-	*	*	*	*	*
SUB mem,reg	*	-	-	-	*	*	*	*	*
SUB reg,immed	*	-	-	-	*	*	*	*	*
SUB mem,immed	*	-	-	-	*	*	*	*	*
SBB reg,reg	*	-	-	-	*	*	*	*	*
SBB reg,mem	*	-	-	-	*	*	*	*	*
SBB mem,reg	*	-	-	-	*	*	*	*	*
SBB reg,immed	*	-	-	-	*	*	*	*	*
SBB mem,immed	*	-	-	-	*	*	*	*	*
AAS	?	-	-	-	?	?	*	?	*
DAS	?	-	-	-	*	*	*	*	*
DEC reg	*	-	-	-	*	*	*	*	-
DEC mem	*	-	-	-	*	*	*	*	-
NEG reg	*	-	-	-	*	*	*	*	*
NEG mem	*	-	-	-	*	*	*	*	*
CMP reg,reg	*	-	-	-	*	*	*	*	*
CMP reg,mem	*	-	-	-	*	*	*	*	*
CMP mem,reg	*	-	-	-	*	*	*	*	*
CMP reg,immed	*	-	-	-	*	*	*	*	*
CMP mem,immed	*	-	-	-	*	*	*	*	*
Multiplication									
MUL reg	*	-	-	-	?	?	?	?	*
MUL mem	*	-	-	-	?	?	?	?	*
IMUL reg	*	-	-	-	?	?	?	?	*
IMUL mem	*	-	-	-	?	?	?	?	*
IMUL dest-reg,immed	*	-	-	-	?	?	?	?	*
IMUL mem16,immed	*	-	-	-	?	?	?	?	*
IMUL dest-reg, reg16,immed	*	-	-	-	?	?	?	?	*
IMUL dest-reg, mem16,immed	*	-	-	-	?	?	?	?	*
AAM	?	-	-	-	*	*	?	*	?

Assembler Format	Flags								
	OF	DF	IF	TF	SF	ZF	AF	PF	CF
Division									
DIV reg	?	-	-	-	?	?	?	?	?
DIV mem	?	-	-	-	?	?	?	?	?
IDIV reg	?	-	-	-	?	?	?	?	?
IDIV mem	?	-	-	-	?	?	?	?	?
AAD	?	-	-	-	*	*	?	*	?
Sign-Extension									
CBW	-	-	-	-	-	-	-	-	-
CWD	-	-	-	-	-	-	-	-	-

Addition

The *Add (ADD)* and *Add with Carry (ADC)* instructions can add 8-bit or 16-bit operands. ADD adds a source operand to a destination operand. ADC does the same thing, but it includes the Carry Flag (CF) in the addition. These instructions affect six status flags. The most important ones are:

- The Carry Flag (CF) is 1 if the result cannot be contained in the destination operand.
- The Zero Flag (ZF) is 1 if the result is zero.
- The Sign Flag (SF) is 1 if the result is negative.
- The Overflow Flag is 1 if adding two like-signed numbers (both positive or both negative) produces a result that exceeds the two's-complement range of the destination, which changes the sign.

The microprocessor always adds numbers as if they were binary. If they are actually binary-coded decimal (BCD), you must adjust the result to put it into BCD form. The instructions *ASCII Adjust for Addition (AAA)* and *Decimal Adjust for Addition (DAA)* adjust the result in AL of a decimal addition. AAA produces an unpacked decimal digit in the low four bits of AL, while DAA produces two packed decimal digits in AL.

The *Increment Destination by One (INC)* instruction adds 1 to a register or memory operand. Unlike ADD, however, it does not affect the Carry Flag (CF). INC is convenient for increasing a loop counter and increasing an index register when you are accessing consecutive memory locations.

Subtraction

Subtract (SUB) and *Subtract with Borrow (SBB)* are similar to ADD and ADC, but when you subtract, the Carry Flag (CF) acts as a *borrow* indicator. SUB subtracts a source operand from a destination operand and returns the result in the destination. That is,

destination = destination – source

SBB does the same thing, except it also subtracts out the Carry Flag, like this:

destination = *destination* – *source* – CF

SUB and SBB affect six status flags. The most important ones are:

- The Carry Flag (CF) is 1 if a borrow was needed.
- The Zero Flag (ZF) is 1 if the result is zero.
- The Sign Flag (SF) is 1 if the result is negative.
- The Overflow Flag is 1 if you subtract a positive number from a negative number (or vice versa), and the result exceeds the two's-complement range of the destination, which changes the sign.

As with addition, the microprocessor subtracts operands as if they were binary. Thus, if you subtract binary-coded decimal (BCD) numbers, you must adjust the result. The instructions *ASCII Adjust for Subtraction (AAS)* and *Decimal Adjust for Subtraction (DAS)* make this adjustment on the AL register. AAS produces an unpacked decimal digit in the low four bits of AL, while DAS converts AL to two packed decimal digits.

The *Decrement Destination by One (DEC)* instruction subtracts 1 from a register or memory operand. Unlike SUB, however, it does not affect the Carry Flag (CF). DEC is convenient for decreasing a loop counter and decreasing an index register when you are accessing consecutive memory locations.

Negate (NEG) subtracts the destination operand from zero, thereby two's-complementing it. The important flags for NEG are:

- The Carry Flag (CF) and Sign Flag (SF) are 1 if the operand is a nonzero positive number.
- The Zero Flag (ZF) is 1 if the operand is zero.
- The Overflow Flag (OF) is 1 if the operand has the value 80H (byte) or 8000H (word).

Most programs don't execute instructions in the exact order they are stored in memory. Instead, they include jumps, loops, and subroutine calls that make the processor transfer to different parts of a program. I discuss the *control transfer* instructions later in this chapter, but now I will describe *Compare Destination to Source (CMP)*. CMP is used to help the control transfer instructions make their transfer/no-transfer decisions.

Like the SUB instruction, CMP subtracts a source from a destination and describes the result in the flags (see Table 3-4). Unlike SUB, however, CMP does not save the result of the subtraction; its only purpose is to set up the flags for decision making by conditional jump instructions.

Multiplication

There are two multiplication instructions. *Multiply (MUL)* multiplies unsigned numbers, while *Integer Multiply (IMUL)* multiplies signed numbers. They have the general forms

Table 3-4. CMP Instruction Results.

Condition	OF	SF	ZF	CF
Unsigned Operands				
Destination > Source	D	D	0	0
Destination = Source	D	D	1	0
Destination < Source	D	D	0	1
Signed Operands				
Destination > Source	0/1	0	0	D
Destination = Source	0	0	1	D
Destination < Source	0/1	1	0	D

Note: "D" means Don't Care; "0/1" means the flag may be either 0 or 1, depending on the values of the operands.

        MUL *multiplier*
        IMUL *multiplier*

where *multiplier* is a byte- or word-sized general register or memory location. MUL and IMUL obtain the multiplier from AL for byte operations and from AX for word operations. Multiplying bytes produces a 16-bit product in AX; multiplying words produces a 32-bit product in DX (high word) and AX (low word).

The 80186 and 80286 also provide a version of IMUL that lets you multiply a signed or unsigned operand by an immediate value. The formats are:

        IMUL *dest-reg,immed*
        IMUL *mem16,immed*
        IMUL *dest-reg,reg16,immed*
        IMUL *dest-reg,mem16,immed*

The *ASCII Adjust for Multiplication (AAM)* instruction converts the product of a byte multiplication in AX into two unpacked decimal digits. It puts the high digit in AH and the low digit in AL.

Division

Divide (DIV) divides unsigned numbers, while *Integer Divide (IDIV)* divides signed numbers. Their formats are:

        DIV   *divisor*
        IDIV *divisor*

where *divisor* (the value by which you want to divide) is a byte- or word-sized general register or memory location. DIV and IDIV obtain the dividend from AX if the divisor is a byte or from DX (high) and AX (low) if it is a word. For byte operations, the quotient and remainder are returned in AL and AH, respectively; for word operations, they are returned in AX and DX.

Both instructions leave the flags undefined. If, however, the quotient cannot fit in AL or AX, the processor generates a type 0 (divide by zero) interrupt. The following conditions can cause overflow:

1. The divisor is zero.
2. For an unsigned byte divide, the dividend is at least 256 times larger than the divisor.
3. For an unsigned word divide, the dividend is at least 65,536 times larger than the divisor.
4. For a signed byte divide, the quotient exceeds $+127$ or -128.
5. For a signed word divide, the quotient exceeds $+32,767$ or $-32,768$.

There is also an *ASCII Adjust for Division (AAD)* instruction that converts an unpacked dividend to a binary value in AL. To do this, it multiplies the high-order digit in AH by 10 and adds the result to the low-order digit in AL. Then it clears AH to zero. Unlike the decimal adjust instructions I described earlier, you must execute AAD *before* you divide, not after.

Sign-Extension

Two instructions let you operate on mixed-size data, by doubling the length of a signed operand. *Convert Byte to Word (CBW)* reproduces the sign bit (7) of AL throughout AH, while *Convert Word to Doubleword (CWD)* reproduces bit 15 of AX throughout DX. Thus, CBW lets you add a byte to a word, subtract a word from a byte, and so on. Similarly, CWD lets you divide a word by a word.

BIT-MANIPULATION INSTRUCTIONS

The bit-manipulation instructions manipulate bit patterns within registers and memory locations. Table 3-5 divides them into three groups: logical, shift, and rotate.

Table 3-5. Bit Manipulation Instructions.

Assembler Format	Flags								
	OF	DF	IF	TF	SF	ZF	AF	PF	CF
Logical									
AND reg,reg	0	-	-	-	*	*	?	*	0
AND reg,mem	0	-	-	-	*	*	?	*	0
AND mem,reg	0	-	-	-	*	*	?	*	0
AND reg,immed	0	-	-	-	*	*	?	*	0
AND mem,immed	0	-	-	-	*	*	?	*	0

Assembler Format	OF	DF	IF	TF	SF	ZF	AF	PF	CF
Logical									
OR reg,reg	0	-	-	-	*	*	?	*	0
OR reg,mem	0	-	-	-	*	*	?	*	0
OR mem,reg	0	-	-	-	*	*	?	*	0
OR reg,immed	0	-	-	-	*	*	?	*	0
OR mem,immed	0	-	-	-	*	*	?	*	0
XOR reg,reg	0	-	-	-	*	*	?	*	0
XOR reg,mem	0	-	-	-	*	*	?	*	0
XOR mem,reg	0	-	-	-	*	*	?	*	0
XOR reg,immed	0	-	-	-	*	*	?	*	0
XOR mem,immed	0	-	-	-	*	*	?	*	0
NOT reg	-	-	-	-	-	-	-	-	-
NOT mem	-	-	-	-	-	-	-	-	-
TEST reg,reg	0	-	-	-	*	*	?	*	0
TEST reg,mem	0	-	-	-	*	*	?	*	0
TEST reg,immed	0	-	-	-	*	*	?	*	0
TEST mem,immed	0	-	-	-	*	*	?	*	0
Shift									
SAL/SHL reg,1	*	-	-	-	*	*	?	*	*
SAL/SHL reg,CL	?	-	-	-	*	*	?	*	*
SAL/SHL mem,1	*	-	-	-	*	*	?	*	*
SAL/SHL reg,CL	?	-	-	-	*	*	?	*	*
SAL/SHL reg,count	?	-	-	-	*	*	?	*	*
SAL/SHL mem,count	?	-	-	-	*	*	?	*	*
SAR reg,1	0	-	-	-	*	*	?	*	*
SAR reg,CL	?	-	-	-	*	*	?	*	*
SAR mem,1	0	-	-	-	*	*	?	*	*
SAR reg,CL	?	-	-	-	*	*	?	*	*
SAR reg,count	?	-	-	-	*	*	?	*	*
SAR mem,count	?	-	-	-	*	*	?	*	*
SHR reg,1	*	-	-	-	0	*	?	*	*
SHR reg,CL	?	-	-	-	0	*	?	*	*
SHR mem,1	*	-	-	-	0	*	?	*	*
SHR reg,CL	?	-	-	-	0	*	?	*	*
SHR reg,count	?	-	-	-	0	*	?	*	*
SHR mem,count	?	-	-	-	0	*	?	*	*
Rotate									
ROL/ROR reg,1	*	-	-	-	-	-	-	-	*
ROL/ROR reg,CL	?	-	-	-	-	-	-	-	*
ROL/ROR mem,1	*	-	-	-	-	-	-	-	*

Rotate

ROL/ROR reg,CL	?	-	-	-	-	-	-	-	*
ROL/ROR reg,count	?	-	-	-	-	-	-	-	*
ROL/ROR mem,count	?	-	-	-	-	-	-	-	*
RCL/RCR reg,1	*	-	-	-	-	-	-	-	*
RCL/RCR reg,CL	?	-	-	-	-	-	-	-	*
RCL/RCR mem,1	*	-	-	-	-	-	-	-	*
RCL/RCR reg,CL	?	-	-	-	-	-	-	-	*
RCL/RCR reg,count	?	-	-	-	-	-	-	-	*
RCL/RCR mem,count	?	-	-	-	-	-	-	-	*

Logical

Logical instructions obey the rules of formal logic, rather than those of mathematics. For example, the rule that states, "If A is true and B is true, then C is true" has an assembly language counterpart in the *Logical AND (AND)* instruction. AND applies that rule to corresponding bits in two operands.

Specifically, for each bit position where both operands are 1 (true), AND sets the bit in the destination operand to 1. For any other combination, AND sets the bit in the destination to 0. Note that any bit ANDed with 0 becomes 0, while any bit ANDed with 1 retains its original value.

The *Logical Inclusive-OR (OR)* instruction produces a 1 in the destination for each bit position in which either or both operands contain 1. OR is useful for forcing specific bits to 1.

The *Logical Exclusive-OR (XOR)* instruction puts a 1 in the destination for every bit position in which the operands differ; that is, where one operand has 0 and the operand has 1. Table 3-6 shows how AND, OR, and XOR operate.

Table 3-6. AND, OR, and XOR Bit Combinations.

		Result		
Source	**Destination**	**AND**	**OR**	**XOR**
0	0	0	0	0
0	1	0	1	1
1	0	0	1	1
1	1	1	1	0

The *Logical NOT (NOT)* instruction reverses the state of each bit in a register or memory location, but does not affect the flags. That is, NOT changes each 1 to 0 and each 0 to 1. In technical terminology, it *one's-complements* the operand.

Test (TEST) ANDs two operands, but affects only the flags, not the operands.

Shift

There are four instructions that displace the contents of a general register or memory location to the left or right. Here, the Carry Flag (CF) serves as a "ninth bit" (byte operations) or "17th bit" (word operations) extension of the operand. That is, CF receives the value of the bit that has been displaced out of one end of the operand. A right shift puts the value of bit 0 into CF; a left shift puts the value of bit 7 (byte) or bit 15 (word) into CF.

There are two kinds of shifts. *Logical* shifts displace an operand without regard to its sign; they operate on unsigned numbers. *Arithmetic* shifts preserve the most-significant bit, the sign bit. Figure 3-1 shows how these instructions work. I have also illustrated the similar rotate instructions, which I describe in the next section.

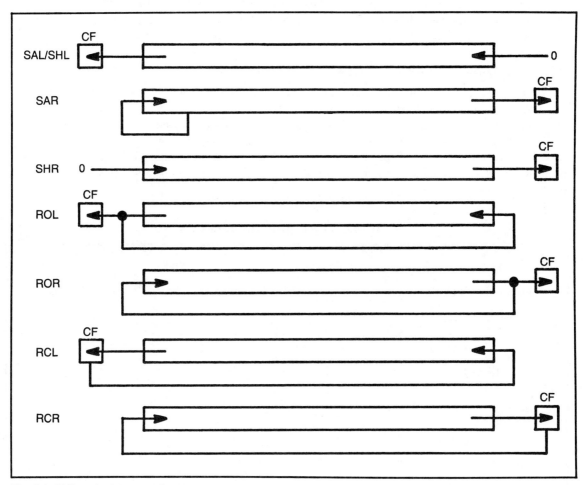

Fig. 3-1. Shift and rotate operations.

Shift Arithmetic Left (SAL) and *Shift Arithmetic Right (SAR)* shift signed numbers. SAR preserves the operand's sign by replicating the sign bit throughout the shift operation. SAL does not preserve the sign bit, but it sets the Overflow Flag (OF) to 1 if the sign ever changes. Whenever SAL shifts an operand, the vacated bit position 0 receives 0.

Shift Logical Left (SHL) and *Shift Logical Right (SHR)* shift unsigned numbers. SHL does the same thing as SAL. SHR is similar, but it shifts operands right instead of left. Whenever SHR shifts an operand, the vacated high-order bit position receives 0.

The shift instructions can also serve as fast multiply and divide instructions, because shifting an operand one bit position to the left doubles its value (multiplies it by two) and shifting it one bit position to the right halves its value (divides it by two).

Rotate

The rotate instructions are similar to the shifts, but rotates put displaced bits back into the operand. For *Rotate Left (ROL)* and *Rotate Right (ROR)*, the bit displaced out of one end enters the opposite end. For *Rotate Left through Carry (RCL)* and *Rotate Right through Carry (RCR)*, the value of CF goes into the opposite end of the operand.

CONTROL TRANSFER INSTRUCTIONS

As I mentioned earlier, instructions are stored consecutively in memory, but programs rarely execute in that exact order. All but the simplest programs include jumps and subroutine calls that alter the execution path the microprocessor takes.

The control transfer instructions can make the microprocessor transfer from one part of a program to another. Table 3-7 divides them into three groups: unconditional transfer, conditional transfer, and loop. Note that none of these instructions affect the flags.

Table 3-7. Control Transfer Instructions.

	Flags								
Assembler Format	OF	DF	IF	TF	SF	ZF	AF	PF	CF
Unconditional Transfer									
CALL procedure-name	-	-	-	-	-	-	-	-	-
CALL memptr	-	-	-	-	-	-	-	-	-
CALL regptr16	-	-	-	-	-	-	-		
RET	-	-	-	-	-	-	-	-	-
RET pop-value	-	-	-	-	-	-	-	-	-
JMP SHORT short-label	-	-	-	-	-	-	-	-	-
JMP label	-	-	-	-	-	-	-	-	-
JMP memptr	-	-	-	-	-	-	-	-	-
JMP regptr16	-	-	-	-	-	-	-	-	-
Conditional Transfer									
JA/JNBE short-label	-	-	-	-	-	-	-	-	-
JAE/JNB/JNC short-label	-	-	-	-	-	-	-	-	-
JB/JNAE/JC short-label	-	-	-	-	-	-	-	-	-
JBE/JNA short-label	-	-	-	-	-	-	-	-	-

JCXZ	short-label	-	-	-	-	-	-	-	-	-
JE/JZ	short label									
JG/JNLE	short-label									
JG/JNLE	short-label									
JGE/JNL	short-label	-	-	-	-	-	-	-	-	-
JL/JNGE	short-label	-	-	-	-	-	-	-	-	-
JLE/JNG	short-label	-	-	-	-	-	-	-	-	-
JNE/JNZ	short-label	-	-	-	-	-	-	-	-	-
JNO	short-label	-	-	-	-	-	-	-	-	-
JNP/JPO	short-label	-	-	-	-	-	-	-	-	-
JNS	short-label	-	-	-	-	-	-	-	-	-
JO	short-label	-	-	-	-	-	-	-	-	-
JP/JPE	short-label	-	-	-	-	-	-	-	-	-
JS	short-label	-	-	-	-	-	-	-	-	-
Loop										
LOOP	short-label	-	-	-	-	-	-	-	-	-
LOOPE/Z	short-label	-	-	-	-	-	-	-	-	-
LOOPNE/NZ	short-label	-	-	-	-	-	-	-	-	-

Unconditional Transfer

The first two instructions in this group, *Call a Procedure (CALL)* and *Return from Procedure (RET)* do exactly the same things that GOSUB and RETURN do in BASIC. That is, CALL transfers control from the current location in a program to a subroutine or *procedure*. (Subroutines and procedures are similar, but a subroutine must end with an RET instruction, while a procedure can end with something else, such as an interrupt instruction.) Conversely, RET makes the processor leave the subroutine and return to the instruction that follows the CALL.

Note that CALL has three different formats. The one you normally use is CALL *procedure name*, in which *procedure name* can be either the name of a procedure or the name of a subroutine. For example, CALL MYSUB transfers control to a subroutine named MYSUB. You can also make an *indirect* call through a register or memory location. For example, if MYSUB's offset is in the BX register, CALL WORD PTR [BX] does the same thing as CALL MYSUB.

The *Jump (JMP)* instruction does the same thing as GOTO in BASIC: it makes the processor obtain the next instruction from some place other than the next consecutive memory location. The operand is generally a label. For example, JMP THERE makes the processor transfer to the instruction labeled THERE.

If the label lies within – 128 bytes or + 127 bytes from the JMP instruction, you can use the form JMP SHORT short label. The SHORT operator makcs the assembler construct JMP as a two-byte instruction. Without it, JMP is three to five bytes long. SHORT JMPs also execute faster.

Conditional Transfer

There are 17 different instructions that let the microprocessor make an execution "decision" based on some prescribed condition, such as a subtraction result being zero or the Carry Flag being set to 1. If the condition is satisfied, the processor jumps to a specified label; otherwise, it continues to the next instruction in the program.

As Table 3-7 shows, the assembler recognizes most conditional transfer instructions by two or three different mnemonics. For example, JA TARGET and JNBE TARGET are identical instructions. These particular instructions test the result of a preceding Compare (CMP) or Subtract (SUB or SBB) instruction.

The mnemonic JA tells the processor to make the jump if the destination is "Above" (i.e., greater than) the source. The mnemonic JNBE says the same thing in a different way; it tells the processor to make the jump if the destination is "Not Below Nor Equal" to the source.

The conditional transfer instructions have the general format

Jcc short-label

where *cc* is a one- to three-letter condition code. The operand form *short-label* indicates that the target label must be no farther than − 128 bytes or + 127 bytes from the Jcc instruction.

Table 3-8 summarizes the conditional transfer instructions, and shows which conditions cause a jump. I have listed the mnemonics individually to save you from searching through a list of alternates. Note that the instructions for signed arithmetic operations are different from those for unsigned arithmetic operations. The table shows why: they base the jump/no-jump decision on different status flags.

Table 3-8. Conditional Transfer Instructions.

Mnemonic	Jump if Destination is . . . Source	Flags for Jump
JA	Above	CF = 0 and ZF = 0
JAE	Above or Equal to	CF = 0
JB	Below	CF = 1
JBE	Below or Equal to	CF = 1 or ZF = 1
JE	Equal to	ZF = 1
JNA	not Above	CF = 1 or ZF = 1
JNAE	not Above nor Equal to	CF = 1
JNB	not Below	CF = 0
JNBE	not Below nor Equal to	CF = 0 and ZF = 0
JNE	not Equal to	ZF = 0
*JG	Greater than	ZF = 0 and ZF = OF
*JGE	Greater than or Equal to	SF = OF
*JL	Less than	SF not = OF
*JLE	Less than or Equal to	ZF = 1 or SF not = OF
*JNG	not Greater than	ZF = 1 or SF not = OF
*JNGE	not Greater than nor Equal to	SF not = OF
*JNL	not Less than	SF = OF
*JNLE	not Less than nor Equal to	ZF = 0 and SF = OF

Mnemonic	Jump On . . .	Flags for Jump
JCXZ	CX Equal to Zero	(CX) = 0
JC	Carry	CF = 1
*JO	Overflow	OF = 1
JP	Parity (Even)	PF = 1
JPE	Parity Even	PF = 1
*JS	Sign (Negative)	SF = 1
JZ	Zero	ZF = 1
JNC	no Carry	CF = 0
*JNO	no Overflow	OF = 0
JNP	no Parity (Odd)	PF = 0
JPO	Parity Odd	PF = 0
*JNS	no Sign (Positive)	SF = 0
JNZ	not Zero	ZF = 0

*means pertinent for signed arithmetic.

Conditional transfer instructions are usually preceded with a Compare (CMP) instruction. Table 3-4 under "Arithmetic Instructions" shows how CMP affects the flags for various combinations of the source and destination operands. Now, with the wide variety of conditional transfer instructions at your disposal, it is worthwhile to look at a more practical table—one that shows which Jcc to use with various operand combinations. Table 3-9 is the one you need.

Table 3-9. Using Conditional Transfers with CMP.

	Follow CMP with	
To jump if . . .	for unsigned numbers	for signed numbers
Destination > source	JA	JG
Destination = source	JE	JE
Destination not = source	JNE	JNE
Destination < source	JB	JL
Destination < or = source	JBE	JLE
Destination is > or =	JAE	JGE

Loop

The loop instructions make the processor repeat sections of a program like a FOR-NEXT structure does in BASIC. Here, the CX register serves as the repetition counter. Each loop instruction decreases CX by 1 and then makes a repeat/quit decision based on its new value.

Loop (LOOP) continues looping until CX has been decremented to 0. *Loop If Equal (LOOPE)* continues until CX is 0 or the Zero Flag (ZF) is 0. Its opposite, *Loop If Not*

If Not Equal (LOOPNE), continues looping until CX is 0 or ZF is 1. LOOPE and LOOPNE are normally used to find the first nonzero result and the first zero result in a series of operations, respectively. They are also available under the alternate names *Loop If Zero (LOOPZ)* and *Loop If Not Zero (LOOPNZ)*.

STRING INSTRUCTIONS

The string instructions let you operate on blocks of consecutive bytes or words in memory. These blocks, or *strings*, may be up to 64K bytes long and may consist of numeric values (either binary or BCD) or text characters.

As Table 3-10 shows, there are seven types of string instructions: move, compare, scan, load, store, input, and output. Table 3-10 also lists direction instructions and repeat prefixes. The direction instructions determine whether a string instruction works forward or backward through a string. The repeat prefixes make a string instruction operate on a block of consecutive bytes or words.

Table 3-10. String Instructions.

Assembler Format	Flags								
	OF	DF	IF	TF	SF	ZF	AF	PF	CF
Direction									
CLD	-	0	-	-	-	-	-	-	-
STD	-	1	-	-	-	-	-	-	-
Repeat Prefixes									
REP	-	-	-	-	-	-	-	-	-
REPE/REPZ	-	-	-	-	-	-	-	-	-
REPNE/REPNZ	-	-	-	-	-	-	-	-	-
Move String									
MOVS dest$,source$	-	-	-	-	-	-	-	-	-
MOVSB	-	-	-	-	-	-	-	-	-
MOVSW	-	-	-	-	-	-	-	-	-
Compare Strings									
CMPS dest$,source$	*	-	-	-	*	*	*	*	*
CMPSB	*	-	-	-	*	*	*	*	*
CMPSW	*	-	-	-	*	*	*	*	*
Scan String									
SCAS dest$	*	-	-	-	*	*	*	*	*
SCASB	*	-	-	-	*	*	*	*	*
SCASW	*	-	-	-	*	*	*	*	*
Load and Store String									
LODS source$	-	-	-	-	-	-	-	-	-

Load and Store String

LODSB	•	•	•	•	•	•	•	•	•
LODSW	•	•	•	•	•	•	•	•	•
STOS dest$	•	•	•	•	•	•	•	•	•
STOSB	•	•	•	•	•	•	•	•	•
STOSW	•	•	•	•	•	•	•	•	•
Input and Output String									
INS dest$,DX	•	•	•	•	•	•	•	•	•
INSB	•	•	•	•	•	•	•	•	•
INSW	•	•	•	•	•	•	•	•	•
OUTS DX,source$	•	•	•	•	•	•	•	•	•
OUTSB	•	•	•	•	•	•	•	•	•
OUTSW	•	•	•	•	•	•	•	•	•

Direction

Because the string instructions are designed to operate on a series of elements (bytes or words), they automatically update their element pointer(s) to point to the next element in the string. The Direction Flag (DF) bit in the flags register determines whether an element pointer is increased or decreased at the end of a string instruction. That is, it determines whether the processor works forward or backward through a string.

If DF is 0, the processor increases the pointer, thereby addressing the next element. Conversely, if DF is 1, the processor decreases the pointer, to address the preceding element. The *Clear Direction Flag (CLD)* instruction makes DF 0, while *Set Direction Flag (STD)* makes it 1.

Repeat Prefixes

While the string instructions update their pointers automatically alone, they only operate on a single element. To make a string instruction operate on a series of elements, you must precede it with a *repeat prefix*. This makes the processor repeat the instruction based on a count in the CX register. For example, the sequence

```
        MOV   CX,500
REP     MOVS  DEST,SOURCE
```

makes the processor execute the Move String (MOVS) instruction 500 times, and decrement the CX register after each repetition. In effect, the *REP (Repeat)* prefix tells the processor "repeat MOVS until you reach the end of the string;" that is, repeat until CX reaches 0.

The remaining repeat prefixes involve the Zero Flag (ZF) in the repeat/quit decision. You can only apply them to the Compare String (CMPS) and Scan String (SCAS) instructions, which affect ZF. *Repeat While Equal (REPE)* repeats the instruction as long as CX is not 0 and ZF is 1. *Repeat While Not Equal (REPNE)* repeats as long as CX is not 0 and ZF is 0.

Move String

Move String (MOVS) copies a byte or word from one place in memory to another. It has the general format

```
MOVS dest$,source$
```

where *dest$* and *source$* are the names of the destination and source strings.

MOVS uses DI to point to the destination and SI to point to the source. Thus, if you want to move forward through a string (DF = 0), you must make SI and DI point to the beginning of the source and destination strings, respectively. To move backward through a string (DF = 1), you must make SI and DI point to the end of their respective strings. These rules for the initial pointer values apply to all string instructions, so I will not repeat them each time.

The following sequence copies the first 100 elements (bytes or words) of a string called OLD$ to a location labeled NEW$:

```
        CLD                ;Set DF to 0, to move forward
        LEA    SI,OLD$     ;Load OLD$ offset into SI
        LEA    DI,NEW$     ; and NEW$ offset into DI
        MOV    CX,100      ;Load element count into CX
REP     MOVS   NEW$,OLD$   ;Do the copy operation
```

Note that this program copies either bytes or words. How does the assembler know which you want to copy? It finds out from the labels you enter in the MOVS instruction. If they are defined with DB (Define Byte) directives, it puts a *Move Byte String (MOVSB)* instruction in memory; if they are defined with DW (Define Word) directives, it puts a *Move Word String (MOVSW)* string in memory.

Compare Strings

Like the Compare (CMP) instruction I discussed earlier, *Compare Strings (CMPS)* compares a source operand to a destination operand and returns the results in the flags. However, while CMP subtracts the source from the destination, CMPS does just the opposite: it subtracts the destination from the source! This means the conditional transfer instruction that follows a CMPS must be different from the one that follows a CMP. Table 3-11 shows what you need with CMPS.

To compare more than one element, you must precede CMPS with an REPE or REPNE prefix. REPE makes the processor compare until CX is zero or it finds two unalike elements. REPNE makes it compare the strings until CX is zero or it finds two identical elements.

The assembler translates CMPS to either CMPSB (for bytes) or CMPSW (for words).

Scan String

The Scan String (SCAS) instruction searches a string for a specific byte value (in AL) or word value (in AX), starting at the offset in DI. A scan is simply a compare-

46

Table 3-11. Using Conditional Transfers with CPMS.

	Follow CMPS with	
To jump if . . .	for unsigned numbers	for signed numbers
Destination > source	JB	JL
Destination = source	JE	JE
Destination not = source	JNE	JNE
Destination < source	JA	JG
Destination < or = source	JAE	JGE
Destination is > or =	JBE	JLE

with-accumulator operation, so it affects the flags in the same way as Compare Strings (CMPS).

As with CMPS, to operate on more than one element, apply the repeat prefix REPE or REPNE. For example, this sequence searches up to 100 elements of the byte string B$ looking for an element other than a space:

```
        CLD                 ;Search forward
        LEA     DI,B$       ;Load offset of B$ into DI
        MOV     AL,' '      ;Scan for a space
        MOV     CX,100      ;Search 100 bytes
REPE    SCAS    B$
```

If it finds a nonspace element, it returns the offset of the *next* element in DI and sets DI to 0. A subsequent JCXZ instruction indicates whether the element was found (no jump) or not found (jump).

The assembler translates SCAS to either SCASB (for bytes) or SCASW (for words).

Load and Store String

Load String (LODS) copies a string element addressed by SI to AL (byte) or AX (word) and then makes SI point to the next element. LODS increases SI if DF = 0 or decreases SI if DF = 1. As usual, LODS has the optional shorter forms LODSB and LODSW.

Store String (STOS) copies the byte in AL or word in AX to the string location addressed by DI and then makes DI point to the next element (if DF = 0) or the preceding element (if DF = 1).

Input and Output String

The new 80186/80286 instructions *Input String (INS)* and *Output String (OUTS)* are similar to IN and OUT, except they transfer data to or from a memory location rather than a register. The general forms are:

```
INS   dest$,DX
OUTS  DX,source$
```

where DX contains the port number. INS obtains the string's starting offset from DI; OUTS obtains it from SI. INS and OUTS are available in the size-specific forms INSB, INSW, OUTSB, and OUTSW.

INTERRUPT INSTRUCTIONS

Like a procedure call, an *interrupt* makes the processor save return information on the stack and then jump to an instruction sequence elsewhere in memory. A procedure call, however, makes the processor execute a procedure, while an interrupt makes it execute an *interrupt service routine* or *interrupt handler.*

An interrupt always makes an indirect jump to its handler. It does this by obtaining the handler's address from an *interrupt vector*, a 32-bit location in memory. In addition to saving the return address on the stack, it also saves the flags, as a PUSHF instruction does.

Interrupts can be activated by external devices in the system or by special interrupt instructions in the program. There are three interrupt-related instructions; two "calls" and one "return," as summarized in Table 3-12.

Table 3-12. Interrupt Instructions.

				Flags					
Assembler Format	**OF**	**DF**	**IF**	**TF**	**SF**	**ZF**	**AF**	**PF**	**CF**
INT immed8	-	-	0	0	-	-	-	-	-
INTO	-	-	0	0	-	-	-	-	-
IRET	*	*	*	*	*	*	*	*	*

The interrupt instruction has the general form

        INT   *immed8*

where *immed8* is the identification number of one of 256 interrupts in memory. When the processor executes an INT instruction, it does the following:

1. Pushes the flags register onto the stack.
2. Clears the Trap Flag (TF) and the Interrupt Enable Flag (IF), thereby disabling single-stepping and locking out other maskable interrupts.
3. Pushes the CS register onto the stack.
4. Calculates the address of the interrupt vector by multiplying the interrupt number in *immed8* by 4.
5. Copies the second word (segment number) of the interrupt vector into CS.
6. Pushes the IP onto the stack.
7. Copies the first word (offset) of the interrupt vector into IP.

In summary, INT saves the flags, CS, and IP on the stack, sets TF and IF to 0, and makes CS:IP point to the starting address of the interrupt handler.

As I mentioned earlier, the 256 interrupt vectors are located in the lowest locations in memory. Each vector is four bytes long, so they occupy the first 1K bytes, addresses 0 through 3FFH. For example, the instruction INT 1AH makes the processor calculate the vector address 68H (4 × 1AH). Thus, it obtains the 16-bit segment number and offset values from locations 68H and 6AH, respectively.

Interrupt if Overflow (INTO) is a conditional interrupt instruction; it generates an interrupt only if the Overflow Flag (OF) is 1. When that happens, INTO activates the type 4 interrupt.

Interrupt Return (IRET) is to interrupts what RET is to procedure calls; that is, it undoes the work of the original operation and makes the processor return to the calling program. For this reason, IRET must be the last instruction the processor executes in an interrupt handler. IRET pops three 16-bit values off the stack and loads them into the instruction pointer (IP), code segment (CS) register, and flags register, respectively.

PROCESSOR CONTROL INSTRUCTIONS

These instructions let you regulate the processor from within a program. As Table 3-13 shows, there are three kinds of processor control instructions: flag operations, external synchronization, and the do-nothing instruction, *No Operation (NOP)*.

Table 3-13. Processor Control Instructions.

Assembler Format	OF	DF	IF	TF	SF	ZF	AF	PF	CF
Flag Operations									
CLC	-	-	-	-	-	-	-	-	0
STC	-	-	-	-	-	-	-	-	1
CMC	-	-	-	-	-	-	-	-	*
CLI	-	-	0	-	-	-	-	-	-
STI	-	-	1	-	-	-	-	-	-
External Synchronization									
HLT	-	-	-	-	-	-	-	-	-
WAIT	-	-	-	-	-	-	-	-	-
ESC immed6,mem	-	-	-	-	-	-	-	-	-
ESC immed6,reg	-	-	-	-	-	-	-	-	-
LOCK	-	-	-	-	-	-	-	-	-
No Operation									
NOP	-	-	-	-	-	-	-	-	-

Flag Operations

There are five instructions that let you change the Carry Flag (CF) and Interrupt Enable Flag (IF). *Clear Carry Flag (CLC)* and *Set Carry Flag (STC)* force CF to a 0 or 1 state, respectively. These are useful to prepare CF for a rotate-with-carry (RCL or RCR) operation. *Complement Carry Flag (CMC)* makes CF 0 if it is 1, or vice versa.

Clear Interrupt Flag (CLI) puts 0 in IF, which makes the processor ignore maskable interrupts from external devices. You generally disable interrupts when the processor is performing some time-critical or high-priority task that must not be interrupted. The processor will still process nonmaskable interrupts while IF is 0, however. *Set Interrupt Flag (STI)* sets IF to 1, which lets the processor process maskable interrupts from external devices.

External Synchronization

These instructions synchronize the processor with external events. *Halt (HLT)* puts the processor in a halt state, in which it sits idle and executes no instructions. It leaves the halt state only if you reset it or it receives an external interrupt.

Wait (WAIT) puts the processor in an idle state, in which it halts, but also checks an input line called TEST every five clock intervals. While waiting, the processor services interrupts, but goes idle again upon returning from the interrupt handler.

Escape (ESC) makes the processor put the contents of a specified operand on its data bus. Thus, ESC provides a way for other processors (i.e., *coprocessors*) in the system to receive their instructions.

Lock the Bus (LOCK) is a one-byte prefix that may precede any instruction. LOCK makes the processor activate its LOCK line while the LOCKed instruction is executing. While LOCK is active, no other processor can use the bus.

No Operation

No Operation (NOP) does exactly what its name implies: it performs no operation whatsoever. NOP affects no flags, registers, or memory locations; it only increases the instruction pointer (IP).

NOP has a variety of uses. For example, you can use its opcode (90H) to patch object code when you want to delete an instruction without reassembling. NOP is also convenient for testing sequences of instructions. That is, you can put it at the end of a test program—a convenient spot at which to stop a trace.

80186/286 HIGH-LEVEL INSTRUCTIONS

There are three instructions that are intended for use by programmers who are writing compilers and interpreters for high-level languages such as BASIC, Pascal, or C (see Table 3-14). Since they aren't very useful to the average programmer, I won't spend much time on them.

The ENTER and LEAVE instructions are used to reserve and unreserve blocks of bytes on the stack for nested subroutines. ENTER takes two operands; the first specifies how many bytes are to be reserved, the second specifies the nesting level. LEAVE undoes ENTER's work by restoring the stack pointer to its original, pre-ENTER value.

The BOUND instruction is used to ensure that the user's attempt to access an element in a signed array is valid. Signed arrays begin with two word values that specify the array's boundaries. The first word contains the offset of the array's first element, the second word contains the offset of its last element.

Table 3-14. High-Level Instructions.

					Flags				
Assembler Format	OF	DF	IF	TF	SF	ZF	AF	PF	CF
ENTER immed16,0	-	-	-	-	-	-	-	-	-
ENTER immed16,1	-	-	-	-	-	-	-	-	-
ENTER immed16,level	-	-	-	-	-	-	-	-	-
LEAVE	-	-	-	-	-	-	-	-	-
BOUND reg16,mem32	-	-	-	-	-	-	-	-	-

80286 PROTECTED MODE INSTRUCTIONS

Besides the instructions I have just described, the 80286 recognizes several more that deal with its protected mode. To use these instructions, your program must precede them with a .286P directive. The protected mode is only for very experienced programmers. Hence, I simply list the protected mode instructions in Table 3-15. For details, refer to Intel Corporation's *iAPX 286 Programmer's Reference Manual.*

Table 3-15. 80286 Protected Mode Instructions.

Mnemonic	Description
ARPL	Adjust Requested Privilege Level
CLTS	Clear Task Switched Flag
LAR	Load Access Rights
LGDT	Load Global Descriptor Table Register
LIDT	Load Interrupt Descriptor Table Register
LLDT	Load Local Descriptor Table Register
LMSW	Load Machine Status Word
LSL	Load Segment Limit
LTR	Load Task Register
SGDT	Store Global Descriptor Table Register
SIDT	Store Interrupt Descriptor Table Register
SLDT	Store Local Descriptor Table Register
SMSW	Store Machine Status Word
STR	Store Task Register
VERR	Verify Read Access
VERW	Verify Write Access

Chapter 4

Program Models

The remaining chapters in this book present assembly language subroutines written in the COM (Command) format. Because they are subroutines, rather than complete programs, you need a *calling program* to use them. A calling program is the main program module, the one you run by mentioning its name to DOS or a debugger program (e.g., DEBUG or SYMDEB). Calling programs must do at least two things: they must call the subroutine and they must make a return to DOS or the debugger.

This chapter lists two models that you can use in your everyday work. These models are simply skeletons; that is, they contain the "boilerplate" that establishes the proper format for assembling (the COM format, in this case), but not the instructions. It's your job to insert the instructions. The first model is for a main module; use it to construct your calling programs. The second model is for a secondary module; use it to construct subroutines of your own design. (The subroutines in this book are complete secondary modules;'you needn't add the skeletal material.)

MAIN MODULE

Figure 4-1 shows the model for a source module that will contain a complete program or act as a calling program that will be linked with one or more secondary modules to form a program.

SECONDARY MODULE

Figure 4-2 shows the model for a secondary module that must be linked with the main module in Fig. 4-1 to form a program. Note that I have inserted *PNAME* to mark

```
(Insert EXTRN statements, if appropriate.)

CSEG   SEGMENT PARA PUBLIC 'CODE'
          ASSUME   CS:CSEG,DS:CSEG,ES:CSEG,SS:CSEG

          ORG    100H              ;Skip to end of the PSP
ENTRY:    JMP    START             ;Skip data

(Insert data here, if any.)

START     PROC   NEAR

(Insert instructions here.)

          RET                      ;Return to DOS or DEBUG
START     ENDP
CSEG  ENDS
          END    ENTRY
```

Fig. 4-1. Model for a main COM module.

```
          PUBLIC   PNAME
(Insert PUBLIC for data variables, if required.)
(Insert EXTRNs, if this module calls others.)

CSEG   SEGMENT  PARA PUBLIC 'CODE'
          ASSUME   CS:CSEG,DS:CSEG,ES:CSEG,SS:CSEG
          JMP    PNAME      ;Skip past data area

(Insert data here, if any.)

PNAME     PROC   NEAR

(Insert instructions here.)

          RET                      ;Return to calling program
PNAME     ENDP
CSEG  ENDS
          END
```

Fig. 4-2. Model for secondary COM module.

the place where the procedure (or subroutine) name belongs. When you create your own module, use your editor to replace PNAME with the name you want.

USING THE MODELS

You can create these models just as you would any other program: use EDLIN, an editor, or any word processing program that can produce pure ASCII text. Then, when you want to construct a new calling program or subroutine, copy the appropriate model and give the copy the name you want; then use the editor to insert your instructions and data.

Remember, too, that if your program consists of more than one module, the main module must contain an EXTRN directive that lists each subroutine it calls (e.g., EXTRN SUB1:NEAR,SUB2:NEAR). Similarly, each subroutine module must declare itself PUBLIC to allow other modules to call it. For example, a subroutine called SUB1 must include the directive PUBLIC SUB1.

Once you have created the main and secondary modules for your program, assemble them individually and then link them to form the EXE run file. Finally, use EXE2BIN to convert the run file to a COM file.

The code (program) segment in my models is named *CSEG*, but you can substitute another name. Just be sure to use the same name in every module. (The word NEAR in EXTRN directives and the PNAME PROC NEAR directive in the secondary module promises consistent names. It tells the linker that all modules are in the same code segment. Perhaps SAME would have been a more descriptive term, but the people who designed the assembler chose NEAR.)

54

Chapter 5

Memory Operations

This chapter provides subroutines that operate on blocks of bytes or words in memory. These subroutines are convenient for processing data tables.

FILL A MEMORY BLOCK WITH A BYTE VALUE (FILLMEMB)

FILLMEMB stores a selected value in each byte of a block of memory, starting at a given offset.

Operation

The subroutine repeatedly stores the byte value in AL, based on a repetition count in CX. After each store operation, the STOSB instruction increases the location pointer in DI by 1 and decreases the count in CX by 1.

Entry Values

DI =   Offset of the starting address
AL =   Byte value
CX =   Number of bytes to fill

Results

The block is filled with specified byte. The registers are unaffected.

Link Command

```
link callprog+fillmemb;
```

Special Case

A block size of zero causes an immediate exit with no memory locations changed.

Example

Fill a 100-byte table (BTABLE) with ASCII "space" characters:

```
                EXTRN   FILLMEMB:NEAR
ENTRY:          JMP     START           ;Skip past data area
BTABLE          DB      100 DUP(?)      ;Set up 100-byte table
START           PROC    NEAR

                MOV     CX,SEG BTABLE   ;Load segment number into ES
                MOV     ES,CX
                LEA     DI,BTABLE       ; and offset into DI
                MOV     AL,' '          ;Load "space" into AL
                MOV     CX,100          ; and byte count into CX ·
                CALL    FILLMEMB        ;Do the fill operation
```

Subroutine Listing

```
; FILLMEMB - Fills memory with a specified byte value.
; Inputs: DI = Offset of the starting address
```

```
;           AL = Byte value
;           CX = Number of bytes to fill
; Result: Block is filled with specified byte.
;           Registers are unaffected.

            PUBLIC  FILLMEMB
CSEG  SEGMENT  PARA PUBLIC 'CODE'
            ASSUME  CS:CSEG,DS:CSEG,ES:CSEG,SS:CSEG

FILLMEMB    PROC  NEAR
            JCXZ  EXIT        ;Exit if CX = 0
            PUSH  DI          ;Save affected registers
            PUSH  CX
            CLD               ;Work forward
REP         STOSB             ;Repeat STOS to fill memory
            POP   CX          ;Restore registers
            POP   DI
EXIT:       RET               ;Return to calling program
FILLMEMB    ENDP
CSEG  ENDS
            END
```

FILL A MEMORY BLOCK WITH A WORD VALUE (FILLMEMW)

FILLMEMW stores a selected value in each word of a block of memory, starting at a given offset.

Operation

The subroutine repeatedly stores the word value in AX, based on a repetition count in CX. After each store operation, the STOSW instruction increases the location pointer in DI by 2 (because word are two bytes long) and decreases the count in CX by 1.

Entry Values

DI = Offset of the starting address
AX = Word value
CX = Number of words to fill

Results

The block is filled with specified word. The registers are unaffected.

Link Command

```
link callprog+fillmemw;
```

Special Case

A block size of zero causes an immediate exit with no memory locations changed.

Example

Fill a 100-word table (WTABLE) with zeroes:

```
            EXTRN   FILLMEMW:NEAR
ENTRY:      JMP     START           ;Skip past data area
WTABLE      DW      100 DUP(?)      ;Set up 100-word table
START       PROC    NEAR

            MOV     CX,SEG WTABLE   ;Load segment number into ES
            MOV     ES,CX
            LEA     DI,WTABLE       ; and offset into DI
            MOV     AX,0            ;Load zero into AX
            MOV     CX,100          ; and word count into CX
            CALL    FILLMEMW        ;Do the fill operation
```

Subroutine Listing

```
; FILLMEMW - Fills memory with a specified word value.
; Inputs: DI = Offset of the starting address
;         AX = Word value
;         CX = Number of words to fill
; Result: Block is filled with specified word.
```

58

```
          PUBLIC  FILLMEMW
CSEG   SEGMENT  PARA PUBLIC 'CODE'
          ASSUME   CS:CSEG,DS:CSEG,ES:CSEG,SS:CSEG

FILLMEMW   PROC   NEAR
           JCXZ   EXIT        ;Exit if CX = 0
           PUSH   DI          ;Save affected registers
           PUSH   CX
           CLD                ;Work forward
REP        STOSW              ;Repeat STOS to fill memory
           POP    CX          ;Restore registers
           POP    DI
EXIT:      RET                ;Return to calling program
FILLMEMW   ENDP
CSEG   ENDS
           END
```

MOVE BLOCK OF BYTES (MOVBLOCK)

MOVBLOCK copies a block of bytes from one memory location to another.

Operation

The subroutine begins by checking whether the final location of the block (destination) is higher or lower in memory than its original location (source). If the destination is higher, the subroutine copies the block starting with the final byte; if the destination is lower, it copies the block from the beginning.

Using two different procedures guards against overwriting bytes that have not yet been moved. For example, if the block is to be moved one byte higher, starting at the beginning would cause the second byte to be overwritten when the first byte is copied. Thus, moving higher requires working from the end of the block, rather than the beginning.

Entry Values

SI = Offset of the source block
DI = Offset of the target block
CX = Number of bytes to move

Result

The block is copied to the destination location.

Link Command

```
link callprog+movblock;
```

Subroutine Listing

```
; MOVBLOCK - Moves a block of bytes in memory.
; Inputs: SI = Offset of the source address
;         DI = Offset of the destination address
;         CX = Number of bytes to move
; Result: The specified number of bytes are copied from
;         the source to the destination.
;         Registers are unaffected.

        PUBLIC  MOVBLOCK
CSEG    SEGMENT PARA PUBLIC 'CODE'
        ASSUME  CS:CSEG,DS:CSEG,ES:CSEG,SS:CSEG

MOVBLOCK PROC   NEAR
        PUSH    DI          ;Save affected registers
        PUSH    SI
        PUSH    CX
        CMP     DI,SI       ;Is destination higher in memory?
        JBE     LOWER
        STD                 ; Yes.  Work from end of block.
```

```
            ADD     SI,CX       ;  End Addr. = Start Addr. + CX - 1
            DEC     SI
            ADD     DI,CX
            DEC     DI
            JMP     MOVEM
LOWER:      CLD                 ; No.  Work from beginning of block.
MOVEM:
REP         MOVSB               ;Repeat MOVS to move bytes
            POP     CX          ;Restore registers
            POP     SI
            POP     DI
            RET                 ;Return to calling program
MOVBLOCK    ENDP
CSEG   ENDS
            END
```

COMPARE BLOCKS OF BYTES (COMPMEMB)

COMPMEMB compares the bytes in two blocks of memory, starting at given offsets.

Operation

The subroutine compares the bytes pointed to by SI and DI until a mismatch is encountered or the repetition count in CX has been decremented to 0. After each compare operation, the CMPSB instruction increases both location pointers by 1 and decreases CX by 1. If a mismatch is found, a SUB DI, 1 instruction "backs up" DI to make it point to the mismatching byte.

Entry Values

SI = Offset of the source block
DI = Offset of the target block
CX = Number of bytes to compare

Results

The Zero Flag (ZF) indicates the result of the compare. If ZF = 1, the blocks are identical and DI is unchanged. If ZF = 0, a mismatching byte was found and DI points to it. SI and CX are unaffected in either case.

Link Command

```
link callprog+compmemb;
```

Special Case

A byte count of zero causes an immediate exit with no memory locations compared.

Example

Compare two 100-byte tables, BTABLE1 and BTABLE2:

```
             EXTRN   COMPMEMB:NEAR
ENTRY:       JMP     START             ;Skip past data area
BTABLE1      DB      ..                ;Set up 100-byte tables
                     ..
BTABLE2      DB      ..
                     ..
START        PROC    NEAR

             MOV     CX,SEG BTABLE1 ;Point to source table with DS
             MOV     DS,CX
             LEA     SI,BTABLE1        ; and SI
             MOV     CX,SEG            ;Point to dest. table with ES
             MOV     ES,CX
             LEA     DI,BTABLE2        ; and DI
             MOV     CX,100            ;Load byte count into CX
```

```
            CALL    COMPMEMB        ;Do the compare operation
            JNE     MISMATCH        ;Are the blocks identical?
            ..                      ; If so, continue here
            ..
            RET
MISMATCH:   ..                      ; If not, continue here
            ..
            RET
```

Subroutine Listing

```
; COMPMEMB - Compares two blocks of bytes in memory.
; Inputs: SI = Offset of the source block
;         DI = Offset of the target block
;         CX = Number of bytes to compare
; Results: If the blocks compare, DI is unchanged and ZF = 1.
;          If a mismatching byte is found, DI holds its offset
;          and ZF = 0.
;          SI and CX are unchanged in either case.
            PUBLIC  COMPMEMB
CSEG   SEGMENT    PARA PUBLIC 'CODE'
            ASSUME  CS:CSEG,DS:CSEG,ES:CSEG,SS:CSEG

COMPMEMB    PROC    NEAR
            JCXZ    QUIT            ;Quit if CX = 0
            PUSH    CX              ;Save input values
            PUSH    SI
            PUSH    DI
            CLD                     ;Work forward
REPE        CMPSB                   ;Compare the blocks
            JZ      MATCH           ;Do the blocks match?
            PUSHF                   ; No.  Save Zero Flag on stack,
            SUB     DI,1            ;  point to the mismatched byte,
            POPF                    ;  restore Zero Flag,
            POP     CX              ;  and discard old DI value.
            JMP     EXIT
MATCH:      POP     DI              ; Yes.  Restore DI
EXIT:       POP     SI              ;Restore SI
            POP     CX              ; and CX
QUIT:       RET                     ;Return to calling program
COMPMEMB    ENDP
CSEG   ENDS
            END
```

COMPARE BLOCKS OF WORDS (COMPMEMW)

COMPMEMW compares the words in two blocks of memory, starting at given offsets.

Operation

The subroutine compares the words pointed to by SI and DI until a mismatch is encountered or the repetition count in CX has been decremented to 0. After each compare operation, the CMPSW instruction increases both location pointers by 2 (because words are two bytes long) and decreases CX by 1. If a mismatch is found, a SUB DI,2 instruction "backs up" DI to make it point to the mismatching word.

Entry Values

SI = Offset of the source block
DI = Offset of the target block
CX = Number of words to compare

Results

The Zero Flag (ZF) indicates the result of the compare. If ZF = 1, the blocks are identical and DI is unchanged. If ZF = 0, a mismatching word was found and DI points to it. SI and CX are unaffected in either case.

Link Command

```
link callprog+compmemw;
```

Special Case

A word count of zero causes an immediate exit with no memory locations compared.

Subroutine Listing

```
; COMPMEMW - Compares two blocks of words in memory.
; Inputs: SI = Offset of the source block
;         DI = Offset of the target block
;         CX = Number of words to compare
; Results: If the blocks compare, DI is unchanged and ZF = 1.
;          If a mismatching word is found, DI holds its offset
;            and ZF = 0.
;          SI and CX are unchanged in either case.

        PUBLIC  COMPMEMW
CSEG    SEGMENT  PARA PUBLIC 'CODE'
        ASSUME  CS:CSEG,DS:CSEG,ES:CSEG,SS:CSEG

COMPMEMW    PROC NEAR
        JCXZ    QUIT  ;Exit if CX = 0
        PUSH    CX    ;Save input values
        PUSH    SI
```

```
        PUSH   DI
        CLD            ;Work forward
REPE  CMPSW            ;Compare the blocks
        JZ     MATCH   ;Do the blocks match?
        PUSHF          ;No.  Save Zero Flag on stack,
        SUB    DI,2    ;point to the mismatched word,
        POPF           ;restore Zero Flag,
        POP    CX      ;and discard old DI value.
        JMP    EXIT
MATCH:        POP    DI; Yes.  Restore DI
EXIT:         POP    SI;Restore SI
              POP    CX   ; and CX
QUIT:         RET    ;Return to calling program
COMPMEMW      ENDP
CSEG   ENDS
        END
```

FIND A BYTE VALUE IN A MEMORY BLOCK (FINDBYTE)

FINDBYTE searches for a selected byte value in a block of memory, starting at a given offset.

Operation

The subroutine searches for the byte value in AL in the block pointed to by DI. It continues searching until it finds the byte or CX has been decremented to 0. After each search, or scan, operation, the SCASB instruction increases the location pointer in DI by 1 and decreases the count in CX by 1. If the byte is found, a SUB DI,1 instruction "backs up" DI to make it point to the byte.

Entry Values

DI = Offset of the starting address
AL = Byte value
CX = Number of bytes to search

Results

The Zero Flag (ZF) indicates the result of the search. If the search is unsuccessful, DI is unchanged and ZF = 0. If the byte is found, DI points to it and ZF = 1. AL and CX are unaffected in either case.

Link Command

```
link callprog+findbyte;
```

Special Case

A byte count of zero causes an immediate exit with no memory locations searched.

Example

Search a 100-byte table (TEXT) for the first $ character:

```
            EXTRN   FINDBYTE:NEAR
ENTRY:      JMP     START           ;Skip past data area
TEXT        DB      ..              ;Table to be searched
                    ..
START       PROC    NEAR

            MOV     CX,SEG TEXT     ;Load segment number into ES
            MOV     ES,CX
            LEA     DI,TEXT         ; and offset into DI
            MOV     AL,'$'          ;Load "$" into AL
            MOV     CX,100          ; and byte count into CX
            CALL    FINDBYTE        ;Do the search operation
```

Subroutine Listing

```
;  FINDBYTE - Searches memory for a specified byte value.
;  Inputs: DI = Offset of the starting address
;          AL = Byte value
;          CX = Number of bytes to search
;  Results: If byte is found, DI holds its offset and ZF = 1.
;           If byte is not found, DI is unchanged and ZF = 0.
;           AL and CX are unaffected in either case.

          PUBLIC  FINDBYTE
CSEG    SEGMENT  PARA PUBLIC 'CODE'
          ASSUME   CS:CSEG,DS:CSEG,ES:CSEG,SS:CSEG

FINDBYTE  PROC   NEAR
          JCXZ   QUIT       ;Exit if CX = 0
          PUSH   CX         ;Save input values
          PUSH   DI
          CLD               ;Search forward
REPNE     SCASB             ;Scan memory block for byte

          JNZ    NOT_FOUND  ;Was the byte found?
          PUSHF             ; Yes.  Save Zero Flag on stack,
          SUB    DI,1       ;  point to the byte,
          POPF              ;  restore Zero Flag,
          POP    CX         ;  and discard old DI value.
          JMP    EXIT
NOT_FOUND: POP   DI         ; No.  Restore DI
EXIT:     POP    CX         ;Restore CX
QUIT:     RET               ;Return to calling program
FINDBYTE  ENDP
CSEG    ENDS
          END
```

FIND A WORD VALUE IN A MEMORY BLOCK (FINDWORD)

FINDWORD searches for a selected word value in a block of memory, starting at a given offset.

Operation

The subroutine searches for the word value in AX in the block pointed to by DI. It continues searching until it finds the word or CX has been decremented to 0. After each search, or scan, operation, the SCASW instruction increases the location pointer in DI by 2 (because words are two bytes long) and decreases the count in CX by 1. If the word is found, a SUB DI,2 instruction "backs up" DI to make it point to the word.

Entry Values

DI = Offset of the starting address
AX = Word value
CX = Number of words to search

Results

The Zero Flag (ZF) indicates the result of the search. If the search is unsuccessful, DI is unchanged and ZF = 0. If the word is found, DI points to it and ZF = 1. AL and CX are unaffected in either case.

Link Command

```
link callprog+findword;
```

Special Case

A word count of zero causes an immediate exit with no memory locations searched.

Subroutine Listing

```
; FINDWORD - Searches memory for a specified word value.
; Inputs: DI = Offset of the starting address
;         AX = Word value
;         CX = Number of words to search
; Results: If word is found, DI holds its offset and ZF = 1.
;          If word is not found, DI is unchanged and ZF = 0.

      PUBLIC  FINDWORD
CSEG  SEGMENT  PARA PUBLIC 'CODE'
      ASSUME  CS:CSEG,DS:CSEG,ES:CSEG,SS:CSEG

FINDWORD   PROC NEAR
     JCXZ   QUIT ;Exit if CX = 0
     PUSH   CX    ;Save input values
     PUSH   DI
     CLD          ;Search forward
REPNE       SCASW;Scan memory block for word
```

```
        JNZ    NOT_FOUND   ;Was the word found?
        PUSHF            ; Yes.  Save Zero Flag on stack,
        SUB    DI,2 ;  point to the word,
        POPF             ;  restore Zero Flag,
        POP    CX    ;  and discard old DI value.
        JMP    EXIT
NOT_FOUND: POP  DI; No.  Restore DI
EXIT:      POP  CX;Restore CX
QUIT:      RET  ;Return to calling program
FINDWORD   ENDP
CSEG ENDS
        END
```

TAKE THE AVERAGE OF UNSIGNED WORDS (AVERAGEU)

AVERAGEU takes the average of a specified number of consecutive unsigned words in memory.

Operation

The subroutine uses the 32-bit register combination DX (high part) and AX (low part) to hold the sum of the words, because these are the registers required by the DIV (unsigned divide) instruction. A loop at ADD__W adds each word to the total, propagates any carry into DX, and increases the word pointer BX by 2 (because words are two bytes long). When all words have been added, the total in DX:AX is divided by the word count in CX, to produce the average. The integer part of the result is returned in AX, while the remainder is returned in DX.

Entry Values

BX =   Offset of the first word
CX =   Number of words to average

Results

AX = Integer portion of the average
DX = Fractional remainder
BX and CX are unaffected.

Link Command

```
link callprog+averageu;
```

Special Case

A word count of zero causes an immediate exit with no memory locations averaged.

Example

Take the average of the first 10 words in the table WTABLEU:

```
          EXTRN   AVERAGEU:NEAR
ENTRY:    JMP     START             ;Skip past data area
WTABLEU   DW      ..                ;The table goes here
                  ..
START     PROC    NEAR

          LEA     BX,WTABLEU        ;Load offset into BX
          MOV     CX,10             ; and word count into CX
          CALL    AVERAGEU          ;Do the average operation
```

Subroutine Listing

```
; AVERAGEU - Takes the average of a specified number of
; unsigned word values.
; Inputs: BX = Offset of first word
;         CX = Word count
; Results: AX = Integer portion of the average
;          DX = Fractional remainder
; BX and CX are unaffected.

          PUBLIC  AVERAGEU
CSEG  SEGMENT  PARA PUBLIC 'CODE'
          ASSUME  CS:CSEG,DS:CSEG,ES:CSEG,SS:CSEG

AVERAGEU  PROC  NEAR
          JCXZ  EXIT              ;Exit if CX = 0
          PUSH  BX                ;Save starting offset
          SUB   AX,AX             ;Clear dividend to start
          SUB   DX,DX
          PUSH  CX                ;Save word count on stack
ADD_W:    ADD   AX,[BX]           ;Add word to total
          ADC   DX,0
          ADD   BX,2              ; and point to next word
          LOOP  ADD_W             ;All words now totaled?
          POP   CX                ; Yes. Retrieve word count
          DIV   CX                ;  and take the average
          POP   BX                ;Restore offset
EXIT:     RET
AVERAGEU ENDP
CSEG  ENDS
          END
```

TAKE THE AVERAGE OF SIGNED WORDS (AVERAGES)

AVERAGES takes the average of a specified number of consecutive signed words in memory.

Operation

The subroutine uses the 32-bit register combination DX (high part) and AX (low part) to hold the sum of the words, because these are the registers required by the IDIV (signed divide) instruction. A loop at ADD__W adds each word to the total, propagates any carry into DX, and increases the word pointer BX by 2 (because words are two bytes long). If the sum ever goes negative, the value in DX is forced negative by adding FFFF (-1) to it. When all words have been added, the total in DX:AX is divided by the word count in CX, to produce the average. The integer part of the result is returned in AX, while the remainder is returned in DX.

Entry Values

BX =   Offset of the first word
CX =   Number of words to average

Results

AX = Integer portion of the average
DX = Fractional remainder
BX and CX are unaffected.

Link Command

```
link callprog+averages;
```

Special Case

A word count of zero causes an immediate exit with no memory locations averaged.

Subroutine Listing

```
; AVERAGES - Takes the average of a specified number of
; signed word values.
; Inputs: BX = Offset of first word
;         CX = Word count
; Results: AX = Integer portion of the average
;          DX = Fractional remainder
; BX and CX are unaffected.

        PUBLIC  AVERAGES
CSEG   SEGMENT  PARA PUBLIC 'CODE'
        ASSUME  CS:CSEG,DS:CSEG,ES:CSEG,SS:CSEG
AVERAGES  PROC  NEAR
        JCXZ   EXIT            ;Exit if CX = 0
```

```
            PUSH    BX              ;Save starting offset
            SUB     AX,AX           ;Clear dividend to start
            SUB     DX,DX
            PUSH    CX              ;Save word count on stack
ADD_W:      ADD     AX,[BX]         ;Add next word to total
            JS      NEGATIVE        ;Is result positive?
            ADC     DX,0            ; Yes.  Add carry to DX
            JMP     NEXT_WORD
NEGATIVE:   CMP     DX,0            ; No.  Make DX negative
            JS      NEXT_WORD       ;   if it isn't already
            ADD     DX,0FFFFH
NEXT_WORD:  ADD     BX,2            ;Point to next word
            LOOP    ADD_W           ;All words now totaled?
            POP     CX              ; Yes.Retrieve word count
            IDIV    CX              ;   and take the average
            POP     BX              ;Restore offset
EXIT:       RET
AVERAGES    ENDP
CSEG   ENDS
            END
```

Chapter 6

32-Bit Binary Arithmetic

As I mentioned earlier, the 8086, 8088, and 80286 microprocessors can process only two sizes of data directly: 8-bit bytes and 16-bit words. A byte can represent unsigned numbers from 0 to 255 or signed numbers from -128 to $+127$. A word can represent unsigned numbers from 0 to 65535 or signed numbers from -32768 to $+32767$. Bytes and words are adequate for most applications, but scientific, statistical, and financial applications often involve processing numbers that are larger than 32767. To work with large numbers using assembly language, you can combine some of the available byte- and word-size instructions.

This chapter lists subroutines that add, subtract, multiply, and compare 32-bit numbers, both unsigned and signed. It also includes a subroutine that extracts the square root of a 32-bit integer. All numbers are in binary format; the next chapter presents subroutines that operate on binary-coded decimal (BCD) numbers.

The subroutines in this chapter obtain 32-bit operands from pairs of 16-bit registers that are treated as if they were connected. For example, a 32-bit addition subroutine called ADDU32 obtains one operand from the AX and BX registers and the other operand from the CX and DX registers. (Here, AX and CX contain the high-order 16 bits, while BX and DX contain the low-order 16 bits.) A basic problem in working with 32-bit numbers is how to get them into the registers in the first place.

LOADING 32-BIT NUMBERS INTO REGISTERS

Since the microprocessor's registers are only 16 bits wide, the assembler does not provide instructions that let you load larger numbers into them directly. How, then, can you set up the registers for use by our 32-bit subroutines?

If your numbers are in *hexadecimal* form, dividing them between the registers is easy. You simply enter the four leftmost digits into the high-order register and enter the four rightmost digits into the low-order register. For example, to load 1234ABCDH into the register pair AX:BX, you would enter 1234 into AX and ABCD into BX.

Entering 32-bit *decimal* numbers is somewhat more difficult, because unless the numbers are no more than 16 bits long, you'll have trouble deciding how much goes in each register. If, however, the numbers are stored as 32-bit data items in memory (they are defined with DD directives), you can let the assembler divide them between the registers. To do this, you use MOV instructions with the PTR operand in the source operand field. For example, if the 32-bit variable MILLION is defined as

```
MILLION   DD   1000000
```

you can read its value into AX (high part) and BX (low part) with

```
MOV   AX,WORD PTR MILLION+2
MOV   BX,WORD PTR MILLION
```

These instructions load 0FH (decimal 983040) into AX and 4240H (decimal 16960) into BX.

Incidentally, note that I used MILLION + 2 to obtain the high-order portion. This reflects the backward way the microprocessor stores data in memory: with the most-significant half *preceding* (rather than following) the least-significant half.

UNSIGNED BINARY ADDITION (ADDU32)

ADDU32 adds two 32-bit unsigned operands in registers and returns the sum in the second operand.

Operation

The subroutine adds the operand in AX:BX to the operand in CX:DX, 16 bits at a time, and returns the result in CX:DX. If the result is too large to fit in CX:DX, the add operation produces a carry, which sets the Carry Flag (CF) to 1.

Entry Values

CX:BX =   First operand
CX:DX =   Second operand

Results

AX:DX =   Result

If the result cannot fit in CX:DX, then CF = 1.
AX and BX are unaffected.

Link Command

```
link callprog+addu32;
```

Comment

Generally, you should follow CALL ADDU32 with an instruction of the form JC ERROR, where ERROR is a set of instructions that processes an invalid result.

Subroutine Listing

```
; ADDU32 - Adds two unsigned 32-bit numbers.
; Inputs: AX:BX = First operand
;         CX:DX = Second operand
; Results: CX:DX = Result
;          If the result cannot fit in CX:DX, then CF = 1.
;          AX and BX are unaffected.

        PUBLIC  ADDU32
CSEG    SEGMENT PARA PUBLIC 'CODE'
        ASSUME  CS:CSEG,DS:CSEG,ES:CSEG,SS:CSEG

ADDU32    PROC  NEAR
          ADD   DX,BX    ;Add the low-order 16 bits
          ADC   CX,AX    ;Add the high-order 16 bits
```

```
            RET                ;Return to calling program
ADDU32      ENDP
CSEG   ENDS
            END
```

UNSIGNED BINARY SUBTRACTION (SUBU32)

SUBU32 subtracts two 32-bit unsigned operands in registers and returns the difference in the minuend (the operand from which the subtrahend is subtracted).

Operation

The subroutine subtracts the subtrahend in AX:BX from the minuend in CX:DX, 16 bits at a time, and returns the result in CX:DX. If the number in AX:BX is greater than the number in CX:DX, the result will be negative. In that case, the subtract operation produces a borrow, which sets the Carry Flag (CF) to 1.

Entry Values

AX:BX =   Subtrahend (number to be subtracted)
CX:DX =   Minuend

Results

CX:DX =   Result
If the result is negative, then CF = 1.
AX and BX are unaffected.

Link Command

```
link callprog+subu32;
```

Comment

Generally, you should follow CALL SUBU32 with an instruction of the form JC ERROR, where ERROR is a set of instructions that processes an invalid result.

Subroutine Listing

```
; SUBU32 - Subtracts unsigned 32-bit numbers.
; Inputs: AX:BX = Number to be subtracted from second operand.
;         CX:DX = Second operand
; Results: CX:DX = Result
;          If the result is negative (AX:BX > CX:DX), CF = 1.
;          AX and BX are unaffected.

        PUBLIC  SUBU32
CSEG    SEGMENT PARA PUBLIC 'CODE'
        ASSUME  CS:CSEG,DS:CSEG,ES:CSEG,SS:CSEG

SUBU32    PROC  NEAR
          SUB   DX,BX     ;Subtract the low-order 16 bits
          SBB   CX,AX     ;Subtract the high-order 16 bits
          RET             ;Return to calling program
SUBU32    ENDP
CSEG    ENDS
        END
```

UNSIGNED BINARY MULTIPLICATION (MULU32)

MULU32 multiplies two 32-bit unsigned operands in registers and returns the 64-bit product in the same registers.

Operation

To multiply the multiplicand in DX:AX by the multiplier in CX:BX, the subroutine calculates a series of *cross products* and then combines them to form the final 64-bit product. Figure 6-1 illustrates how the subroutine derives the four cross products and aligns them to calculate the 64-bit final product. The four circled numbers indicate the 16-bit additions that are to form the product. (For example, Addition 1 adds the high 16 bits of Product #1 to the low 16 bits of Product #2.)

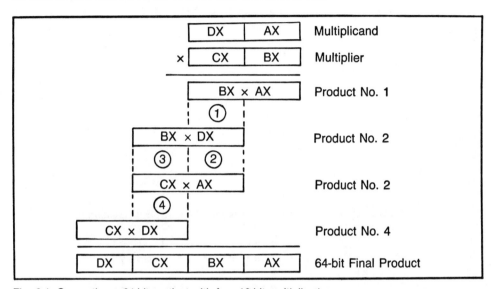

Fig. 6-1. Generating a 64-bit product with four 16-bit multiplications.

The subroutine uses two word-size memory locations to hold each cross product as it is calculated; the first locations hold the high-order 16 bits, the second hold the low-order 16 bits. For example, locations HI_PP1 and LOW_PP1 are used to store Product #1.

Entry Values

CX:BX = Multiplier
DX:AX = Multiplicand

Results

Product in DX, CX, BX, and AX (high to low order).

Link Command

```
link callprog+mulu32;
```

Subroutine Listing

```
;  MULU32  -  Multiplies  two  32-bit  unsigned  numbers  and  generates
;    a  64-bit  product.
;  Inputs:  CX:BX  =  Multiplier
;           DX:AX  =  Multiplicand
;  Result:  Product  in  DX,  CX,  BX,  and  AX  (high  to  low  order).

                PUBLIC    MULU32
CSEG    SEGMENT   PARA  PUBLIC  'CODE'
                ASSUME    CS:CSEG,DS:CSEG,SS:CSEG,ES:CSEG

                JMP     MULU32            ;Skip  past  data  area
HI_MCND    DW      ?
LO_MCND    DW      ?
HI_PP1     DW      ?
LO_PP1     DW      ?
HI_PP2     DW      ?
LO_PP2     DW      ?
HI_PP3     DW      ?
LO_PP3     DW      ?
HI_PP4     DW      ?
LO_PP4     DW      ?

MULU32     PROC   NEAR

                MOV     HI_MCND,DX        ;Save  multiplicand  in  memory
                MOV     LO_MCND,AX
                MUL     BX                ;Form  partial  product  #1
                MOV     HI_PP1,DX         ;  and  save  it  in  memory
                MOV     LO_PP1,AX
                MOV     AX,HI_MCND        ;Form  partial  product  #2
                MUL     BX
                MOV     HI_PP2,DX         ;  and  save  it  in  memory
                MOV     LO_PP2,AX
                MOV     AX,LO_MCND        ;Form  partial  product  #3
                MUL     CX
                MOV     HI_PP3,DX         ;  and  save  it  in  memory
                MOV     LO_PP3,AX
                MOV     AX,HI_MCND        ;Form  partial  product  #4
                MUL     CX
                MOV     HI_PP4,DX         ;  and  save  it  in  memory
                MOV     LO_PP4,AX

;  Add  the  partial  products  to  form  the  final  64-bit  product.

                MOV     AX,LO_PP1         ;Low  16  bits
                MOV     BX,HI_PP1         ;Form  mid-lower  16  bits
                ADD     BX,LO_PP2         ;  with  sum  #1
                ADC     HI_PP2,0
                ADD     BX,LO_PP3         ;  and  sum  #2
```

```
        MOV     CX,HI_PP2          ;Form mid-upper 16 bits
        ADC     CX,HI_PP3          ; with sum #3
        ADC     HI_PP4,0
        ADD     CX,LO_PP4          ; and sum #4
        MOV     DX,HI_PP4          ;Form high 16 bits
        ADC     DX,0               ; including propagated carry
        RET                        ;Return to calling program
MULU32  ENDP
CSEG  ENDS
        END
```

UNSIGNED BINARY COMPARISON (COMPU32)

COMPU32 compares two 32-bit unsigned operands in registers and reports the result in status flags.

Operation

The subroutine compares the operands in AX:BX and CX:DX, 16 bits at a time, and reports the result in the Zero Flag (ZF) and Carry Flag (CF). If the high words differ, it must make only one comparison; if they match, it must make a second comparison to determine whether or not the low words also match.

Entry Values

AX:BX =   First operand
CX:DX =   Second operand

Results

If the operands are identical, then ZF = 1.
If operand 1 is greater, then ZF = 0 and CF = 0.
If operand 2 is greater, then ZF = 0 and CF = 1.
The registers are unaffected.

Link Command

```
link callprog+compu32;
```

Example

Compare two 32-bit unsigned operands:

```
          EXTRN  COMPU32:NEAR
          CALL   COMPU32   ;Make the comparison
          JE     SAME      ;Are the operands identical?
          JNC    OP1GRTR   ; No. Check Carry Flag.
          ..               ;Continue here if op. 2 > op. 1
          ..
SAME:     ..               ;Continue here if op. 1 = op. 2
          ..
OP1GRTR:  ..               ;Continue here if op. 1 > op. 2
          ..
```

Subroutine Listing

```
; COMPU32 - Compares two unsigned 32-bit numbers.
; Inputs: AX:BX = First operand
;         CX:DX = Second operand
; Results: If the operands are identical, then ZF = 1.
```

```
;              If operand 1 is greater, then ZF = 0 and CF = 0.
;              If operand 2 is greater, then ZF = 0 and CF = 1.
;              Registers are unaffected.

           PUBLIC   COMPU32
CSEG   SEGMENT  PARA PUBLIC 'CODE'
           ASSUME   CS:CSEG,DS:CSEG,ES:CSEG,SS:CSEG

COMPU32    PROC  NEAR
           CMP   AX,CX     ;Compare high 16 bits
           JNZ   EXIT
           CMP   BX,DX     ;Compare low 16 bits
EXIT:      RET             ;Return to calling program
COMPU32    ENDP
CSEG   ENDS
           END
```

SQUARE ROOT (SQRT32)

SQRT32 extracts the square root of a 32-bit integer.

Operation

The subroutine calculates the square root using Newton's Method, which states that if A is an approximation for the square root of a number N, then

$$A1 = (N/A + A)/2$$

is a better approximation.

To get the first approximation, the subroutine uses the formula (N/200) + 2, where N is the contents of DX:AX and the value 200 is arbitrary. To get the second approximation, it divides N by the first approximation and then averages the two results. To get the third approximation, it divides N by the second approximation, then averages, and so on. It repeats this procedure until it encounters two approximations that are identical or differ by only 1.

The loop at NXT_APP extends to the label DONE. With each pass, it calculates a new approximation by dividing the 32-bit source number (read from the stack) by the preceding approximation and then averaging the two results. To average results, it shifts AX to the right, which effectively divides it by 2.

The subroutine checks each new approximation against the preceding one, looking for approximations that are identical or differ by only 1 (+1 or −1). If either of these conditions occurs, it transfers to DONE; otherwise, it returns to NXT_APP to calculate the next approximation. At DONE, it puts the final square root in BX, and then pops the source number (AX and DX) and the original value of BP off the stack.

Entry Value

DX:AX = Integer

Results

BX = Square root
DX and AX are unaffected.

Link Command

```
link callprog+sqrt32;
```

Subroutine Listing

```
;   SQRT32 - Calculates the square root of a 32-bit integer.
;   Input: DX:AX = Integer
;   Result: BX = Square root
;   The original number in DX:AX is unaffected.

        PUBLIC  SQRT32
CSEG    SEGMENT  PARA PUBLIC 'CODE'
```

```
        ASSUME   CS:CSEG,DS:CSEG,ES:CSEG,SS:CSEG

SQRT32      PROC   NEAR
            PUSH   BP                 ;Save contents of BP
            PUSH   DX                 ; and source number DX:AX
            PUSH   AX
            MOV    BP,SP              ;BP points to AX on the stack
            MOV    BX,200             ;As a first approximation,
            DIV    BX                 ; divide source number by 200,
            ADD    AX,2               ; then add 2
NXT_APP:    MOV    BX,AX              ;Save this approx. in BX
            MOV    AX,[BP]            ;Read source number again
            MOV    DX,[BP+2]
            DIV    BX                 ;Divide by last approx.
            ADD    AX,BX              ;Average last two approxs.
            SHR    AX,1
            CMP    AX,BX              ;Last two approxs. identical?
            JE     DONE
            SUB    BX,AX              ; No. Check for diff. of 1
            CMP    BX,1
            JE     DONE
            CMP    BX,-1
            JNE    NXT_APP
DONE:       MOV    BX,AX              ;Put result in BX
            POP    AX                 ;Restore source number
            POP    DX
            POP    BP                 ; and scratch register BP
            RET
SQRT32      ENDP
CSEG  ENDS
            END
```

SIGNED BINARY ADDITION (ADDS32)

ADDS32 adds two 32-bit signed operands in registers and returns the sum in the second operand.

Operation

The subroutine adds the operand in AX:BX to the operand in CX:DX, 16 bits at a time, and returns the result in CX:DX. If the result cannot fit in CX:DX, the add operation produces a carry, which sets the Carry Flag (CF) to 1. If adding two like-signed numbers (both positive or both negative) produces a result that exceeds the two's complement range of CX:DX, which changes the sign, then the Overflow Flag (OF) is set to 1.

The subroutine operates only on positive numbers. If either operand (or both operands) is negative, the subroutine two's complements it before doing the addition. Two's complementing is done by a macro called COMP, which takes parameters that have the general names "hireg" and "loreg." To complement the first operand, the subroutine substitutes AX and BX for hireg and loreg; to complement the second, it substitutes CX and DX.

Entry Values

AX:BX = First operand
CX:DX = Second operand

Results

CX:DX = Result
If the result cannot fit in CX:DX, then CF = 1.
If the operation changes the sign illegally, then OF = 1.
AX and BX are unaffected.

Link Command

```
link callprog+adds32;
```

Comment

Generally, you should follow CALL ADDS32 with instructions of the form

```
JC   OUT_OF_RANGE
JC   OVERFLOW
```

where OUT_OF_RANGE is a set of instructions that processes a too-large or too-small result and OVERFLOW is a set of instructions that deals with overflow (i.e., an unexpected change of sign).

Subroutine Listing

```
; ADDS32 - Adds two signed 32-bit numbers.
; Inputs: AX:BX = First operand
```

```
;            CX:DX = Second operand
; Results: CX:DX = Result
;            If the result cannot fit in CX:DX, then CF = 1.
;            If the result exceeds the two's complement range
;             of CX:DX, which changes the sign, then OF = 1.
;            AX and BX are unaffected.


; The following macro two's-complements the register
; combination hireg:lowreg

COMP  MACRO  hireg,loreg
        NOT   loreg
        ADD   loreg,1
        NOT   hireg
        ADC   hireg,0
      ENDM


        PUBLIC  ADDS32
CSEG  SEGMENT  PARA PUBLIC 'CODE'
        ASSUME  CS:CSEG,DS:CSEG,ES:CSEG,SS:CSEG

ADDS32    PROC  NEAR
        PUSH  AX         ;Preserve first operand
        PUSH  BX

; If both operands are positive, add them directly.

        PUSH  CX
        OR    CX,AX
        POP   CX
        JS    NEGS       ;Jump if not positive
        ADD   DX,BX      ;Add the low-order 16 bits
        ADC   CX,AX      ;Add the high-order 16 bits
        JMP   EXIT

; If both operands are negative, complement them, then
; add and complement the result.

NEGS:     TEST  AX,CX
        JNS   OPP_SIGNS
        COMP  AX,BX      ;Complement both operands
        COMP  CX,DX
        ADD   DX,BX      ;Add the low-order 16 bits
        ADC   CX,AX      ;Add the high-order 16 bits
        JMP   COMP_RES ;Go complement the result

; The operands have opposite signs.  Before adding them,
; we must make them both positive.

OPP_SIGNS: TEST AX,8000H ;Is operand 1 negative?
        JNS   OP2_NEG
```

```
                COMP    AX,BX       ; Yes. Two's-complement it
                SUB     DX,BX       ;Subtract the low 16 bits
                SBB     CX,AX       ;Subtract the high 16 bits
                JMP     EXIT
OP2_NEG:        COMP    CX,DX       ;Two's-complement operand 2
                SUB     DX,BX       ;Subtract the low 16 bits
                SBB     CX,AX       ;Subtract the high 16 bits
                CMP     CX,0        ;If CX = 0 and DX = 0, exit
                JNZ     COMP_RES    ; otherwise, complement the result
                CMP     DX,0
                JZ      EXIT
COMP_RES:       COMP    CX,DX       ;Two's-complement the result
EXIT:           POP     BX          ;Restore saved registers
                POP     AX
                RET                 ;Return to calling program
ADDS32          ENDP
CSEG    ENDS
                END
```

SIGNED BINARY SUBTRACTION (SUBS32)

SUBS32 subtracts two 32-bit signed operands in registers and returns the difference in the minuend (the number from which the subtrahend is subtracted).

Operation

The subroutine subtracts the subtrahend in AX:BX from the minuend in CX:DX, 16 bits at a time, and returns the result in CX:DX. If the subtract operation gives a negative result that is too large to fit in CX:DX, it produces a borrow, which sets the Carry Flag (CF) to 1. If subtracting a positive number from a negative number (or vice versa) produces a result that exceeds the two's complement range of CX:DX, which changes the sign, the Overflow Flag (OF) is set to 1.

The subroutine operates only on positive numbers. If either operand (or both operands) is negative, the subroutine two's complements it before subtracting the operands. Two's complementing is done by a macro called COMP, which takes parameters that have the general names "hireg" and "loreg." To complement the first operand, the subroutine substitutes AX and BX for hireg and loreg; to complement the second operand, it substitutes CX and DX.

Entry Values

AX:BX = Subtrahend (number to be subtracted)
CX:DX = Minuend

Results

CX:DX = Result
If the result is negative, then CF = 1.
If the result is a too-large negative number, then OF = 1.
AX and BX are unaffected.

Link Command

```
link callprog+subs32;
```

Comment

Generally, you should follow CALL SUBS32 with instructions of the form

```
JC   BORROW
JC   OVERFLOW
```

where BORROW is a set of instructions that processes a too-large negative result and OVERFLOW is a set of instructions that deals with overflow (i.e., an unexpected change of sign).

Subroutine Listing

```
; SUBS32 - Subtracts signed 32-bit numbers.
; Inputs: AX:BX = Number to be subtracted from second operand.
```

```
;               CX:DX = Second operand
; Results:  CX:DX = Result
;               If the result generates a borrow, then CF = 1.
;               If the result exceeds the two's complement range
;                 of AX:DX, which changes the sign, then OF = 1.
;               AX and BX are unaffected.


; The following macro two's-complements the register
; combination hireg:lowreg

COMP   MACRO  hireg,loreg
        NOT    loreg
        ADD    loreg,1
        NOT    hireg
        ADC    hireg,0
       ENDM


        PUBLIC  SUBS32
CSEG   SEGMENT PARA PUBLIC 'CODE'
        ASSUME  CS:CSEG,DS:CSEG,ES:CSEG,SS:CSEG

SUBS32     PROC  NEAR
           PUSH  AX          ;Preserve first operand
           PUSH  BX

; If both operands are positive, subtract them directly.

           PUSH  CX
           OR    CX,AX
           POP   CX
           JS    NEGS         ;Jump if not positive
           SUB   DX,BX        ;Subtract the low 16 bits
           SBB   CX,AX        ;Subtract the high 16 bits
           JMP   EXIT

; If both operands are negative, complement them, then
; subtract.  If the result is zero, exit; otherwise,
; complement the result.

NEGS:      TEST  AX,CX
           JNS   OPP_SIGNS
           COMP  AX,BX        ;Complement both operands
           COMP  CX,DX
           SUB   DX,BX        ;Subtract the low 16 bits
           SBB   CX,AX        ;Subtract the high 16 bits
           CMP   CX,0         ;If CX = 0 and DX = 0, exit
           JNZ   COMP_RES     ; otherwise, complement the result
           CMP   DX,0
           JNZ   COMP_RES
           JZ    EXIT
```

```
; The operands have opposite signs.  If operand 1 is
; negative, two's-complement it and add.  If operand 2
; is negative, two's-complement it, then add and two's-
; complement the result.

OPP_SIGNS: TEST AX,8000H ;Is operand 1 negative?
           JNS   OP2_NEG
           COMP  AX,BX    ; Yes. Two's-complement it
           ADD   DX,BX    ;Add the low 16 bits
           ADC   CX,AX    ;Add the high 16 bits
           JMP   EXIT
OP2_NEG:   COMP  CX,DX    ;Two's-complement operand 2
           ADD   DX,BX    ;Add the low 16 bits
           ADC   CX,AX    ;Add the high 16 bits
COMP_RES:  COMP  CX,DX    ;Two's-complement the result
EXIT:      POP   BX       ;Restore saved registers
           POP   AX
           RET            ;Return to calling program
SUBS32     ENDP
CSEG  ENDS
           END
```

SIGNED BINARY MULTIPLICATION (MULS32)

MULS32 multiplies two 32-bit signed operands in registers and returns the 64-bit product sum in the same registers.

Operation

The subroutine makes both operands positive (as necessary), and uses a memory location called NEG__IND to keep track of the sign of the result. It then calls the Unsigned Binary Multiplication subroutine MULU32 to multiply the operands (MULU32 is described earlier in this chapter) and changes the sign of the result if NEG__IND is nonzero.

Entry Values

CX:BX = Multiplier
DX:AX = Multiplicand

Results

The product in DX, CX, BX, and AX (high to low order).

Link Command

```
link callprog+mulu32+muls32;
```

Subroutine Listing

```
; MULS32 -  Multiplies two 32-bit signed numbers and
; generates a 64-bit product.
; Inputs: CX:BX = Multiplier
;         DX:AX = Multiplicand
; Result: Product in DX, CX, BX, and AX (high to low order).
; Link Instructions: Calls MULU32, so link using the form
;                    LINK callprog+MULS32+MULU32;

          EXTRN MULU32:NEAR
          PUBLIC  MULS32
CSEG  SEGMENT  PARA PUBLIC 'CODE'
          ASSUME  CS:CSEG,DS:CSEG,ES:CSEG,SS:CSEG

          JMP     MULS32          ;Skip past data
NEG_IND   DB      ?

MULS32    PROC    NEAR
          MOV     NEG_IND,0       ;Negative indicator = 0
          CMP     DX,0            ;Multiplicand negative?
          JNS     CHKCX           ; No.  Go check multiplier
          NOT     AX              ; Yes.  2s-comp. multiplicand
          NOT     DX
          ADD     AX,1
          ADC     DX,0
          NOT     NEG_IND         ;  and invert indicator
```

```
CHKCX:      CMP    CX,0          ;Multiplier negative?
            JNS    GOMUL         ; No.  Go multiply
            NOT    BX            ; Yes. 2s-comp. multiplier
            NOT    CX
            ADD    BX,1
            ADC    CX,0
            NOT    NEG_IND       ;  and 1s-comp. indicator
GOMUL:      CALL   MULU32        ;Do unsigned multiplication
            CMP    NEG_IND,0     ;Does product have right sign?
            JZ     DONE          ; Yes. Exit.
            NOT    AX            ; No.  2s-comp. product
            NOT    BX
            NOT    CX
            NOT    DX
            ADD    AX,1
            ADC    BX,0
            ADC    CX,0
            ADC    DX,0
DONE:       RET
MULS32      ENDP
CSEG   ENDS
            END
```

SIGNED BINARY COMPARISON (COMPS32)

COMPS32 compares two 32-bit signed operands in registers and reports the result in status flags.

Operation

The subroutine compares the operand in AX:BX with the operand in CX:DX, 16 bits at a time, and reports the result in the Zero Flag (ZF) and the Carry Flag (CF). If the high words differ, it must make only one comparison; if they match, it must make a second comparison to determine whether or not the low words also match.

Entry Values

AX:BX = First operand
CX:DX = Second operand

Results

If the operands are identical, then ZF = 1.
If operand 1 is greater, then ZF = 0 and SF = 0.
If operand 2 is greater, then ZF = 0 and SF = 1.
The registers are unaffected.

Link Command

```
callprog+muls32;
```

Example

Compare two 32-bit signed operands:

```
          EXTRN COMPS32:NEAR
          CALL  COMPS32   ;Make the comparison
          JE    SAME      ;Are the operands identical?
          JNS   OP1GRTR   ; No. Check Sign Flag.
          ..              ;Continue here if op. 2 > op. 1
          ..
SAME:     ..              ;Continue here if op. 1 = op. 2
          ..
OP1GRTR:  ..              ;Continue here if op. 1 > op. 2
          ..
```

Subroutine Listing

```
; COMPS32 - Compares two signed 32-bit numbers.
; Inputs: AX:BX = First operand
;         CX:DX = Second operand
; Results: If the operands are identical, then ZF = 1.
;          If operand 1 is greater, then ZF = 0 and SF = 0.
;          If operand 2 is greater, then ZF = 0 and SF = 1.
```

```
;             Registers are unaffected.

          PUBLIC  COMPS32
CSEG   SEGMENT  PARA PUBLIC 'CODE'
          ASSUME  CS:CSEG,DS:CSEG,ES:CSEG,SS:CSEG

COMPS32   PROC  NEAR
          CMP   AX,CX      ;Compare high 16 bits
          JNZ   EXIT
          CMP   BX,DX      ;Compare low 16 bits
EXIT:     RET              ;Return to calling program
COMPS32   ENDP
CSEG   ENDS
          END
```

Chapter 7

16-Bit Decimal Arithmetic

This chapter presents subroutines that add, subtract, multiply, and divide 16-bit decimal numbers. (To compare 16-bit decimal numbers, use the regular CMP instruction.) Decimal numbers are represented in the so-called binary-coded decimal (BCD) format, in which each decimal digit occupies four bits in a register or memory location. BCD numbers may be stored in *unpacked* or *packed* form.

For unpacked numbers, each byte holds one BCD digit, in the lower four bits. Therefore, a byte can represent values from 0 to 9. For packed numbers, each byte holds two BCD digits, with the most-significant digit in the upper four bits. Thus, a packed byte can represent values from 00 to 99.

ENTERING BCD NUMBERS

Packed BCD numbers are easiest to enter, because you simply type them consecutively, as you would any decimal number—except you attach an H (for Hexadecimal) at the end. For example, these instructions enter the packed BCD value 371567 into the 32-bit register pair DX:AX:

```
MOV    DX,37H
MOV    AX,1567H
```

Entering unpacked BCD numbers is a little trickier (and thus a little more error-prone), because you must load the digits into the low four bits of each byte. For example, these instructions enter the unpacked BCD value 1567 into DX:AX:

```
MOV     DX,105H
MOV     AX,607H
```

The main point is that you must remember to put zeroes between the digits when you enter unpacked BCD numbers.

UNPACKED DECIMAL ADDITION (ADDUD16)

ADDUD16 adds two unpacked 16-bit BCD operands in registers and returns the sum in the second operand.

Operation

The subroutine adds the operand in BX to the operand in AX, one byte at a time, and returns the result in AX. If the result is too large to fit in AX (i.e., if it is larger than 99), the add operation produces a carry, which sets the Carry Flag (CF) to 1.

Entry Values

BX = First operand
AX = Second operand

Results

AX = Result
If the result cannot fit in AX, then CF = 1.
BX is unaffected.

Link Command

```
link callprog+addu16;
```

Comment

Generally, you should follow CALL ADDUD16 with an instruction of the form JC ERROR, where ERROR is a set of instructions that processes a too-large result.

Subroutine Listing

```
; ADDUD16 - Adds two 16-bit "unpacked" binary-coded decimal
; (BCD) numbers.
; Unpacked BCD numbers are stored one digit per byte.
; Thus, a 16-bit unpacked BCD number holds two digits.
; Inputs: BX = First operand
;         AX = Second operand
; Result: AX = Result
;         If the result cannot fit in AX, then CF = 1.
;         BX is unaffected.


        PUBLIC  ADDUD16
CSEG    SEGMENT PARA PUBLIC 'CODE'
        ASSUME  CS:CSEG,DS:CSEG,ES:CSEG,SS:CSEG

ADDUD16 PROC    NEAR
        PUSH    CX          ;Save working register
        MOV     CH,AH       ;Save AH in CH
        ADD     AL,BL       ;Add the low-order bytes
```

```
            AAA                     ; and unpack the result
            XCHG    AL,CH           ;Get ready for second addition
            ADC     AL,BH           ;Add the high-order bytes
            AAA                     ; and unpack the result
            MOV     AH,AL           ;Put bytes in proper order
            MOV     AL,CH
            POP     CX              ;Restore CX
            RET                     ;Return to calling program
ADDUD16     ENDP
CSEG    ENDS
            END
```

UNPACKED DECIMAL SUBTRACTION (SUBUD16)

SUBUD16 subtracts two unpacked 16-bit BCD operands in registers and returns the difference in the second operand.

Operation

The subroutine subtracts the operand in BX from the operand in AX, one byte at a time, and returns the result in AX. If BX is greater than AX, the subtract operation produces a borrow, which sets the Carry Flag (CF) to 1.

Entry Values

BX = Subtrahend (number to be subtracted)
AX = Minuend

Results

AX = Result
If the result is negative, then CF = 1.
BX is unaffected.

Link Command

```
link callprog+subud16;
```

Comment

Generally, you should follow CALL SUBUD16 with an instruction of the form JC ERROR, where ERROR is a set of instructions that processes a negative result.

Subroutine Listing

```
; SUBUD16 - Subtracts 16-bit "unpacked" binary-coded decimal
; (BCD) numbers.
; Unpacked BCD numbers are stored one digit per byte.
; Thus, a 16-bit unpacked BCD number holds two digits.
; Inputs: BX = First operand
;         AX = Second operand
; Result: AX = Result
;         If the result is negative (BX > AX), then CF = 1.
;         BX is unaffected.

            PUBLIC   SUBUD16
CSEG    SEGMENT  PARA PUBLIC 'CODE'
            ASSUME   CS:CSEG,DS:CSEG,ES:CSEG,SS:CSEG

SUBUD16     PROC  NEAR
            PUSH  CX          ;Save working register
            MOV   CH,AH       ;Save AH in CH
            SUB   AL,BL       ;Subtract the low bytes
            AAS               ; and unpack the result
```

```
              XCHG    AL,CH       ;Get ready for 2nd subtraction
              SBB     AL,BH       ;Subtract the high bytes
              AAS                 ; and unpack the result
              MOV     AH,AL       ;Put bytes in proper order
              MOV     AL,CH
              POP     CX          ;Restore CX
              RET                 ;Return to calling program
SUBUD16       ENDP
CSEG   ENDS
              END
```

UNPACKED DECIMAL MULTIPLICATION (MULUD16)

MULUD16 multiplies two unpacked 16-bit BCD operands in registers and returns a 32-bit product.

Operation

The subroutine converts the BCD operands in AX and BX to binary values in AL and BL and then performs the multiplication. The subroutine divides the 16 bit product in AX by 1000 to calculate the "thousands" digit and then divides the remainder by 100 to calculate the "hundreds" digit; it places these digits in DX. Finally, it divides the remainder by 10 to calculate the "tens" digit, and places it, along with the final "ones" digit remainder, in AX.

Entry Values

BX = Multiplier
AX = Multiplicand

Results

DX:AX = Product
BX is unaffected.

Link Command

```
link callprog+mulud16;
```

Subroutine Listing

```
; MULUD16 - Multiplies two 16-bit unpacked binary-coded decimal
;   numbers and generates a 32-bit product.
; Inputs: BX = Multiplier
;         AX = Multiplicand
; Result: Product in DX (high part) and AX (low part).
;         BX is unaffected.

        PUBLIC  MULUD16
CSEG    SEGMENT PARA PUBLIC 'CODE'
        ASSUME  CS:CSEG,DS:CSEG,SS:CSEG,ES:CSEG

MULUD16 PROC  NEAR

; Convert the BCD multiplicand in AX to a binary number
; in AL.

        PUSH    BX          ;Save affected registers
        PUSH    CX
        MOV     CH,AL       ;Save AL in CH
        MOV     AL,AH       ;Multiply AH by 10
        MOV     CL,10
```

```
                MUL     CL
                ADD     AL,CH       ; and add original AL to it
                MOV     CH,AL       ;Save multiplicand in CH

; Convert the BCD multiplier in BX to a binary number
; in BL.

                MOV     AL,BH       ;Multiply BH by 10
                MUL     CL
                ADD     BL,AL       ; and add it to BL

; Multiply the operands to produce a 16-bit binary product
; in AX, then convert the product to unpacked BCD in DX:AX.

                MOV     AL,CH       ;Retrieve the multiplicand
                MUL     BL          ;Do the multiplication
                CWD                 ;Make product a 32-bit value in DX:AX
                MOV     CX,1000     ;Calculate the thousands digit
                DIV     CX
                XCHG    AX,DX       ;Put remainder in AX
                MOV     DH,DL       ; and thousands digit in DH
                MOV     CL,100      ;Calculate the hundreds digit
                DIV     CL
                MOV     DL,AL       ; and put it in DL
                MOV     AL,AH       ;Move remainder to AL
                CBW                 ; and extend it to 16 bits
                MOV     CL,10       ;Calculate tens and ones digits
                DIV     CL
                XCHG    AH,AL       ;Put digits in proper order
                POP     CX          ;Restore working registers
                POP     BX
                RET                 ;Return to calling program
MULUD16         ENDP
CSEG    ENDS
                END
```

UNPACKED DECIMAL DIVISION (DIVUD16)

DIVUD16 divides a 32-bit unpacked BCD dividend by a 16-bit unpacked BCD divisor and returns a 16-bit unpacked quotient and remainder.

Operation

The subroutine converts the dividend DX:AX and divisor BX to binary values in CX and BL, respectively, and then performs the binary division. If the divisor is zero or the dividend is at least 256 times larger than the divisor, the computer activates a divide-by-zero interrupt, which displays a message such as "Divide Overflow."

After the divide operation, the subroutine checks the size of the quotient (AL) and remainder (AH). If either value is larger than 99 (the size of the result registers, in unpacked BCD), it exits immediately. Otherwise, it unpacks the remainder and quotient by dividing them by 10 and putting the digits in proper order in AX and DX.

Entry Values

DX:AX = 32-bit (four-digit) dividend
BX = 16-bit (two-digit) divisor

Results

AX = 16-bit (two-digit) quotient
DX = 16-bit (two-digit) remainder
BX is unaffected.

Link Command

```
link callprog+divud16;
```

Example

Divide 156 by 89:

```
        EXTRN   DIVUD16:NEAR
        MOV     DX,1        ;Load dividend
        MOV     AX,506H
        MOV     BX,809H     ;Load divisor
        CALL    DIVUD16     ;Perform the division
        JC      ERROR       ;Invalid result?
        . .                 ; No. Continue here
        . .
ERROR:  . .                 ; Yes. Result is too large
        . .
```

Subroutine Listing

```
; DIVUD16 -  Divides unpacked binary-coded decimal numbers
; Inputs: DX:AX = 32-bit dividend
;         BX = 16-bit divisor
```

104

```
; Results: AX = Quotient
;         DX = Remainder
;         If the quotient or remainder is greater than 99, then
;           CF = 1.
;         If divisor is zero or dividend is 256 times larger
;           than divisor, the microprocessor activates a
;           divide-by-zero interrupt.
;         BX is unaffected.

        PUBLIC  DIVUD16
CSEG  SEGMENT  PARA PUBLIC 'CODE'
        ASSUME  CS:CSEG,DS:CSEG,SS:CSEG,ES:CSEG

DIVUD16   PROC   NEAR

; Convert the BCD dividend in DX:AX to a binary number in CX.
        PUSH  BX          ;Save affected registers
        PUSH  CX
        AAD               ;Convert low half to binary in AL,
        MOV   CX,AX       ; and save it in CX
        MOV   AX,DX       ;Move high half to AX
        AAD               ;Convert it to binary in AL
        MOV   DL,100      ; and multiply it by 100
        MUL   DL          ; (product is in AX)
        ADD   CX,AX       ;Put the final dividend in CX

; Convert the BCD divisor in BX to a binary number in BL.

        MOV   AX,BX       ;Move divisor to AX
        AAD               ;Convert it to binary in AL
        MOV   BL,AL       ; and put it in BL

; Divide AX by BL to produce an 8-bit binary quotient and
; remainder in AL and AH, then convert them to unpacked BCD
; values in AX and DX.

        MOV   AX,CX       ;Put the dividend in AX
        DIV   BL          ;Do the division
        MOV   BL,99       ;Check for too-large results
        CMP   BL,AL
        JC    EXIT
        CMP   BL,AH
        JC    EXIT
        MOV   BL,AL       ;Save the quotient in BL
        MOV   AL,AH       ;Unpack the remainder
        SUB   AH,AH
        MOV   CL,10       ; by dividing it by 10
        DIV   CL
        MOV   DX,AX       ;Move remainder to DX
        XCHG  DH,DL       ; and put digits in correct order
        MOV   AL,BL       ;Unpack the quotient
```

```
            SUB     AH,AH
            DIV     CL
            XCHG    AH,AL     ; and put digits in correct order
EXIT:       POP     CX        ;Restore working registers
            POP     BX
            RET               ;Return to calling program
DIVUD16     ENDP
CSEG    ENDS
            END
```

16-BIT BINARY TO PACKED BCD CONVERSION (B2BCDW)

B2BCDW converts the binary contents of a 16-bit register to four packed binary-coded decimal digits.

Operation

The subroutine converts the binary value in AX to four BCD digits, and packs the two high-order digits into AH and the two low-order digits into AL. To calculate the digits, the subroutine divides the original binary value by 1000, then 100, and then 10. Each divide operation produces a quotient that is a BCD digit. That is, the first divide produces the "thousands" digit; the second, the "hundreds" digit; and the last, the "tens" digit (with the "ones" digit as the remainder).

The subroutine uses DX to accumulate the digits, adding the new digit and shifting DX left each time. When all four digits are in DX, the subroutine simply copies the contents of DX into AX, restores the working registers, and exits.

Entry Value

AX = 16-bit binary value

Result

If CF = 0, the input was valid and AX = four packed BCD digits.
If CF = 1, the input was invalid and AX is unaffected.

Link Command

```
link callprog+b2bcdw;
```

Comments

Generally, you should follow CALL B2BCDW with an instruction of the form JC TOO_BIG, where TOO_BIG is a set of instructions that display a message if the binary number was larger than 9999.

Chapter 9 contains a subroutine that converts an 8-bit binary number to packed BCD.

Subroutine Listing

```
; B2BCDW - Converts a 16-bit binary number to packed
;   binary-coded decimal.
; Input: AX = 16-bit binary value
; Result: If CF = 0, then AX = Four-digit BCD number
;         If CF = 1, then the number was too large to
;         be converted and AX contains the original
;         binary value.

        PUBLIC  B2BCDW
CSEG    SEGMENT  PARA PUBLIC 'CODE'
        ASSUME   CS:CSEG,DS:CSEG,SS:CSEG,ES:CSEG
```

```
B2BCDW      PROC    NEAR
            CMP     AX,9999     ;Number too large?
            JBE     PUSHCX
            STC                 ; If so, set CF
            JC      EXIT        ;  and exit
PUSHCX:     PUSH    CX          ;Save affected registers
            PUSH    DX
            SUB     DX,DX       ;Prepare for divide operation
            MOV     CX,1000     ;Calculate the thousands digit
            DIV     CX
            XCHG    AX,DX       ;Put remainder in AX and digit in DX
            MOV     CL,4        ;Shift partial total left four bits
            SHL     DX,CL
            MOV     CL,100      ;Calculate the hundreds digit

            DIV     CL
            ADD     DL,AL       ; and add it to total
            MOV     CL,4        ;Shift partial total left four bits
            SHL     DX,CL
            XCHG    AL,AH       ;Put remainder in AL
            SUB     AH,AH       ; and clear AH
            MOV     CL,10       ;Calculate tens digit
            DIV     CL
            ADD     DL,AL       ; and add it to total
            MOV     CL,4        ;Shift partial total left four bits
            SHL     DX,CL
            ADD     DL,AH       ; and add ones digit to total
            MOV     AX,DX       ;Put final answer in AX
            POP     DX          ;Restore working registers
            POP     CX
EXIT:       RET                 ;Return to calling program
B2BCDW      ENDP
CSEG   ENDS
            END
```

16-BIT PACKED BCD TO BINARY CONVERSION (BCDW2B)

BCDW2B converts the four packed binary-coded-decimal digits in a 16-bit register to binary.

Operation

The subroutine converts the four BCD digits in AX to binary. To do this, it copies the contents of AX to SI and then clears AX so that it can be used to accumulate the binary values. After that, the subroutine calls a subroutine named ADDDIG four times, to convert each digit to binary and add it to the total.

ADDDIG converts each digit to binary by shifting the contents of SI to the left four times (i.e., one digit position), and rotating each displaced bit into DI. Once the digit is in DI, ADDDIG multiplies the total (in AX) by 10 and adds the new digit to it.

Entry Value

AX = 16-bit BCD value (four digits)

Result

AX = 16-bit binary value

Link Command

```
link callprog+bcdw2b;
```

Comment

Chapter 9 contains a subroutine that converts two packed BCD digits to an 8-bit binary number.

Subroutine Listing

```
; BCDW2B - Converts a 16-bit packed binary-coded decimal
;   number to binary.
; Input: AX = 16-bit BCD value
; Result: AX = 16-bit binary value

        PUBLIC  BCDW2B
CSEG    SEGMENT PARA PUBLIC 'CODE'
        ASSUME  CS:CSEG,DS:CSEG,SS:CSEG,ES:CSEG

BCDW2B    PROC  NEAR

        PUSH  CX          ;Save affected registers
        PUSH  DX
        PUSH  DI
        PUSH  SI
        MOV   SI,AX        ;Save BCD value in SI
        SUB   AX,AX        ;Set total to zero
```

```
          CALL    ADDDIG      ;Convert the high digit
          CALL    ADDDIG      ;Convert the upper-middle digit
          CALL    ADDDIG      ;Convert the lower-middle digit
          CALL    ADDDIG      ;Convert the low digit
          POP     SI          ;Restore working registers
          POP     DI
          POP     DX
          POP     CX
          RET                 ;Return to calling program
BCDW2B    ENDP


; This subroutine converts a BCD digit to binary (in DI) and
; adds it to the total in AX.

ADDDIG    PROC    NEAR
          MOV     DI,0        ;Clear DI
          MOV     CX,4        ;Shift next digit into DI
NEXTDIG:  SHL     SI,1        ; one bit at a time
          RCL     DI,1
          LOOP    NEXTDIG
          MOV     CX,10       ;Multiply total by 10,
          MUL     CX
          ADD     AX,DI       ; and add new digit to it
          RET
ADDDIG    ENDP
CSEG      ENDS
                  END
```

PACKED DECIMAL ADDITION (ADDPD16)

ADDPD16 adds two packed 16-bit BCD operands in registers and returns the sum in the second operand.

Operation

The subroutine adds the operand in BX to the operand in AX, one byte at a time, and returns the result in AX. If the result is too large to fit in AX (i.e., if it is larger than 99), the add operation produces a carry, which sets the Carry Flag (CF) to 1.

Entry Values

BX = First operand
AX = Second operand

Results

AX = Result
If the result cannot fit in AX, then CF = 1.
BX is unaffected.

Link Command

```
link callprog+addpd16;
```

Comment

Generally, you should follow CALL ADDPD16 with an instruction of the form JC ERROR, where ERROR is a set of instructions that processes a too-large result.

Subroutine Listing

```
; ADDPD16 - Adds two 16-bit "packed" binary-coded decimal
; (BCD) numbers.
; Packed BCD numbers are stored two digits per byte.
; Thus, a 16-bit packed BCD number holds four digits.
; Inputs: BX = First operand
;         AX = Second operand
; Result: AX = Result
;         If the result cannot fit in AX, then CF = 1.
;         BX is unaffected.

        PUBLIC  ADDPD16
CSEG    SEGMENT PARA PUBLIC 'CODE'
        ASSUME  CS:CSEG,DS:CSEG,ES:CSEG,SS:CSEG

ADDPD16 PROC    NEAR
        PUSH    CX          ;Save working register
        MOV     CH,AH       ;Save AH in CH
        ADD     AL,BL       ;Add the low-order bytes
        DAA                 ; and pack the result
```

```
            XCHG   AL,CH      ;Get ready for second addition
            ADC    AL,BH      ;Add the high-order bytes
            DAA               ; and pack the result
            MOV    AH,AL      ;Put bytes in proper order
            MOV    AL,CH
            POP    CX         ;Restore CX
            RET               ;Return to calling program
ADDPD16     ENDP
CSEG   ENDS
            END
```

PACKED DECIMAL SUBTRACTION (SUBPD16)

SUBPD16 subtracts two packed 16-bit BCD operands in registers and returns the difference in the second operand.

Operation

The subroutine subtracts the operand in BX from the operand in AX, one byte at a time, and returns the result in AX. If BX is greater than AX, the subtraction produces a borrow, which sets the Carry Flag (CF) to 1.

Entry Values

BX = Subtrahend (number to be subtracted)
AX = Minuend

Results

AX = Result
If the result is negative, then CF = 1.
BX is unaffected.

Link Command

```
link callprog+subpd16;
```

Comment

Generally, you should follow CALL SUBPD16 with an instruction of the form JC ERROR, where ERROR is a set of instructions that processes a negative result.

Subroutine Listing

```
; SUBPD16 - Subtracts 16-bit "packed" binary-coded decimal
; (BCD) numbers.
; Packed BCD numbers are stored two digits per byte.
; Thus, a 16-bit packed BCD number holds four digits.
; Inputs: BX = First operand
;         AX = Second operand
; Result: AX = Result
;         If the result is negative (BX > AX), then CF = 1.
;         BX is unaffected.

        PUBLIC  SUBPD16
CSEG    SEGMENT PARA PUBLIC 'CODE'
        ASSUME  CS:CSEG,DS:CSEG,ES:CSEG,SS:CSEG

SUBPD16 PROC  NEAR
        PUSH  CX        ;Save working register
        MOV   CH,AH     ;Save AH in CH
        SUB   AL,BL     ;Subtract the low bytes
```

```
            DAS                     ; and pack the result
            XCHG    AL,CH           ;Get ready for 2nd subtraction
            SBB     AL,BH           ;Subtract the high bytes
            DAS                     ; and pack the result
            MOV     AH,AL           ;Put bytes in proper order
            MOV     AL,CH
            POP     CX              ;Restore CX
            RET                     ;Return to calling program
SUBPD16     ENDP
CSEG   ENDS
            END
```

PACKED DECIMAL MULTIPLICATION (MULPD16)

MULPD16 multiplies two packed 16-bit (four-digit) BCD operands in registers and returns a 32-bit (eight-digit) product.

Operation

To begin, the subroutine calls the earlier BCDW2B subroutine to convert the BCD operands in AX and BX to binary values, and then performs the multiplication. After that, it makes a series of calls to a subroutine named SIDIG, which performs successive subtractions to calculate the high four digits of the product; that is, the "ten-millions," "millions," "hundred-thousands," and "ten-thousands" digit. To do this, SIDIG makes a trial subtraction by calling COMPU32 (see Chapter 6). If a digit can be obtained, SIDIG calculates it by calling SUBU32 (also in Chapter 6); with each subtraction, it increments the SI register. Upon return from the subroutine, SI holds the digit.

To calculate the low four digits of the product, MULPD16 makes a series of calls to a subroutine named DIDIG, which calculates a digit by dividing. DIDIG returns the digit in DI and the remainder in DX:AX. Finally, MULPD16 moves the final product from SI:DI to DX:AX.

Entry Values

    BX = Multiplier (four digits)
    AX = Multiplicand (four digits)

Results

    DX:AX = Product (eight digits)
    BX is unaffected.

Link Command

```
link callprog+mulpd16+bcdw2b+compu32+subu32;
```

Subroutine Listing

```
; MULPD16 - Multiplies two 16-bit packed binary-coded decimal
;   numbers and generates a 32-bit product.
; Inputs: BX = Multiplier
;         AX = Multiplicand
; Result: Product in DX (high part) and AX (low part).
;         BX is unaffected.
; Link With: LINK callprog+MULPD16+BCDW2B+COMPU32+SUBU32;

            EXTRN   BCDW2B:NEAR,COMPU32:NEAR,SUBU32:NEAR
            PUBLIC  MULPD16
CSEG   SEGMENT  PARA PUBLIC 'CODE'
            ASSUME  CS:CSEG,DS:CSEG,SS:CSEG,ES:CSEG
```

```
MULPD16    PROC   NEAR

; Convert both operands to binary.

         PUSH   BX        ;Save affected registers
         PUSH   CX
         PUSH   BP
         PUSH   DI
         PUSH   SI
         CALL   BCDW2B    ;Convert multiplicand to binary
         PUSH   AX        ; and save it on the stack
         MOV    AX,BX     ;Convert multiplier to binary,
         CALL   BCDW2B
         MOV    BX,AX     ; then return it to BX
         POP    AX        ;Retrieve the multiplicand

; Multiply the operands to produce a 32-bit binary product
; in DX:AX, then convert the product to packed BCD.
         SUB    SI,SI     ;SI will hold the high digits
         SUB    DI,DI     ;DI will hold the low digits
         MUL    BX        ;Do the multiplication
         MOV    CX,DX     ;Move DX:AX to CX:DX
         MOV    DX,AX
         MOV    AX,98H    ;Load 10,000,000 into AX:BX
         MOV    BX,9680H
         CALL   SIDIG     ; and calculate the ten-millions digit
         MOV    AX,0FH    ;Load 1,000,000 into AX:BX
         MOV    BX,4240H
         CALL   SIDIG     ; and calculate the millions digit
         MOV    AX,1      ;Load 100,000 into AX:BX
         MOV    BX,86A0H
         CALL   SIDIG     ; and calculate the hund-thous digit
         MOV    AX,0      ;Load 10,000 into AX:BX
         MOV    BX,2710H
         CALL   SIDIG     ; and calculate the ten-thousands digit
         MOV    AX,DX     ;Move CX:DX to DX:AX
         MOV    DX,CX

; At this point, SI holds the high four digits and the remainder
; is in DX:AX.

         MOV    BP,1000   ;Calculate the thousands digit
         CALL   DIDIG
         MOV    BP,100    ;Calculate the hundreds digit
         CALL   DIDIG
         MOV    BP,10     ;Calculate the tens digit
         CALL   DIDIG
         ADD    AX,DI     ;Form final low word in AX
         MOV    DX,SI     ; and move final high word to DX
         POP    SI        ;Restore working registers
         POP    DI
```

```
            POP    BP
            POP    CX
            POP    BX
            RET                    ;Return to calling program
MULPD16     ENDP

; This subroutine shifts SI (the high-word accumulator) left by
; four bits, then calculates the next packed digit by successive
; subtractions.

SIDIG       PROC   NEAR
            SHL    SI,1    ;Shift SI left four bits
            SHL    SI,1
            SHL    SI,1
            SHL    SI,1
NEXTSUB:    CALL   COMPU32 ;Calculate the digit
            JA     RETURN
            CALL   SUBU32  ; by successive subtractions
            INC    SI
            JMP    NEXTSUB
RETURN:     RET
SIDIG       ENDP

; This subroutine shifts DI (the low-word accumulator) left by
; four bits, then calculates the next packed digit and adds it
; to DI.

DIDIG       PROC   NEAR
            MOV    CL,4    ;Shift DI left four bits
            SHL    DI,CL
            DIV    BP      ;Calculate the digit
            ADD    DI,AX   ; and add it to DI
            MOV    AX,DX   ;Move remainder to AX
            SUB    DX,DX   ; and clear DX
            RET
DIDIG       ENDP
CSEG  ENDS
            END
```

PACKED DECIMAL DIVISION (DIVPD16)

DIVPD16 divides a 32-bit packed BCD dividend by a 16-bit packed BCD divisor and returns a 16-bit packed quotient and remainder.

Operation

The subroutine converts the dividend DX:AX and divisor BX to binary values, using the earlier BCDW2B subroutine. It then performs the binary division. If the divisor is zero or the dividend is at least 256 times larger than the divisor, the computer activates a divide-by-zero interrupt, which displays a message such as "Divide Overflow." Following the divide operation, the subroutine packs the remainder and quotient using the earlier B2BCDW subroutine.

Entry Values

        DX:AX = 32-bit (four-digit) dividend
           BX = 16-bit (two-digit) divisor

Results

        AX = 16-bit (two-digit) quotient
        DX = 16-bit (two-digit) remainder
        If the divisor is zero or the dividend is 256 times larger than the divisor, the
            microprocessor activates a divide-by-zero interrupt.
        BX is unaffected.

Link Command

    link callprog+divpd16+bcdw2b+b2bcdw;

Subroutine Listing

```
; DIVPD16 -  Divides packed binary-coded decimal numbers
; Inputs: DX:AX = 32-bit (eight-digit) dividend
;         BX = 16-bit (four-digit) divisor
; Results: AX = Four-digit quotient
;          DX = Four-digit remainder
;          If divisor is zero or dividend is 256 times larger
;             than divisor, the microprocessor activates a
;             divide-by-zero interrupt.
;          BX is unaffected.
; Link With: LINK callprog+divpd16+bcdw2b+b2bcdw;

          EXTRN   BCDW2B:NEAR,B2BCDW:NEAR
          PUBLIC  DIVPD16
CSEG    SEGMENT  PARA PUBLIC 'CODE'
          ASSUME   CS:CSEG,DS:CSEG,SS:CSEG,ES:CSEG

DIVPD16   PROC    NEAR
; Convert the BCD divisor to binary.
```

```
                PUSH    BX          ;Save affected registers
                PUSH    CX
                PUSH    SI
                PUSH    AX          ;Save low dividend on the stack
                MOV     AX,BX       ;Move divisor to AX,
                CALL    BCDW2B      ; convert it to binary,
                MOV     BX,AX       ; and return it to BX

; Convert the BCD dividend in DX:AX to binary.

                MOV     AX,DX       ;Move high dividend to AX,
                CALL    BCDW2B      ; convert it to binary,
                MOV     CX,10000    ; and multiply it by 10000
                MUL     CX          ; (result is in DX:AX)
                MOV     SI,AX       ;Save low result in SI
                POP     AX          ;Retrieve low dividend
                CALL    BCDW2B      ; and convert it to binary
                ADD     AX,SI       ;Form binary dividend in DX:AX
                ADC     DX,0

; Divide DX:AX by BX to produce a 16-bit binary quotient and
; remainder in AX and DX, then convert them to packed BCD.

                DIV     BX          ;Do the division
                MOV     CX,AX       ;Save the quotient in CX
                MOV     AX,DX       ;Move the remainder to AX,
                CALL    B2BCDW      ; pack it,
                MOV     DX,AX       ; and return it to DX
                MOV     AX,CX       ;Move the quotient to AX
                CALL    B2BCDW      ; and pack it
                POP     SI          ;Restore working registers
                POP     CX
                POP     BX
                RET                 ;Return to calling program
DIVPD16     ENDP
CSEG    ENDS
                END
```

Chapter 8

32-Bit Shift and Rotate Operations

The 8086, 8088, and 80286 microprocessors provide instructions that let you shift or rotate the contents of an 8-bit or 16-bit register. This chapter provides subroutines that perform the same operations on 32-bit numbers. As in previous chapters, 32-bit operands are comprised of two 16-bit registers that are treated as though they are connected. Here, I use DX:AX to hold operands. Figure 8-1 shows what each subroutine does.

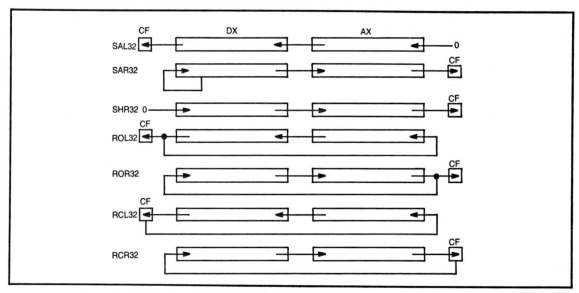

Fig. 8-1. 32-bit shift and rotate operations.

SHIFT LEFT (SAL32)

SAL32 shifts a 32-bit number left by a specified number of bit positions.

Operation

If the shift count in CL is zero, the subroutine exits immediately, without shifting; otherwise, it clears CH to form a 16-bit shift count in CX. This value serves as a counter for the loop that starts at SHIFT. With each pass through the loop, the subroutine shifts AX to the left one bit position and rotates the displaced bit into DX.

The subroutine also keeps track of whether rotating DX changes the sign bit. Specifically, the subroutine uses DI as an Overflow Flag holder and makes it 0 initially. If rotating DX ever changes the sign bit, which sets OF = 1, the subroutine sets bit 11 of DI (because OF is bit 11 of the Flags register). Just before exiting, the subroutine copies the flags to SI, ORs DI with SI, and then copies SI back to the Flags register. This makes OF = 1 if overflow occurred, and OF = 0 otherwise.

Entry Values

DX:AX = Number to be shifted
CL = Shift count (0-30)

Results

DX:AX = Shifted number
If the sign bit ever changes, OF = 1.
The Carry Flag (CF) holds the last bit to be shifted out of DX.
CL is unaffected.

Link Command

```
link callprog+sal32;
```

Special Case

A shift count of zero causes an immediate exit with no shifting.

Comment

Like the regular SAL and SHL instructions, the SAL32 subroutine can shift either signed or unsigned operands. With signed operands, however, you must check the status of the Overflow Flag upon return. To do this, follow CALL SAL32 with an instruction of the form

```
JO  OVERFLOW
```

where OVERFLOW is a set of instructions that deals with overflow (i.e., an unexpected sign change.)

Subroutine Listing

```
; SAL32 - Shifts a 32-bit number left by a specified number
; of bit positions.
; Inputs: DX:AX = Number to be shifted
;         CL = Shift count (0-30)
; Results: DX:AX = Number after shift operation
;          If the sign bit ever changes, OF = 1.
;          CL is unaffected.


            PUBLIC  SAL32
CSEG   SEGMENT  PARA PUBLIC 'CODE'
            ASSUME  CS:CSEG,DS:CSEG,ES:CSEG,SS:CSEG

SAL32       PROC  NEAR

            CMP    CL,0        ;If CL = 0, leave
            JE     EXIT
            PUSH   CX          ;Preserve shift count
            PUSH   DI          ; and working registers
            PUSH   SI
            SUB    DI,DI       ;Clear status flag holder
            SUB    CH,CH       ;Clear high byte of CX
SHIFT:      SAL    AX,1        ;Shift AX left one bit
            RCL    DX,1        ;Put displaced bit into DX
            JNO    CONTINUE
            MOV    DI,800H     ;On overflow, set bit 11 in DI
CONTINUE:   LOOP   SHIFT       ;Keep shifting until done
            PUSHF              ;Adjust Overflow Flag, if needed
            POP    SI
            OR     SI,DI
            PUSH   SI
            POPF
            POP    SI          ;Restore registers
            POP    DI
            POP    CX
EXIT:       RET                ;Return to calling program
SAL32       ENDP
CSEG   ENDS
            END
```

SHIFT ARITHMETIC RIGHT (SAR32)

SAR32 shifts a 32-bit signed number right by a specified number of bit positions.

Operation

If the shift count in CL is 0, the subroutine exits immediately, without shifting; otherwise, it clears CH to form a 16-bit shift count in CX. This value serves as a counter for the loop that starts at SHIFT. With each pass through the loop, the subroutine shifts DX to the right one bit position and rotates the displaced bit into AX.

Entry Values

DX:AX = Number to be shifted
CL = Shift count (0-30)

Results

DX:AX = Shifted number
The Carry Flag (CF) holds the last bit to be shifted out of AX.
CL is unaffected.

Link Command

```
link callprog+sar32;
```

Special Case

A shift count of zero causes an immediate exit with no shifting.

Subroutine Listing

```
; SAR32 - Shifts a signed 32-bit number right by a specified
; number of bit positions.
; Inputs: DX:AX = Number to be shifted
;         CL = Shift count (0-30)
; Results: DX:AX = Number after shift operation
;          CL is unaffected.

        PUBLIC  SAR32
CSEG    SEGMENT  PARA PUBLIC 'CODE'
        ASSUME  CS:CSEG,DS:CSEG,ES:CSEG,SS:CSEG

SAR32   PROC  NEAR

        CMP   CL,0      ;If CL = 0, leave
        JE    RTRN
        PUSH  CX        ;Preserve shift count
        SUB   CH,CH     ;Clear high byte of CX
SHIFT:  SAR   DX,1      ;Shift DX right one bit
        RCR   AX,1      ;Put displaced bit into AX
        LOOP  SHIFT     ;Keep shifting until done
        POP   CX        ;Restore shift count
```

```
RTRN:      RET              ;Return to calling program
SAR32      ENDP
CSEG  ENDS
           END
```

SHIFT LOGICAL RIGHT (SHR32)

SHR32 shifts a 32-bit unsigned number right by a specified number of bit positions.

Operation

If the shift count in CL is zero, the subroutine exits immediately, without shifting; otherwise, it clears CH to form a 16-bit shift count in CX. This value serves as a counter for the loop that starts at SHIFT. With each pass through the loop, the subroutine shifts DX to the right one bit position and rotates the displaced bit into AX.

Entry Values

DX:AX = Number to be shifted
   CL = Shift count (0-30)

Results

DX:AX = Shifted number
The Carry Flag (CF) holds the last bit to be shifted out of AX.
CL is unaffected.

Link Command

```
link callprog+shr32;
```

Special Case

A shift count of zero causes an immediate exit with no shifting.

Subroutine Listing

```
; SHR32 - Shifts an unsigned 32-bit number right by a
; specified number of bit positions.
; Inputs: DX:AX = Number to be shifted
;         CL = Shift count
; Results: DX:AX = Number after shift operation
;         CL is unaffected.

          PUBLIC  SHR32
CSEG  SEGMENT  PARA PUBLIC 'CODE'
          ASSUME  CS:CSEG,DS:CSEG,ES:CSEG,SS:CSEG

SHR32     PROC  NEAR

          CMP   CL,0      ;If CL = 0, leave
          JE    RTRN
          PUSH  CX        ;Preserve shift count
          SUB   CH,CH     ;Clear high byte of CX
SHIFT:    SHR   DX,1      ;Shift DX right one bit
          RCR   AX,1      ;Put displaced bit into AX
          LOOP  SHIFT     ;Keep shifting until done
```

```
                POP     CX              ;Restore shift count
RTRN:           RET                     ;Return to calling program
SHR32           ENDP
CSEG    ENDS
                END
```

ROTATE LEFT (ROL32)

ROL32 rotates a 32-bit operand left by a specified number of bit positions.

Operation

If the rotate count in CL is zero, the subroutine exits immediately, without rotating; otherwise, it clears CH to form a 16-bit count in CX. This value serves as a counter for the loop that starts at ROT. With each pass through the loop, the subroutine shifts DX to the left one bit position and rotates the displaced bit into AX.

Entry Values

DX:AX = Number to be rotated
    CL = Rotate count (0-30)

Results

DX:AX = Rotated number
The Carry Flag (CF) holds the last bit to be rotated out of DX.
CL is unaffected.

Link Command

```
link callprog+rol32;
```

Special Case

A rotate count of zero causes an immediate exit with no rotating.

Subroutine Listing

```
; ROL32 - Rotates a 32-bit number left by a specified
; number of bit positions.
; Inputs: DX:AX = Number to be rotated
;         CL = Rotate count
; Results: DX:AX = Number after rotate operation
;          CL is unaffected.

        PUBLIC  ROL32
CSEG    SEGMENT PARA PUBLIC 'CODE'
        ASSUME  CS:CSEG,DS:CSEG,ES:CSEG,SS:CSEG

ROL32   PROC    NEAR

        CMP     CL,0     ;If CL = 0, leave
        JE      RTRN
        PUSH    CX       ;Preserve count
        SUB     CH,CH    ;Clear high byte of CX
ROT:    SAL     DX,1     ;Shift DX left one bit
        PUSHF            ;Save CF status
        RCL     AX,1     ;Put displaced bit into AX
        ADC     DX,0     ;Put last AX bit into DX
```

```
               POPF                  ;Restore CF status
               LOOP    ROT           ;Keep rotating until done
               POP     CX            ;Restore count
RTRN:          RET                   ;Return to calling program
ROL32          ENDP
CSEG    ENDS
               END
```

ROTATE RIGHT (ROR32)

ROR32 rotates a 32-bit operand right by a specified number of bit positions.

Operation

If the rotate count in CL is zero, the subroutine exits immediately, without rotating; otherwise, it clears CH to form a 16-bit count in CX. This value serves as a counter for the loop that starts at ROT. With each pass through the loop, the subroutine shifts AX to the right one bit position and rotates the displaced bit into DX.

Entry Values

DX:AX = Number to be rotated
   CL = Rotate count (0-30)

Results

DX:AX = Rotated number
The Carry Flag (CF) holds the last bit to be rotated out of AX.
CL is unaffected.

Link Command

```
link callprog+ror32;
```

Special Case

A rotate count of zero causes an immediate exit with no rotating.

Subroutine Listing

```
; ROR32 - Rotates a 32-bit number right by a specified
; number of bit positions.
; Inputs: DX:AX = Number to be rotated
;         CL = Rotate count
; Results: DX:AX = Number after rotate operation
;         CF holds last bit rotated.
;         CL is unaffected.

        PUBLIC  ROR32
CSEG  SEGMENT PARA PUBLIC 'CODE'
        ASSUME  CS:CSEG,DS:CSEG,ES:CSEG,SS:CSEG

ROR32   PROC  NEAR

        CMP   CL,0      ;If CL = 0, leave
        JE    RTRN
        PUSH  CX        ;Preserve count
        SUB   CH,CH     ;Clear high byte of CX
ROT:    SHR   AX,1      ;Shift AX right one bit
        PUSHF           ;Save CF status
        RCR   DX,1      ;Put displaced bit into DX
```

129

```
              JNC     GET_CF      ;Put last DX bit into AX
              OR      AX,8000H
GET_CF:       POPF                ;Restore CF status
              LOOP    ROT         ;Keep rotating until done
              POP     CX          ;Restore count
RTRN:         RET                 ;Return to calling program
ROR32         ENDP
CSEG   ENDS
              END
```

ROTATE LEFT THROUGH CARRY (RCL32)

RCL32 rotates a 32-bit operand left through Carry by a specified number of bit positions.

Operation

If the rotate count in CL is zero, the subroutine exits immediately, without rotating; otherwise, it clears CH to form a 16-bit count in CX. This value serves as a counter for the loop that starts at ROT. With each pass through the loop, the subroutine rotates AX to the left one bit position and rotates the displaced bit into DX.

Entry Values

DX:AX = Number to be rotated
   CL = Rotate count (0-30)
The Carry Flag (CF) must hold the bit value to be rotated into bit 1 of AX.

Results

DX:AX = Rotated number
The Carry Flag (CF) holds the last bit to be displaced out of DX.
CL is unaffected.

Link Command

```
link callprog+rcl32;
```

Special Case

A rotate count of zero causes an immediate exit with no rotating.

Warning

Before calling RCL32, remember to set or clear the Carry Flag, depending on whether you want to rotate a 1 or a 0 into the low bit of AX. An STC instruction sets the Carry Flag; a CLC instruction clears it.

Subroutine Listing

```
; RCL32 - Rotates a 32-bit number left, through the
; Carry Flag (CF), by a specified number of bit positions.
; number of bit positions.
; Inputs: DX:AX = Number to be rotated
;         CL = Rotate count
;         CF holds initial value to be rotated into AX.
; Results: DX:AX = Number after rotate operation
;         CF holds last bit rotated out of DX.
;         CL is unaffected.

        PUBLIC  RCL32
CSEG  SEGMENT  PARA PUBLIC 'CODE'
        ASSUME  CS:CSEG,DS:CSEG,ES:CSEG,SS:CSEG
```

```
RCL32       PROC   NEAR

            PUSHF             ;Save initial CF value
            CMP    CL,0       ;Does CL = 0?
            JNE    GO
            POPF              ; If so, restore CF
            RET               ;  and leave
GO:         PUSH   CX         ;Preserve count
            SUB    CH,CH      ;Clear high byte of CX
            POPF              ;Restore initial CF value
ROT:        RCL    AX,1       ;Rotate AX left one bit
            RCL    DX,1       ;Rotate DX left one bit
            LOOP   ROT        ;Keep rotating until done
            POP    CX         ;Restore count
            RET               ;Return to calling program
RCL32       ENDP
CSEG   ENDS
            END
```

ROTATE RIGHT THROUGH CARRY (RCR32)

RCR32 rotates a 32-bit operand right through Carry by a specified number of bit positions.

Operation

If the rotate count in CL is zero, the subroutine exits immediately, without rotating; otherwise, it clears CH to form a 16-bit count in CX. This value serves as a counter for the loop that starts at ROT. With each pass through the loop, the subroutine rotates DX to the right one bit position and rotates the displaced bit into AX.

Entry Values

DX:AX = Number to be rotated
    CL = Rotate count (0-30)
The Carry Flag (CF) must hold the bit value to be rotated into bit 15 of DX.

Results

DX:AX = Rotated number
The Carry Flag (CF) holds the last bit to be displaced out of AX.
CL is unaffected.

Link Command

```
link callprog+rcr32;
```

Special Case

A rotate count of zero causes an immediate exit with no rotating.

Warning

Before calling RCR32, remember to set or clear the Carry Flag, depending on whether you want to rotate a 1 or a 0 into the high bit of DX. An STC instruction sets the Carry Flag; a CLC instruction clears it.

Subroutine Listing

```
; RCR32 - Rotates a 32-bit number right, through the
; Carry Flag (CF), by a specified number of bit positions.
; Inputs: DX:AX = Number to be rotated
;         CL = Rotate count
;         CF holds initial value to be rotated into DX.
; Results: DX:AX = Number after rotate operation
;          CF holds last bit rotated out of AX.
;          CL is unaffected.

        PUBLIC  RCR32
CSEG  SEGMENT  PARA PUBLIC 'CODE'
        ASSUME  CS:CSEG,DS:CSEG,ES:CSEG,SS:CSEG
```

```
RCR32       PROC  NEAR

            PUSHF             ;Save initial CF value
            CMP   CL,0        ;Does CL = 0?
            JNE   GO
            POPF              ; If so, restore CF
            RET               ;  and leave
GO:         PUSH  CX          ;Preserve count
            SUB   CH,CH       ;Clear high byte of CX
            POPF              ;Restore initial CF value
ROT:        RCR   DX,1        ;Rotate DX right one bit
            RCR   AX,1        ;Rotate AX right one bit
            LOOP  ROT         ;Keep rotating until done
            POP   CX          ;Restore count
            RET               ;Return to calling program
RCR32       ENDP
CSEG  ENDS
            END
```

Chapter 9

Code Conversion

Sometimes your data is not in the form you want. When that happens, you can certainly write a special program that manipulates the data as-is, but that approach is often too time consuming and error prone to warrant the effort. Generally, it's easier to convert the data to a form that's more convenient to use, do the operation, and then convert the result back to the original form. The subroutines in this chapter provide a variety of code conversion operations.

The first two subroutines convert between binary and BCD, the two numeric forms on which Intel microprocessors can operate. The rest of the subroutines perform conversions to and from a code convention called *ASCII* (short for American Standard Code for Information Interchange). ASCII is the form in which data is transferred between a computer and its peripherals. For example, when you read characters in from the keyboard, they arrive in ASCII. Similarly, characters the computer sends to the display or printer must also be in ASCII form. Appendix B summarizes the ASCII character set. You will encounter ASCII extensively in the later chapters of this book, starting with Chapter 14.

BINARY TO PACKED BCD CONVERSION (BIN2BCD)

BIN2BCD converts an eight-bit binary number to two binary-coded-decimal (BCD) digits.

Operation

The subroutine converts the binary value in AL to two BCD digits. To begin, it checks whether the number is greater than 99; if so, it sets the Carry Flag (CF) to 1 and exits. Otherwise, it extends AL to a 16-bit number and divides it by 10. The quotient in AL is the high digit; the remainder in AH is the low digit. The subroutine then aligns the high digit in the upper four bits by shifting AL to the left. Finally, it combines the digits to form the result.

Entry Value

AL = 8-bit binary value

Result

If CF = 0, the input was valid and AL = two packed BCD digits.
If CF = 1, the input was invalid and AL is unaffected.

Link Command

```
link callprog+bin2bcd;
```

Comments

Generally, you should follow CALL BIN2BCD with an instruction of the form JC TOO_BIG, where TOO_BIG is a set of instructions that display a message if the binary number was larger than 99.

Chapter 7 contains a subroutine that converts a 16-bit binary number to packed BCD.

Subroutine Listing

```
; BIN2BCD - Converts an eight-bit binary number to packed BCD
; Input: AL = Eight-bit binary number.
; Results: If CF = 0, then AL = Two-digit BCD number
;          If CF = 1, then the number is too large to be
;                     converted and AL contains the original binary value.

        PUBLIC   BIN2BCD
CSEG    SEGMENT  PARA PUBLIC 'CODE'
        ASSUME   CS:CSEG,DS:CSEG,ES:CSEG,SS:CSEG
        JMP      BIN2BCD    ;Skip past data area
AHLOC   DB       ?          ;Save AH here
CLLOC   DB       ?          ;Save CL here

BIN2BCD PROC     NEAR
        CMP      AL,99      ;Number out of range?
        JBE      SAVEAH
        STC                 ; If so, set CF
```

```
                JC      EXIT        ;  and exit
SAVEAH:         MOV     AHLOC,AH    ;Save working registers in memory
                MOV     CLLOC,CL
                CBW                 ;Extend AL through AH
                MOV     CL,10       ;Divide by 10
                DIV     CL          ; (high digit in AL, low in AH)
                MOV     CL,4        ;Shift high digit left four bits
                SHL     AL,CL
                OR      AL,AH       ; and combine it with low digit
                MOV     AH,AHLOC    ;Restore working registers
                MOV     CL,CLLOC
EXIT:           RET                 ;Return to calling program
BIN2BCD         ENDP
CSEG    ENDS
                END
```

PACKED BCD TO BINARY CONVERSION (BCD2BIN)

BCD2BIN converts two packed binary-coded-decimal (BCD) digits in a register to binary.

Operation

The subroutine converts the two BCD digits in AL to binary. To do this, it saves the lower digit in CH, and then shifts the high digit to the rightmost bit positions and multiplies it by 10. From here, it simply adds CH to AL to obtain the binary result.

Entry Value

AL = two-digit packed BCD value

Result

AL = 8-bit binary value

Link Command

```
link callprog+bcd2bin;
```

Comment

Chapter 7 contains a subroutine that converts four packed BCD digits to a 16-bit binary number.

Subroutine Listing

```
; BCD2BIN - Converts a packed two-digit BCD number to binary.
; Input: AL = Two-digit BCD value
; Result: AL = Eight-bit binary value

            PUBLIC   BCD2BIN
CSEG    SEGMENT  PARA PUBLIC 'CODE'
            ASSUME   CS:CSEG,DS:CSEG,SS:CSEG,ES:CSEG
            JMP      BCD2BIN   ;Skip the data area
SAVEAH      DB       ?         ;Save AH here
SAVECX      DW       ?         ;Save CX here

BCD2BIN     PROC  NEAR
            MOV      SAVEAH,AH ;Save affected registers
            MOV      SAVECX,CX
            MOV      CH,AL      ;Save low digit in CH
            AND      CH,0FH     ; by clearing the high digit
            MOV      CL,4       ;Shift high digit to low bits
            SHR      AL,CL
            MOV      CL,10      ; and multiply it by 10
            MUL      CL
            ADD      AL,CH      ;Add the digits
            MOV      AH,SAVEAH ;Restore working registers
            MOV      CX,SAVECX
            RET
```

```
BCD2BIN    ENDP
CSEG    ENDS
            END
```

BINARY TO HEXADECIMAL ASCII CONVERSION (BIN2ASC)

BIN2ASC converts a 4-bit binary number to an ASCII character.

Operation

The subroutine converts the binary number in the low four bits of AL to ASCII, using a look-up table. It returns the ASCII character in the lower four bits of AL and puts zeroes in the upper four bits.

Entry Value

Low four bits of AL = Binary number (0-15)

Result

AL = ASCII character (0-F)

Link Command

```
link callprog+bin2asc;
```

Comment

See Appendix B for the ASCII character set.

Subroutine Listing

```
; BIN2ASC -  Converts a hexadecimal number to ASCII
; Input: Low four bits of AL = Binary number (0-15)
, Result: AL = ASCII character (0-F)
          PUBLIC   BIN2ASC
CSEG   SEGMENT  PARA PUBLIC 'CODE'
          ASSUME   CS:CSEG,DS:CSEG,SS:CSEG,ES:CSEG
          JMP      BIN2ASC  ;Skip the look-up table
ASCII     DB       '0123456789ABCDEF'

BIN2ASC   PROC     NEAR
          PUSH     BX          ;Save BX on the stack
          AND      AL,0FH      ;Clear the high four bits of AL
          LEA      BX,ASCII ;Look up the ASCII character
          XLAT     ASCII
          POP      BX          ;Retrieve BX
          RET
BIN2ASC   ENDP
CSEG   ENDS
          END
```

HEXADECIMAL ASCII TO BINARY CONVERSION (ASC2BIN)

ASC2BIN converts an ASCII character between 0 and 9 or A and F to a binary number.

Operation

The subroutine converts the ASCII character in AL to a binary number. If the character is not in the range 0 to 9 or A to F, the subroutine sets the Carry Flag to 1.

Entry Value

ASCII character (0-F)

Result

If CF = 0, then AL = Binary number (0-15).
If CF = 1, then the character was invalid and AL contains its original value.

Link Command

```
link callprog+asc2bin;
```

Comments

Generally, you should follow CALL ASC2BIN with an instruction of the form JC NOT_HEX, where NOT_HEX is a set of instructions that display a message if the ASCII character does not represent a hexadecimal digit.

See Appendix B for the ASCII character set.

Subroutine Listing

```
; ASC2BIN -  Converts an ASCII character to binary
; Input: AL = ASCII character (0-F)
; Result: If CF = 0, then AL = Binary number (0-15)
;         If CF = 1, then the input was invalid and AL is
;         unchanged

        PUBLIC  BIN2ASC
CSEG  SEGMENT  PARA PUBLIC 'CODE'
        ASSUME  CS:CSEG,DS:CSEG,SS:CSEG,ES:CSEG

ASC2BIN PROC  NEAR
        CMP   AL,'0'    ;Check for hex character
        JB    INVALID
        CMP   AL,'9'
        JBE   STRIP
        CMP   AL,'A'
        JB    INVALID
        CMP   AL,'F'
        JA    INVALID
        ADD   AL,9      ;Add nine (char. between A and F)
```

```
STRIP:      AND    AL,0FH    ;Strip off the high four bits
            RET

INVALID:    STC              ;Char. is invalid, set CF = 1
            RET

ASC2BIN    ENDP
CSEG   ENDS
            END
```

UNSIGNED BINARY TO ASCII STRING CONVERSION (UBIN2$)

UBIN2$ converts an unsigned 16-bit binary number to an ASCII string.

Operation

The subroutine converts the unsigned binary number in AX to an ASCII string in memory. To begin, it checks the magnitude of the number. If the number is less than or equal to 9999, the subroutine uses the B2BCDW subroutine in Chapter 7 to convert the number to packed BCD. This number is stored in memory at location BCDS.

The loop that starts at NXTDIG skips leading zeroes by comparing the digit characters, one-by-one, to ASCII 0. Upon finding the first nonzero character, the subroutine stores it in the string buffer (ASC$) in memory and, unless it is all zeroes, jumps to NEXTDIG to store the remaining characters. Finally, the instructions at GETOFF load the string offset into DX and the character count into CX.

The subroutine works similarly for binary numbers greater than 9999, except it first processes the "ten-thousands" digit. To do this, the subroutine divides the entry value by 10,000 to calculate the digit and then uses the BIN2ASC subroutine in this chapter to convert the digit to ASCII. Once the subroutine has extracted this digit, the remainder is less than 9999. Therefore, the subroutine converts the remainder to four-digit packed BCD and stores it in the ASC$ buffer as before.

Entry Value

AX = Unsigned binary number

Results

DX = Offset of string
CX = Character count
AX is unaffected.

Link Command

```
link callprog+ubin2$+bin2asc+b2bcdw;
```

Comment

To convert a signed binary number to a string, use the SBIN2$ subroutine in this chapter.

Subroutine Listing

```
; UBIN2$ - Converts an unsigned 16-bit binary number to an
;   ASCII string
; Input: AX = Unsigned binary number
; Results: DX = Offset of string
;          CX = Character count
;          AX is unaffected.

        EXTRN   BIN2ASC:NEAR,B2BCDW:NEAR
        PUBLIC  UBIN2$
```

```
CSEG    SEGMENT  PARA PUBLIC 'CODE'
                ASSUME  CS:CSEG,DS:CSEG,ES:CSEG,SS:CSEG
                JMP     UBIN2$      ;Skip the data area
ASC$    DB      5 DUP(?)    ;String can be up to 5 characters
BCDS    DW      ?           ;This word holds 4 BCD digits
UBIN2$  PROC  NEAR
                PUSH    AX          ;Save input value
                PUSH    DI          ; and working register DI
                LEA     DI,ASC$     ;Make DI point to string buffer
                CLD                 ;Make string instructions go forward
                CMP     AX,9999     ;Is number < or = 9999?
                JA      GT9999
                CALL    B2BCDW      ; Yes. Convert it to 4 BCD digits
                MOV     BCDS,AX     ; and store it in memory
                MOV     CX,4        ;Skip leading zeroes
NXTDIG:         CALL    ROTAX4L
                CMP     AL,'0'
                LOOPE   NXTDIG
                STOS    ASC$        ;Store remaining digits in the string
                JCXZ    GETOFF
                JMP     NEXTDIG

; The number is greater than 9999.

GT9999:         SUB     DX,DX       ;Form 32-bit dividend DX:AX
                MOV     CX,10000    ;Calculate ten-thousands digit
                DIV     CX
                CALL    BIN2ASC     ;Convert it to ASCII
                STOS    ASC$        ; and store it in the string
                MOV     AX,DX       ;Convert the remainder to 4 BCD digits
                CALL    B2BCDW
                MOV     BCDS,AX     ; and store it in memory
                MOV     CX,4        ;Convert and store those digits
NEXTDIG:        CALL    ROTAX4L
                STOS    ASC$
                LOOP    NEXTDIG
GETOFF:         LEA     DX,ASC$     ;Load string offset into DX
                SUB     DI,DX       ; and character count into CX
                MOV     CX,DI
                POP     DI          ;Retrieve original DI
                POP     AX          ; and the input value
                RET                 ;Return to calling program
UBIN2$  ENDP

; This subroutine rotates the four-digit BCD number in memory
; location BCDS to the left by four bit positions, then reads
; it into AX and converts the low digit to ASCII.

ROTAX4L PROC  NEAR
                ROL     BCDS,1      ;Rotate BCDS left four bits
                ROL     BCDS,1
```

144

```
        ROL    BCDS,1
        ROL    BCDS,1
        MOV    AX,BCDS   ;Load digits into AX
        JMP    BIN2ASC   ; and convert low digit to ASCII
ROTAX4L ENDP
CSEG  ENDS
        END
```

SIGNED BINARY TO ASCII STRING CONVERSION (SBIN2$)

SBIN2$ converts a signed 16-bit binary number to an ASCII string. If the number is negative, the subroutine stores a minus sign ($-$) as the first character of the string.

Operation

The subroutine converts the signed binary number in AX to an ASCII string in memory. If the number is negative, it stores a minus sign at the beginning of the string, then negates (two's-complements) the number to make it positive. Next, the subroutine checks the magnitude of the number. If the number is less than or equal to 9999, the subroutine uses the B2BCDW subroutine in Chapter 7 to convert the number to packed BCD. This number is stored in memory at location BCDS. The loop that starts at NXTDIG skips leading zeroes by comparing the digits, one-by-one, to ASCII 0. Upon finding the first nonzero character, the subroutine stores it in the string buffer (ASC$) in memory and, unless it is all zeroes, jumps to NEXTDIG to store the remaining characters. Finally, the instructions at GETOFF load the string offset into DX and the character count into CX.

The subroutine works similarly for binary numbers greater than 9999, except it first processes the "ten-thousands" digit. To do this, it divides the entry value by 10,000 to calculate the digit and then uses the BIN2ASC subroutine in this chapter to convert the digit to ASCII. Once the subroutine has extracted this digit, the remainder is less than 9999. Therefore, the subroutine converts the remainder to four-digit packed BCD and stores it in the ASC$ buffer as before.

Entry Value

AX = Signed binary number

Results

DX = Offset of string
CX = Character count
AX is unaffected.

Link Command

```
link callprog+sbin2$+bin2asc+b2bcdw;
```

Comment

To convert an unsigned binary number to a string, use the UBIN2$ subroutine in this chapter.

Subroutine Listing

```
; SBIN2$ - Converts a signed 16-bit binary number to an
;   ASCII string
; Input: AX = Signed binary number
; Results: DX = Offset of string
;          CX = Character count
;          AX is unaffected.
```

```
                EXTRN   BIN2ASC:NEAR,B2BCDW:NEAR
                PUBLIC  SBIN2$
CSEG    SEGMENT  PARA PUBLIC 'CODE'
                ASSUME  CS:CSEG,DS:CSEG,ES:CSEG,SS:CSEG
                JMP     SBIN2$        ;Skip the data area
KEEPAX   DW     ?             ;Save the original number here
ASC$     DB     6 DUP(?)      ;String can have be up to 6 characters
                              ; (minus sign plus five digits)
BCDS     DW     ?             ;This word holds 4 BCD digits

SBIN2$   PROC  NEAR
                PUSH  DI            ;Save DI on the stack
                MOV   KEEPAX,AX   ; and save AX in memory
                LEA   DI,ASC$      ;Make DI point to string buffer
                CLD                ;Make string instructions go forward
                OR    AX,AX        ;Is number negative?
                JNS   POS

; The number is negative. Store a minus sign in the string,
; then make the number positive.

                MOV   AL,'-'     ;Store a minus sign (hyphen)
                STOS  ASC$        ; in the string
                MOV   AX,KEEPAX ;Retrieve the original number
                NEG   AX          ; and make it positive

; Convert a positive binary number to a string in ASC$.

POS:            CMP   AX,9999    ;Is number < or = 9999?
                JA    GT9999
                CALL  B2BCDW     ; Yes. Convert it to 4 BCD digits
                MOV   BCDS,AX    ; and store it in memory
                MOV   CX,4       ;Skip leading zeroes
NXTDIG:         CALL  ROTAX4L
                CMP   AL,'0'
                LOOPE NXTDIG
NONZERO:        STOS  ASC$       ;Store the remaining digits in string
                JCXZ  GETOFF
                JMP   NEXTDIG

; The number is greater than 9999.

GT9999:         SUB   DX,DX      ;Form 32-bit dividend DX:AX
                MOV   CX,10000   ;Calculate ten-thousands digit
                DIV   CX
                CALL  BIN2ASC    ;Convert it to ASCII
                STOS  ASC$       ; and store it in the string
                MOV   AX,DX      ;Convert the remainder to 4 BCD digits
                CALL  B2BCDW
                MOV   BCDS,AX    ; and store it in memory
                MOV   CX,4       ;Convert and store those digits
```

147

```
NEXTDIG:    CALL    ROTAX4L
            STOS    ASC$
            LOOP    NEXTDIG
GETOFF:     LEA     DX,ASC$     ;Load string offset into DX
            SUB     DI,DX       ; and character count into CX
            MOV     CX,DI
            POP     DI          ;Retrieve original DI
            MOV     AX,KEEPAX   ; and input value
            RET                 ;Return to calling program
SBIN2$      ENDP
```

```
; This subroutine rotates the four-digit BCD number in memory
; location BCDS to the left by four bit positions, then reads
; it into AX and converts the low digit to ASCII.
```

```
ROTAX4L     PROC    NEAR
            ROL     BCDS,1      ;Rotate BCDS left four bits
            ROL     BCDS,1
            ROL     BCDS,1
            ROL     BCDS,1
            MOV     AX,BCDS     ;Load digits into AX
            JMP     BIN2ASC     ; and convert low digit to ASCII
ROTAX4L     ENDP
CSEG   ENDS
            END
```

ASCII DECIMAL STRING TO UNSIGNED BINARY CONVERSION ($2UBIN)

$2UBIN converts a string of ASCII decimal characters to an unsigned 16-bit binary number.

Operation

The subroutine converts an ASCII string to an unsigned binary number in AX. It obtains the offset of the string from DX and the character count from CX.

The subroutine uses DX to accumulate the binary number, and begins by clearing DX to zero. At NEXTCHAR, it enters a loop in which it multiplies the running total in DX by 10 and then reads the next string character, converts it to binary, and adds it to the total. Multiplying DX by 10 is performed by a subroutine called DXTIMES10.

The DXTIMES10 subroutine uses Shift Left (SHL) instructions to quadruple the contents of DX; then it adds the original value to form the "times 5" product and shifts left again to form the "times 10" product. I have constructed this subroutine instead of using an MUL instruction to avoid using AX as the multiplicand.

Entry Values

DX = Offset of the string
CX = Character count

Results

If CF = 0, then AX = Binary number
If CF = 1, then the string is invalid and AX is unchanged. The conditions that
  set CF to 1 are:
  • CX is greater than 5
  • The total is more than 65,535
  • A string character is not in the range 0 to 9
DX and CX are unaffected.

Link Command

```
link callprog+$2ubin;
```

Comment

To convert a string to a signed binary number, use the $2SBIN subroutine in this chapter.

Subroutine Listing

```
; $2UBIN - Converts an ASCII string to an unsigned 16-bit
;   binary number.
; Inputs: DX = Offset of string
;         CX = Character count
; Results: If CF = 0, then AX = Binary number
;          If CF = 1, then the string is invalid and AX is
;            unchanged.
;          CX and DX are unaffected.
```

```
                PUBLIC   $2UBIN
CSEG    SEGMENT  PARA PUBLIC 'CODE'
                ASSUME   CS:CSEG,DS:CSEG,ES:CSEG,SS:CSEG
                JMP      $2UBIN     ;Skip the data area
SAVEDX          DW       ?          ;Save DX here temporarily
SAVEAX          DW       ?          ;Save AX in case of error


$2UBIN   PROC  NEAR
                PUSH     CX         ;Save affected registers
                PUSH     DX
                PUSH     SI
                MOV      SAVEAX,AX  ; and original value of AX
                CMP      CX,5       ;Too many characters?
                JA       INVALID
                CLD                 ;Make string instructions go forward
                MOV      SI,DX      ;Make SI point to string
                SUB      DX,DX      ;DX will accumulate the result
NEXTCHAR:       CALL     DXTIMES10  ;Multiply the total by 10
                JC       INVALID
                LODSB               ;Read the next string character
                CMP      AL,'0'     ;Is it between 0 and 9?
                JB       INVALID
                CMP      AL,'9'
                JA       INVALID
                AND      AX,0FH     ; Yes. Convert it to binary
                ADD      DX,AX      ;  and add it to the total
                JC       INVALID
                LOOP     NEXTCHAR   ;Process next character
                MOV      AX,DX      ;Move binary result to AX
                JMP      EXIT       ; and leave
INVALID:        STC                 ;On error, set Carry
                MOV      AX,SAVEAX  ; and restore AX
EXIT:           POP      SI         ;Retrieve registers
                POP      DX
                POP      CX
                RET                 ; and return to calling program
$2UBIN   ENDP

; This subroutine multiplies the running total in DX by 10.

DXTIMES10  PROC  NEAR
                MOV      SAVEDX,DX  ;Save DX in memory
                SHL      DX,1       ;Multiply by 2
                SHL      DX,1       ;Multiply by 2 again (x4)
                ADD      DX,SAVEDX  ;Add original value (x5)
                SHL      DX,1       ;Multiply by 2 once more (x10)
                RET
DXTIMES10  ENDP
CSEG    ENDS
                END
```

ASCII DECIMAL STRING TO SIGNED BINARY CONVERSION ($2SBIN)

$2SBIN converts a string of ASCII decimal characters to a signed 16-bit binary number.

Operation

The subroutine converts an ASCII string to a signed binary number in AX. It obtains the offset of the string from DX and the character count from CX.

The subroutine first checks whether the string begins with a minus or plus sign character. A minus sign sets a MINUS indicator to 1. After checking for a sign character, the subroutine clears DX for use as an accumulator. At NEXTCHAR, it enters a loop in which it multiplies the running total in DX by 10 and then reads the next string character, converts it to binary, and adds it to the total. Multiplying DX by 10 is performed by a subroutine called DXTIMES10.

The DXTIMES10 subroutine uses Shift Left (SHL) instructions to quadruple the contents of DX; then it adds the original value to form the "times 5" product and shifts left again to form the "times 10" product. I have constructed this subroutine instead of using an MUL instruction to avoid using AX as the multiplicand.

Entry Values

DX = Offset of the string
CX = Character count

Results

If CF = 0, then AX = Binary number.
If CF = 1, then the string is invalid and AX is unchanged. The conditions that set CF to 1 are:
- CX is greater than 6
- The total is more negative than −32,768 or more positive than 32,767
- A string character is not in the range 0 to 9

DX and CX are unaffected.

Link Command

```
link callprog+$2sbin;
```

Comment

To convert a string to an unsigned binary number, use the $2UBIN subroutine in this chapter.

Subroutine Listing

```
; $2SBIN - Converts an ASCII string to a signed 16-bit binary
;   number.
; Inputs: DX = Offset of string
;         CX = Character count
; Results: If CF = 0, then AX = Binary number
```

```
;              If CF = 1, then the string is invalid and AX is
;                 unchanged.
;              CX and DX are unaffected.

              PUBLIC   $2SBIN
CSEG   SEGMENT  PARA PUBLIC 'CODE'
              ASSUME   CS:CSEG,DS:CSEG,ES:CSEG,SS:CSEG
              JMP      $2SBIN      ;Skip the data area
MINUS         DB       0           ;MINUS = 1 for negative number
SAVEDX        DW       ?           ;Save DX here temporarily
SAVEAX        DW       ?           ;Save AX in case of error

$2SBIN  PROC  NEAR
              PUSH     CX          ;Save affected registers
              PUSH     DX
              PUSH     SI
              MOV      SAVEDX,AX   ; and original value of AX
              CMP      CX,6        ;Too many characters?
              JA       INVALID
              CLD                  ;Make string instructions go forward
              MOV      SI,DX       ;Make SI point to string
              MOV      AL,[SI]     ;Read the first string character
              CMP      AL,'-'      ;Is it a minus sign?
              JNE      CHK4P
              MOV      MINUS,1     ; Yes. Put 1 in MINUS
              JMP      DECSI       ;  and go adjust the count and pointer
CHK4P:        CMP      AL,'+'      ;Is it a plus sign?
              JNE      CLRDX
DECSI:        DEC      CX          ; Yes. Decrease the character count
              INC      SI          ;  and increase the string pointer
CLRDX:        SUB      DX,DX       ;DX will accumulate the result
NEXTCHAR:     CALL     DXTIMES10   ;Multiply the total by 10
              JC       INVALID
              LODSB                ;Read the next string character
              CMP      AL,'0'      ;Is it between 0 and 9?
              JB       INVALID
              CMP      AL,'9'
              JA       INVALID
              AND      AX,0FH      ; Yes. Convert it to binary
              ADD      DX,AX       ;  and add it to the total
              JC       INVALID
              LOOP     NEXTCHAR    ;Process next character
              MOV      AX,DX       ;Move binary result to AX
              CMP      MINUS,1     ;Was string negative?
              JNE      EXIT        ; No. Leave
              NEG      AX          ; Yes. Negate AX
              JMP      EXIT        ;  and then leave
INVALID:      STC                  ;On error, set Carry
              MOV      AX,SAVEAX   ; and restore AX
EXIT:         POP      SI          ;Retrieve registers
              POP      DX
```

```
          POP     CX
          RET                     ; and return to calling program
$2SBIN    ENDP

; This subroutine multiplies the running total in DX by 10.

DXTIMES10 PROC    NEAR
          MOV     SAVEDX,DX ;Save DX in memory
          SHL     DX,1      ;Multiply by 2
          SHL     DX,1      ;Multiply by 2 again (x4)
          ADD     DX,SAVEDX ;Add original value (x5)
          SHL     DX,1      ;Multiply by 2 once more (x10)
          RET
DXTIMES10 ENDP
CSEG  ENDS
          END
```

Chapter 10

String Manipulation

The 8086 and 8088 microprocessors have instructions that move, compare, scan, load, and store strings, and the 80286 provides additional instructions that input and output strings. These instructions are fairly easy to use once you get familiar with the various repeat prefixes. Still, one of my goals in writing this book is to provide subroutines that can help save you from constructing programs one instruction at a time. The subroutines will (hopefully) do much of the work for you!

I have, in fact, already presented three string manipulation subroutines in Chapter 5, although *string* is not in their names. These are *block* manipulation subroutines, but after all, that's all a string is: a block of consecutive locations in memory. The first of these subroutines, Move Block of Bytes (MOVBLOCK), is simply a "smart" variation of the microprocessor's Move Byte String (MOVSB) instruction. MOVBLOCK starts moving from the end of the block (string) if the destination is higher in memory, and from the beginning of the block if it is lower in memory. This guards against data being overwritten.

The other two block/string subroutines in Chapter 5, Compare Blocks of Bytes (COMPMEMB) and Compare Blocks of Words (COMPMEMW), are enhanced versions of the Compare Byte Strings (CMPSB) and Compare Word Strings (CMPSW) instructions. The subroutines return the offset of the mismatched byte or word, while the instructions only return indications in the status flags.

In summary, I could have actually put MOVBLOCK, COMPMEMB, and COMP-MEMW in this chapter, and renamed them, say, Move Byte String, Compare Byte Strings, and Compare Word Strings. I didn't do that, however, because I felt that readers doing memory operations may not think to look here for subroutines they could use.

154

The subroutines in this chapter provide additional operations on byte strings. Thus, they are particularly useful for manipulating text. I begin with two subroutines that combine two strings into one. The first subroutine places the second string immediately after the first in memory, while the other inserts the second string into the first, at a specified location.

The remaining subroutines work with a part of a string, or as it is called, a *substring*. One subroutine finds the location of a substring; the other three delete, copy, and move substrings. Note that these are tasks that word processing programs do. Hence, you could use them to create your own word processor, if you are so inclined.

APPEND ONE STRING TO ANOTHER (APPEND$)

APPEND$ combines two strings by placing the second immediately after the first in memory.

Operation

The subroutine places one string immediately after another in memory by repeating a Move Byte String (MOVSB) instruction.

Entry Values

DI = Offset of the first string
SI = Offset of the second string (the one to be appended)
BX = Length of first string in bytes
CX = Length of second string in bytes

Results

If ZF = 0, SI contains the new offset of the second string and BX contains the new length of the first string.

If ZF = 1, the operation did not take place because one string has a length of zero or the second string is already within the first one; the registers are unaffected.

Link Command

```
link callprog+append$;
```

Subroutine Listing

```
; APPEND$ - Append one string to another.
; Inputs: DI = Offset of first string
;         SI = Offset of second string
;         BX = Length of first string
;         CX = Length of second string
; Results: If the operation is successful, ZF = 0 and
;          SI = New offset of second string
;          BX = New length of first string
;          If either string has zero length or the second
;          string is already within the first one, ZF =1
;          and the registers are unchanged.

           PUBLIC  APPEND$
CSEG   SEGMENT    PARA PUBLIC 'CODE'
           ASSUME  CS:CSEG,DS:CSEG,ES:CSEG,SS:CSEG
           JMP     APPEND$  ;Skip past data area
SIZE2      DW      ?        ;Hold original CX here
OFF1       DW      ?        ;Hold original DI here

APPEND$    PROC    NEAR
           JCXZ    QUIT     ;Quit if either string is empty
           CMP     BX,0
```

```
                JE      QUIT
                MOV     SIZE2,CX  ;Save input values
                MOV     OFF1,DI
                ADD     DI,BX     ;Calculate target location
                CMP     SI,DI     ;Is second string already in first?
                JA      OKAY
                PUSH    SI
                ADD     SI,CX
                CMP     SI,OFF1
                POP     SI
                JBE     OKAY
                SUB     DI,DI     ; Yes. Force Zero Flag 1
                JZ      EXIT      ;  and exit
OKAY:           CLD               ; No. Work forward
REP             MOVSB             ;Move the second string
                MOV     SI,DI     ;Make SI point to new offset
                ADD     BX,SIZE2  ; and update size of first string
EXIT:           MOV     DI,OFF1   ;Restore DI
                MOV     CX,SIZE2  ; and CX
QUIT:           RET               ;Return to calling program
APPEND$         ENDP
CSEG    ENDS
                END
```

INSERT ONE STRING IN ANOTHER (INSERT$)

INSERT$ combines two strings by inserting the second at a specified location within the first in memory.

Operation

To insert the second string, the subroutine first makes room for it by opening a gap in the first string. The gap starts at the insertion point and is the same length as the second string. The subroutine creates the gap by moving the remainder of the first string (every byte from the insertion point on) down by the length of the second string. It moves bytes starting at the end of the string, because starting at the beginning would cause bytes to be overwritten. The subroutine then copies the second string into the gap, but moves forward (i.e., starts at the beginning of the second string) this time.

Entry Values

DI = Offset of the first string
SI = Offset of the second string (the one to be inserted)
BP = Offset of insertion point in first string
BX = Length of first string in bytes
CX = Length of second string in bytes

Results

If ZF = 0, SI contains the new offset of the second string and BX contains the new length of the first string.

If ZF = 1, the operation did not take place because one string has a length of zero, the second string is already within the first one, or the insertion point is not within the first string; the registers are unaffected.

Link Command

```
link callprog+insert$;
```

Comment

You can also use this subroutine to insert a single character in a string. Simply store the character in memory, make SI point to it, and set CX to 1.

Subroutine Listing

```
; INSERT$ - Insert one string into another
; Inputs: DI = Offset of first string
;         SI = Offset of second string
;         BP = Offset of insertion point in first string
;         BX = Length of first string
;         CX = Length of second string
; Results: If the operation is successful, ZF = 0 and
;             SI = New offset of second string
;             BX = New length of first string
;          If either string has zero length, the second
```

```
;                    string is already within the first one, or the
;                    insertion point is not within the first string,
;                    ZF =1 and the registers are unchanged.

             PUBLIC  INSERT$
CSEG  SEGMENT  PARA PUBLIC 'CODE'
             ASSUME  CS:CSEG,DS:CSEG,ES:CSEG,SS:CSEG
             JMP     INSERT$  ;Skip past data area
SIZE2        DW      ?        ;Hold original CX here
OFF1         DW      ?        ;Hold original DI here
INSERT$      PROC    NEAR
             JCXZ    QUIT       ;Quit if either string is empty
             CMP     BX,0
             JE      QUIT
             MOV     SIZE2,CX ;Save input values
             MOV     OFF1,DI
             ADD     DI,BX      ;Get offset of byte following string 1
             CMP     SI,DI      ;Is second string already in first?
             JA      OKAY
             PUSH    SI
             ADD     SI,CX
             CMP     SI,OFF1
             POP     SI
             JBE     OKAY
             SUB     DI,DI    ; Yes. Force Zero Flag 1
             JZ      EXIT     ;   and exit
OKAY:        STD              ; No. Work backward
             PUSH    SI       ;Open a gap for the second string
             DEC     DI
             MOV     SI,DI
             ADD     DI,CX
REP          MOVSB            ; by moving the rest of the first
                             ; string down
             CLD              ;Now move forward
             POP     SI
             MOV     CX,SIZE2
             MOV     DI,BP
REP          MOVSB            ; and make the insertion
             MOV     SI,BP    ;Make SI point to new offset
             ADD     BX,SIZE2 ; and update size of first string
EXIT:        MOV     DI,OFF1  ;Restore DI
             MOV     CX,SIZE2 ; and CX
QUIT:        RET              ;Return to calling program
INSERT$      ENDP
CSEG  ENDS
             END
```

FIND A SUBSTRING IN A STRING (FINDSUB$)

FINDSUB$ searches for the first occurrence of a specified substring within a string. If the substring is found, FINDSUB$ returns its starting location.

Operation

The subroutine searches for the substring using a Compare Byte Strings (CMPSB) instruction with a REPE prefix. It executes this instruction repeatedly, starting one byte higher each time, until it either finds an occurrence of the substring or reaches the point near the end where there is insufficient space for the substring. A successful search returns ZF = 0 and the offset in DX. An unsuccessful search returns ZF = 1 and the offset of the last starting point, plus 1, in DX.

Entry Values

DI = Offset of the string
SI = Offset of the substring
BX = Length of string in bytes
CX = Length of substring in bytes

Results

If the substring is found, ZF = 0 and DX contains the substring's offset.

If the substring is not found, ZF = 1 and DX contains the offset where the last search started, plus one.

If the substring is longer than the string or either has zero length, ZF = 1 and DX is unchanged.

The input registers are unaffected.

Link Command

```
link callprog+findsub$;
```

Comment

To compare two equal-length strings, use the COMPMEMB subroutine in Chapter 5.

Subroutine Listing

```
; FINDSUB$ - Find a substring in a string
; Inputs: DI = Offset of string
;         SI = Offset of substring
;         BX = Length of string
;         CX = Length of substring
; Results: If the substring is found, ZF = 0 and DX
;            contains the substring's offset
;          If the substring is not found, ZF = 1 and DX
;            points to where the last search started, plus 1.
;          If the substring is longer than the string or
;            either has zero length, ZF = 1 and DX is
```

```
                 undefined.
                 Input registers are unchanged.


                 PUBLIC   FINDSUB$
CSEG    SEGMENT   PARA PUBLIC 'CODE'
                 ASSUME   CS:CSEG,DS:CSEG,ES:CSEG,SS:CSEG
                 JMP      FINDSUB$ ;Skip past data area
STOP      DW   ?  ;Location where searching must stop
HERE      DW   ?  ;Current search location
SAVESI    DW   ?  ;Original value of SI
SAVECX    DW   ?  ;Original value of CX


FINDSUB$  PROC   NEAR
                 JCXZ  QUIT        ;Quit if string is empty
                 CMP   BX,0
                 JE    QUIT
                 CMP   CX,BX       ; or substring is too large
                 JBE   OKAY
                 SUB   DX,DX
                 JZ    QUIT
OKAY:     PUSH  BX          ;Save input values
                 PUSH  DI
                 MOV   SAVESI,SI
                 MOV   SAVECX,CX
                 ADD   BX,DI       ;Location to stop searching =
                 SUB   BX,CX       ; end of string - length of sub$
                 INC   BX          ; + 1
                 MOV   STOP,BX     ;Save this location in memory
                 MOV   HERE,DI     ;Save first search location, too
                 CLD               ;Work forward
SEARCH:
REPE      CMPSB              ;Do the search
                 JE    FOUND       ;Substring found?

; The substring has not yet been found. Start searching
; again at the next byte in the string, unless you have
; reached the STOP location.

                 INC   HERE        ;Move to next byte
                 MOV   DI,HERE
                 CMP   DI,STOP     ;Search again?
                 JE    GETREGS     ; No. Leave
                 MOV   CX,SAVECX   ; Yes. Reinitialize registers
                 MOV   SI,SAVESI
                 JNE   SEARCH      ;  and go search again

; The substring has been found. Record its position and
; leave.

FOUND:    CMP   CX,1        ;Found. Set ZF = 0
GETREGS:  MOV   DX,HERE     ;Put matching offset in DX
```

```
            POP    DI          ;  and retrieve the registers
            POP    BX
            MOV    CX,SAVECX
            MOV    SI,SAVESI
QUIT:       RET                 ;Return to calling program
FINDSUB$    ENDP
CSEG   ENDS
            END
```

DELETE A SUBSTRING FROM A STRING (DELSUB$)

DELSUB$ removes a specified substring from a string.

Operation

The subroutine deletes the substring by moving the remaining string bytes up, overwriting the substring.

Entry Values

DI = Offset of the string
SI = Offset of the substring
BX = Length of string in bytes
CX = Length of substring in bytes

Results

If the substring is deleted, ZF = 0 and the byte count in BX reflects the deletion.
If the substring is longer than the string, either byte count is zero, or the substring
    offset is beyond the boundaries of the string, ZF = 1 and BX is unchanged.
DI, SI, and CX are unaffected.

Link Command

```
link callprog+delsub$;
```

Comment

If you don't know the location of the substring you want to delete, find it by first
calling the preceding FINDSUB$ subroutine. The instructions should look like this:

```
CALL    FINDSUB$  ;Search for the substring
JZ      NOTFOUND  ;Found?
MOV     SI,DX     ; Yes. Make SI point to it,
CALL    DELSUB$   ;   then delete it
```

Subroutine Listing

```
; DELSUB$ - Delete a substring from a string
; Inputs: DI = Offset of string
;         SI = Offset of substring
;         BX = Length of string
;         CX = Length of substring
; Results: If the substring is deleted, ZF = 0 and the
;          byte count in BX reflects the deletion.
;          If the substring is longer than the string,
;          either byte count is zero, or the substring
;          offset is beyond the boundaries of the string,
;          ZF = 1 and BX is unchanged.
;          DI, SI, and CX are unaffected.
```

```
                PUBLIC   DELSUB$
CSEG   SEGMENT   PARA PUBLIC 'CODE'
                ASSUME   CS:CSEG,DS:CSEG,ES:CSEG,SS:CSEG
                JMP      DELSUB$      ;Skip past data area
END$            DW       ?           ;Offset of end of string + 1

DELSUB$         PROC     NEAR
                JCXZ     QUIT         ;Quit if zero length,
                CMP      BX,0
                JE       QUIT
                CMP      CX,BX        ; substring is too large,
                JA       SETZF
                CMP      SI,DI        ; or substring is out of bounds
                JB       SETZF
                MOV      END$,DI
                ADD      END$,BX
                CMP      SI,END$
                JB       OKAY
SETZF:          CMP      CX,CX        ;Set ZF = 1
                JZ       QUIT
OKAY:           PUSH     DI           ;Save input values
                PUSH     SI
                PUSH     CX
                CLD                   ;Move from the beginning
                MOV      DI,SI        ;Put destination in DI
                ADD      SI,CX        ; and starting point in SI
                SUB      END$,SI      ; and bytes to move in CX
                MOV      CX,END$
DELETE:
REP             MOVSB                 ;Make the deletion
                POP      CX           ;Retrieve the registers
                POP      SI
                POP      DI
                SUB      BX,CX        ; and update the string length
QUIT:           RET                   ;Return to calling program
DELSUB$         ENDP
CSEG   ENDS
                END
```

COPY A SUBSTRING WITHIN A STRING (COPYSUB$)

COPYSUB$ copies a substring to a specified location in a string.

Operation

To copy the substring, the subroutine makes two calls to the MOVBLOCK subroutine in Chapter 5. The first call makes room for the copy by opening a gap in the string. MOVBLOCK creates this gap by moving the remainder of the string (from the destination on) down by the length of the substring. The second call to MOVBLOCK copies the substring into the gap.

Entry Values

DI = Offset of the string
SI = Offset of the substring
BP = Offset of destination in string
BX = Length of string in bytes
CX = Length of substring in bytes

Results

If ZF = 0, then:
SI = New offset of the substring
BP = Offset of the copied substring
BX = New length of the string
If ZF = 1, the operation did not take place because one string has a length of zero, the substring is larger than the string, or the destination or substring is not within the string; the registers are unaffected.

Link Command

```
link callprog+copysub$+movblock;
```

Comment

To move a substring, use the MOVESUB$ subroutine in this chapter.

Subroutine Listing

```
; COPYSUB$ - Copy a substring within a string
; Inputs: DI = Offset of string
;         SI = Offset of substring
;         BP = Offset of destination in string
;         BX = Length of string
;         CX = Length of substring
; Results: If the operation is successful, ZF = 0 and
;          SI = New offset of substring
;          BP = Offset of the copied substring
;          BX = New length of string
;          If either string has zero length, the substring
;          is larger than the string, or the destination
```

```
;              is not within the string, ZF =1 and the
;              registers are unchanged.
; Calls MOVBLOCK.

              EXTRN   MOVBLOCK:NEAR
              PUBLIC  COPYSUB$
CSEG   SEGMENT    PARA PUBLIC 'CODE'
              ASSUME  CS:CSEG,DS:CSEG,ES:CSEG,SS:CSEG
              JMP     COPYSUB$ ;Skip past data area
SIZE2         DW      ?        ;Hold original CX here
OFF1          DW      ?        ;Hold original DI here

COPYSUB$  PROC   NEAR
              JCXZ    QUIT     ;Quit if $ or sub$ is empty
              CMP     BX,0
              JE      QUIT
              MOV     SIZE2,CX ;Save input values
              MOV     OFF1,DI
              ADD     DI,BX    ;DI points to byte following $
              CMP     CX,BX    ;Be sure sub$ is shorter than $
              JAE     ERROR
              CMP     SI,DI    ;Make sure subs$ is in $
              JAE     ERROR
              CMP     SI,OFF1
              JB      ERROR
              ADD     CX,SI    ;CX points to byte following sub$
              CMP     BP,DI    ;Dest. must be in $
              JAE     ERROR
              CMP     BP,OFF1
              JB      ERROR
              CMP     CX,DI    ;sub$ must not extend beyond $
              JA      ERROR
              CMP     BP,SI    ;Dest. cannot be inside subs$
              JBE     OKAY
              CMP     BP,CX
              JAE     OKAY
ERROR:        SUB     DI,DI    ;Error. Force Zero Flag 1
              JZ      EXIT     ;  and exit
OKAY:         PUSH    SI       ;No error. Open a gap
              MOV     CX,DI
              SUB     CX,BP
              MOV     SI,BP
              MOV     DI,BP
              ADD     DI,SIZE2
              CALL    MOVBLOCK ; using MOVBLOCK
              POP     SI       ;Now copy the string
              MOV     CX,SIZE2
              CMP     SI,BP
              JB      SAVESI
              ADD     SI,CX
SAVESI:       PUSH    SI
```

```
                MOV     DI,BP
                CALL    MOVBLOCK ; using MOVBLOCK again
                MOV     SI,BP    ;Make SI point to new offset,
                POP     BP       ; BP point to old offset,
                ADD     BX,SIZE2 ; and update size of string
EXIT:           MOV     DI,OFF1  ;Restore DI
                MOV     CX,SIZE2 ; and CX
QUIT:           RET              ;Return to calling program
COPYSUB$        ENDP
CSEG   ENDS
                END
```

MOVE A SUBSTRING WITHIN A STRING (MOVESUB$)

MOVESUB$ moves a substring to a specified location in a string.

Operation

To move the substring, the subroutine first copies it using the COPYSUB$ subroutine and then deletes the original using the DELSUB$ subroutine. Both COPYSUB$ and DELSUB$ are defined in this chapter. COPYSUB$ uses a second subroutine, MOV-BLOCK, which is defined in Chapter 5.

Entry Values

DI = Offset of the string
SI = Offset of the substring
BP = Offset of destination in string
BX = Length of string in bytes
CX = Length of substring in bytes

Results

If ZF = 0, SI contains the new offset of the substring and BX contains the new length of the string.

If ZF = 1, the operation did not take place because one string has a length of zero, the substring is larger than the string, or the destination or substring is not within the string; the registers are unaffected.

Link Command

```
link callprog+movesub$+copysub$+movblock+delsub$;
```

Comment

To copy a substring, use the COPYSUB$ subroutine in this chapter.

Subroutine Listing

```
; MOVESUB$ - Move a substring within a string
; Inputs: DI = Offset of string
;         SI = Offset of substring
;         BP = Offset of destination in string
;         BX = Length of string
;         CX = Length of substring
; Results: If the operation is successful, ZF = 0 and
;             SI = New offset of substring
;             BX = New length of string
;          If either string has zero length, the substring
;          is larger than the string, or the destination
;          is within the string, ZF =1 and the registers
;          are unchanged.
; Calls COPYSUB$ and DELSUB$.
; COPYSUB$ calls MOVBLOCK.
```

```
        EXTRN   COPYSUB$:NEAR,DELSUB$:NEAR
        PUBLIC  MOVESUB$
CSEG    SEGMENT  PARA PUBLIC 'CODE'
        ASSUME  CS:CSEG,DS:CSEG,ES:CSEG,SS:CSEG
MOVESUB$ PROC   NEAR
        CALL    COPYSUB$ ;Copy the substring
        JZ      QUIT     ;If an error occurs, leave
        PUSH    SI       ;Otherwise, save the sub$ offset
        MOV     SI,BP    ;Make SI point to the victim
        CALL    DELSUB$  ; and delete it
        POP     SI       ;Retrieve the sub$ offset
QUIT:   RET              ;Return to calling program
MOVESUB$ ENDP
CSEG    ENDS
        END
```

Chapter 11

Unordered
List Manipulation

In our ordered society, where telephone book entries are arranged alphabetically and building numbers increase or decrease as you go up or down a street, unordered *any-things* seem bothersome somehow. Still, not everything can be neatly arranged, so unordered lists remain a fact of life. This is particularly true for applications that involve random data or data that change with time. For example, computerized weather stations may record hourly temperature and humidity readings in unordered lists, and manufacturers may log monthly shipping statistics in them.

This chapter contains subroutines that let you manipulate unordered lists of bytes. (You can easily modify them to manipulate lists of words, however.) Included are subroutines that sum the elements of a list, find the maximum- and minimum-value elements, and add (append) and delete an element. To search for a specific element in an unordered list, you can use the FINDBYTE or FINDWORD subroutine from Chapter 5.

UNSIGNED BYTE LIST SUMMATION (SUMUB)

SUMUB adds a specified number of consecutive unsigned bytes in memory and returns the sum in a register.

Operation

The subroutine uses a loop to add the elements to AX. The Carry Flag (CF) indicates the success (CF = 0) or failure (CF = 1) of the operation.

Entry Values

BX = Offset of the first byte
CX = Number of bytes to add

Results

If the operation is successful, CF = 0 and AX contains the total.
If the total exceeds the capacity of AX, CF = 1 and AX is unchanged.
BX and CX are unaffected.

Link Command

```
link callprog+sumub;
```

Special Case

A byte count of zero causes an immediate exit with no elements summed.

Comment

To add a list of signed bytes, use the SUMSB subroutine in this chapter.

Example

Sum the first 10 bytes in the table BTABLEU:

```
          EXTRN   SUMUB:NEAR
ENTRY:    JMP     START           ;Skip past data area
BTABLEU   DB      ..              ;The table goes here
                  ..
START     PROC    NEAR
          LEA     BX,BTABLEU      ;Load offset into BX
          MOV     CX,10           ; and byte count into CX
          CALL    SUMUB           ;Do the summation
          JC      ERROR           ;Jump on error
```

Subroutine Listing

```
; SUMUB - Adds a specified number of unsigned byte values.
; Inputs: BX = Offset of first byte
;         CX = Byte count
; Result: AX = Sum
; BX and CX are unaffected.
```

```
               PUBLIC  SUMUB
CSEG   SEGMENT  PARA PUBLIC 'CODE'
               ASSUME  CS:CSEG,DS:CSEG,ES:CSEG,SS:CSEG
               JMP     SUMUB      ;Skip past data area
SAVEAX    DW       ?              ;Save AX here

SUMUB    PROC     NEAR
               JCXZ    EXIT       ;Exit if CX = 0
               PUSH    BX         ;Save starting offset
               SUB     AX,AX      ;Clear total to start
               PUSH    CX         ;Save byte count on stack
               MOV     SAVEAX,AX  ;Save AX in memory
NEXT:          ADD     AL,[BX]    ;Add byte to total
               ADC     AH,0
               JNC     INCBX      ;Result too large?
               MOV     AX,SAVEAX  ; Yes. Retrieve AX
               JC      LEAVE      ;  and exit
INCBX:         INC     BX         ; No. point to next byte
               LOOP    NEXT       ;All bytes now totaled?
LEAVE:         POP     CX         ; Yes. Retrieve byte count
               POP     BX         ; and offset
EXIT:          RET
SUMUB    ENDP
CSEG   ENDS
               END
```

SIGNED BYTE LIST SUMMATION (SUMSB)

SUMSB adds a specified number of consecutive signed bytes in memory and returns the sum in a register.

Operation

The subroutine employs a loop to add the elements and uses DX to accumulate the total. At the end of the loop, DX is moved to AX. The Overflow Flag (OF) indicates the success (OF = 0) or failure (OF = 1) of the operation.

Entry Values

BX = Offset of the first byte
CX = Number of bytes to add

Results

If the operation is successful, OF = 0 and AX contains the total.
If adding two positive or negative numbers produces a result that exceeds the two's complement range of AX, OF = 1 and AX is unchanged.
BX and CX are unaffected.

Link Command

```
link callprog+sumsb;
```

Special Case

A byte count of zero causes an immediate exit with no elements summed.

Comment

To add a list of unsigned bytes, use the SUMUB subroutine in this chapter.

Example

Sum the first 10 bytes in the table BTABLES:

```
              EXTRN   SUMSB:NEAR
ENTRY:        JMP     START          ;Skip past data area
BTABLES       DB      . .            ;The table goes here

                      . .
START         PROC    NEAR
              LEA     BX,BTABLES     ;Load offset into BX
              MOV     CX,10          ; and byte count into CX
              CALL    SUMSB          ;Do the summation
              JO      OVERFLOW       ;Jump if overflow occurred
```

Subroutine Listing

```
; SUMSB - Adds a specified number of signed byte values.
; Inputs: BX = Offset of first byte
;         CX = Byte count
; Result: AX = Sum
```

```
; BX and CX are unaffected.

                PUBLIC   SUMSB
CSEG   SEGMENT  PARA PUBLIC 'CODE'
                ASSUME   CS:CSEG,DS:CSEG,ES:CSEG,SS:CSEG
                JMP      SUMSB       ;Skip past data area
SAVEAX     DW      ?           ;Save AX here

SUMSB   PROC       NEAR
                JCXZ     EXIT        ;Exit if CX = 0
                PUSH     BX          ;Save starting offset
                PUSH     DX          ; and working register
                SUB      DX,DX       ;Clear total to start
                PUSH     CX          ;Save byte count on stack
                MOV      SAVEAX,AX   ;Save AX in memory
NEXT:           MOV      AL,[BX]     ;Read the next byte
                CBW                  ;Extend it to a word
                ADD      DX,AX       ; and add it to total
                JNO      INCBX       ;If result has overflow,
                MOV      AX,SAVEAX   ; retrieve AX
                JC       LEAVE       ; and exit
INCBX:          INC      BX          ;Point to next byte
                LOOP     NEXT        ;All bytes totaled?
                MOV      AX,DX       ; Yes. Move total to AX
LEAVE:          POP      CX          ;Retrieve byte count,
                POP      DX          ; working register,
                POP      BX          ; and offset
EXIT:           RET
SUMSB  ENDP
CSEG   ENDS
                END
```

MAXIMUM AND MINIMUM UNSIGNED BYTES (MAXMINU)

MAXMINU returns the maximum and minimum values in an unordered list of unsigned bytes.

Operation

The subroutine uses BH and BL to hold the current maximum and minimum values, and initially sets these registers to the contents of the first byte. At NEXT, the subroutine begins a loop in which it compares each byte in the list to BH and BL, and updates them when necessary. Just before leaving, it moves BH to AH and BL to AL.

Entry Values

SI = Offset of the list
CX = Length of list in bytes

Results

AH = Maximum values
AL = Minimum value
SI and CX are unaffected.

Link Command

```
link callprog+maxminu;
```

Special Case

A byte count of zero causes an immediate exit with no elements compared.

Comment

To find the maximum and minimum values in a list of signed bytes, use the MAXMINS subroutine in this chapter.

Subroutine Listing

```
; MAXMINU - Returns the maximum and minimum values in a
; list of unsigned bytes
; Inputs: SI = Offset of list
;         CX = Byte count
; Results: AH = Maximum
;          AL = Minimum
; SI and CX are unaffected.

        PUBLIC  MAXMINU
CSEG    SEGMENT PARA PUBLIC 'CODE'
        ASSUME  CS:CSEG,DS:CSEG,ES:CSEG,SS:CSEG
MAXMINU PROC    NEAR
        JCXZ    EXIT        ;Exit if CX = 0
        PUSH    SI          ;Save starting offset
        PUSH    CX          ; and byte count,
        PUSH    BX          ; and a working register
        MOV     BH,[SI]     ;Make first byte both maximum
```

```
                MOV     BL,BH       ; and minimum
NEXT:           LODSB               ;Read the next byte
                CMP     AL,BH       ;Is it a new maximum?
                JBE     CHKMIN      ; No. Check for a minimum
                MOV     BH,AL       ; Yes. Replace the old maximum
                JMP     ENDL
CHKMIN:         CMP     AL,BL       ;Is it a new minimum?
                JAE     ENDL        ; No. Continue
                MOV     BL,AL       ; Yes. Replace the old minimum
ENDL:           LOOP    NEXT        ;Continue reading bytes
                MOV     AX,BX       ;Put the results in AH and AL
                POP     BX          ;Restore the working register
                POP     CX          ; the byte count,
                POP     SI          ; and the offset
EXIT:           RET
MAXMINU ENDP
CSEG  ENDS
                END
```

MAXIMUM AND MINIMUM SIGNED BYTES (MAXMINS)

MAXMINS returns the maximum and minimum values in an unordered list of signed bytes.

Operation

The subroutine uses BH and BL to hold the current maximum and minimum values, and initially sets these registers to the contents of the first byte. At NEXT, the subroutine begins a loop in which it compares each byte in the list to BH and BL, and updates them when necessary. Just before leaving, it moves BH to AH and BL to AL.

Entry Values

SI = Offset of the list
CX = Length of list in bytes

Results

AH = Maximum values
AL = Minimum value
SI and CX are unaffected.

Link Command

```
link callprog+maxmins;
```

Special Case

A byte count of zero causes an immediate exit with no elements compared.

Comments

To find the maximum and minimum values in a list of unsigned bytes, use the MAXMINU subroutine in this chapter.

Note that this subroutine is identical to MAXMINU, except it uses JLE and JGE (instead of JBE and JAE) to check the results of Compare (CMP) instructions.

Subroutine Listing

```
; MAXMINS - Returns the maximum and minimum values in a
; list of signed bytes
; Inputs: SI = Offset of list
;         CX = Byte count
; Results: AH = Maximum
;          AL = Minimum
; SI and CX are unaffected.

            PUBLIC  MAXMINS
CSEG    SEGMENT  PARA PUBLIC 'CODE'
            ASSUME  CS:CSEG,DS:CSEG,ES:CSEG,SS:CSEG
MAXMINS  PROC    NEAR
            JCXZ    EXIT        ;Exit if CX = 0
            PUSH    SI          ;Save starting offset
            PUSH    CX          ; and byte count,
```

```
               PUSH   BX          ; and a working register
               MOV    BH,[SI]     ;Make first byte both maximum
               MOV    BL,BH       ; and minimum
NEXT:          LODSB              ;Read the next byte
               CMP    AL,BH       ;Is it a new maximum?
               JLE    CHKMIN      ; No. Check for a minimum
               MOV    BH,AL       ; Yes. Replace the old maximum
               JMP    ENDL
CHKMIN:        CMP    AL,BL       ;Is it a new minimum?
               JGE    ENDL        ; No. Continue
               MOV    BL,AL       ; Yes. Replace the old minimum
ENDL:          LOOP   NEXT        ;Continue reading bytes
               MOV    AX,BX       ;Put the results in AH and AL
               POP    BX          ;Restore the working register
               POP    CX          ; the byte count,
               POP    SI          ; and the offset
EXIT:          RET
MAXMINS ENDP
CSEG   ENDS
               END
```

ADD A BYTE TO AN UNORDERED LIST (ADDB2UL)

ADDB2UL adds a specified byte to the end of an unordered list in memory; that is, it appends the byte.

Operation

To append the byte, the subroutine calculates the address of the location that follows the list, stores the byte there, and increments CX, the byte count register.

Entry Values

SI = Offset of the list
CX = Length of the list in bytes
AL = Byte value

Results

CX = New length of the list
SI and AL are unaffected.

Link Command

```
link callprog+addb2ul;
```

Special Case

A byte count of zero causes an immediate exit with no elements compared.

Subroutine Listing

```
; ADDB2UL - Adds a byte to the end of an unordered list
; Inputs: SI = Offset of list
;         CX = Byte count
;         AL = Byte value
; Results: CX = New byte count
; SI and AL are unaffected.

          PUBLIC   ADDB2UL
CSEG  SEGMENT  PARA PUBLIC 'CODE'
          ASSUME   CS:CSEG,DS:CSEG,ES:CSEG,SS:CSEG
ADDB2UL   PROC     NEAR
          JCXZ     EXIT        ;Exit if CX = 0
          PUSH     SI          ;Save starting offset
          ADD      SI,CX       ;Get offset of end of list + 1
          MOV      [SI],AL     ;Store the byte
          INC      CX          ;Increase byte count
          POP      SI          ; and leave
EXIT:     RET
ADDB2UL ENDP
CSEG  ENDS
          END
```

DELETE A BYTE FROM AN UNORDERED LIST (DELBUL)

DELBUL deletes a specified byte from an unordered list in memory.

Operation

To delete the byte, the subroutine moves all remaining bytes up, thereby overwriting the byte. After making the deletion, the subroutine decrements CX, the byte count register. The Carry Flag (CF) indicates the success (CF = 0) or failure (CF = 1) of the operation.

Entry Values

SI = Offset of the list
DI = Offset of the byte to be deleted
CX = Length of the list in bytes

Results

If the operation is successful, CF = 0 and CX contains the new length of the list. If the specified offset lies beyond the range of the string, CF = 1 and CX is unaffected.
SI and DI are unaffected.

Link Command

```
link callprog+delbul;
```

Special Case

A byte count of zero causes an immediate exit with no elements compared.

Comment

If you don't know the byte's location, use the FINDBYTE (Find Byte Value in a Memory Block) subroutine from Chapter 5 to find it and then delete it. Assuming the offset of the list is in DI, the byte value is in AL, and the length of the list is in CX, the instructions should look like this:

```
PUSH   DI
CALL   FINDBYTE ;Is the byte in the list?
JNZ    NOTFOUND ;No. Process the error
POP    SI       ;Yes. Delete it
CALL   DELBUL
```

Subroutine Listing

```
; DELBUL - Deletes a byte from an unordered list
; Inputs: SI = Offset of list
;         DI = Offset of byte to be deleted
;         CX = Byte count
; Results: If CF = 0, the operation is a success and
```

```
;               CX = New byte count; otherwise, CF = 1.
;               SI and DI are unaffected.

          PUBLIC  DELBUL
CSEG  SEGMENT  PARA PUBLIC 'CODE'
          ASSUME  CS:CSEG,DS:CSEG,ES:CSEG,SS:CSEG
DELBUL  PROC    NEAR
          JCXZ    EXIT        ;Exit if CX = 0
          PUSH    SI          ;Save starting offset
          PUSH    CX          ; and byte count
          ADD     CX,SI       ;Get offset of end of list + 1
          CMP     DI,CX       ;Is byte within list?
          JAE     OKAY
          CMP     DI,SI
          JAE     OKAY
          STC                 ; No. Set CF = 1
          POP     CX          ;   retrieve the count
          JC      LEAVE       ;   and quit
OKAY:     SUB     CX,DI       ;Yes. Bytes to move =
          DEC     CX          ; CX - DI - 1
          MOV     SI,DI       ;Start at DI + 1
          INC     SI
          CLD                 ;Work forward in list
REP       MOVSB               ;Delete the byte,
          POP     CX          ; adjust the count,
          DEC     CX
LEAVE:    POP     SI          ; and leave
EXIT:     RET
DELBUL ENDP
CSEG  ENDS
          END
```

Chapter 12

Sorting

If you want to plot information versus time or process text, you can accept the data in unordered form. For many applications, however, it's better to have data arranged in increasing or decreasing order, because it's easier to analyze that way.

How can one rearrange a list of unordered data? There's a large amount of literature on sorting, but I concentrate on one common technique known as the *bubble sort*. If you want to explore other sorting techniques, D.E. Knuth's classic *The Art of Computer Programming. Volume 3: Sorting and Searching* (Addison-Wesley) makes an excellent starting point.

BUBBLE SORT

The bubble sort technique is so named because it makes list elements "rise" upward in memory (to higher-numbered locations) like soap bubbles rise in the air. A bubble sort program works its way through a list from the beginning, and compares each element with the next one in the list. If the program encounters an element that has a greater value than its neighbor, it exchanges the elements. It then compares the next two elements, exchanges them if necessary, and so on. By the time the program reaches the last element, the highest-valued element will have "bubbled up" to that final list position.

When bubble sorting, the processor usually makes several passes through the list, as you can see from the simple example in Fig. 12-1. Here, the first pass bubbles 50 to the end of the list, while the last two passes bubble 40 and 30 to the next highest positions. Thus, this particular list has been sorted in three passes.

Seeing pass-by-pass "snapshots" of the list, as you do with Fig. 12-1, makes it easy for *you* to know when a list is entirely sorted, but how can a *computer* know this? Unless you give it a specific pass count or tell it when to stop in some other way, the computer will go merrily along, executing passes ad infinitum. Since the number of sorting passes depends on how the list is arranged initially, you have no way of providing an exact pass count in a program. As an alternative, in the subroutines in this chapter, I have set up a special *exchange flag* that the computer uses to find out when to stop sorting.

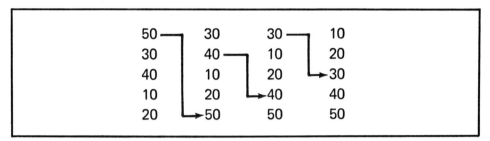

Fig. 12-1. A bubble sort "bubbles" the largest numbers to the end.

Before each sorting pass, the exchange flag is set to 1. Any sorting pass that includes an exchange of elements resets the flag to 0. Thus, after each pass, the state of the exchange flag indicates whether the computer is to continue sorting or quit. A 0 tells it to make another pass through the list; a 1 indicates that the list is sorted and tells the computer to stop.

Bubble Sort Flowchart

Figure 12-2 shows a flowchart of the bubble sort algorithm for sorting lists in ascending order. (For sorting in descending order, the first diamond would read "Element n > Element n – 1?") Here, *n* is the element number and *Count* is the number of comparisons the sort program is to make.

Note that Count is decremented at the beginning of each sorting pass. This is done because, as you probably recall, each pass "bubbles" an element to its final (sorted) position at the end of the list, and the program should exclude it from subsequent passes. In effect then, decrementing Count causes each sorting pass to make one less comparison than its predecessor. That's why the second diamond in Fig. 12-2 reads "More unsorted elements?" rather than "End of list?"

Notice that even if a list is already in order at the outset, it takes the program one pass to realize that fact. If one pass is the minimum, what maximum number of passes may you anticipate? Since the five-number list in Fig. 12-1 was already partially sorted, the program made only three passes to put it in ascending order. One additional pass is needed to detect that the list is indeed sorted, making four passes altogether.

If the list had been in descending order initially (the worst possible case), the program would make five passes through it—four sorting passes and one more to determine that further sorting is unneeded—or, in more general terms, *sorting an N-element list requires from one to N passes, with (N + 1)/2 passes being the average.*

There are only two subroutines in this chapter. They bubble sort a list of unsigned

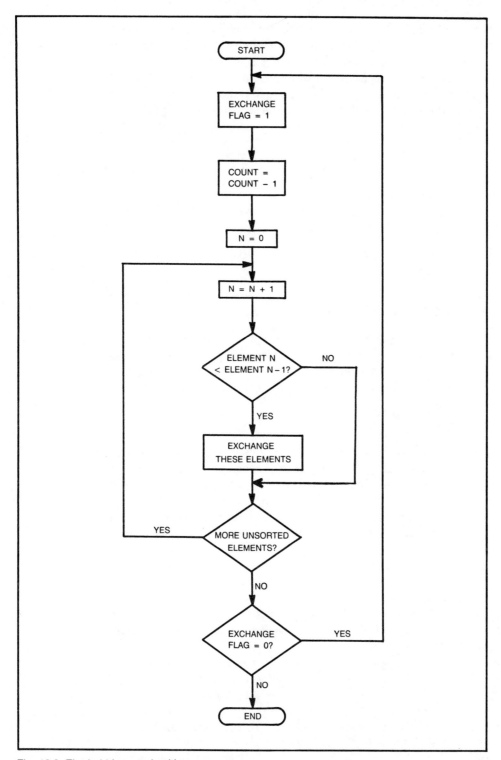

Fig. 12-2. The bubble sort algorithm.

bytes or words in ascending order. My "Comments" within the subroutine descriptions describe how to create subroutines that sort lists of unsigned bytes or words in descending order and other subroutines that sort lists of signed bytes or words.

ASCENDING SORT OF UNSIGNED BYTES (BUBBLEBA)

BUBBLEBA arranges a list of unsigned bytes in ascending order, using the bubble sort technique.

Operation

To begin, the subroutine stores the offset of the list (DI) and the element count (CX) in memory locations OFFL and COUNT, respectively. It then establishes BX as an exchange flag; this will contain either 1 (if the list is entirely sorted) or 0 (the list needs more sorting). The subroutine sets BX to 1 initially.

After reading the contents of COUNT and OFFL into SI and CX, the subroutine loads the first element into AL and compares it with the next element. If the elements are out of order, the subroutine exchanges them and then clears BX to 0. The LOOP instruction at CONT transfers control back to NEXT until the entire list has been processed.

When a sorting pass finishes, a CMP instruction finds out whether or not the exchange flag (BX) is 0. A 0 here means at least one exchange occurred, so the subroutine jumps back to INIT to begin another sorting pass. When BX = 1 after a pass, the list is finally sorted, so the subroutine restores the registers and exits.

Entry Values

SI = Offset of the list
CX = Length of the list in bytes

Results

None.
SI and CX are unaffected.

Link Command

```
link callprog+bubbleba;
```

Special Case

If the element count in CX is 1 or 0, the subroutine exits immediately with no sorting.

Comments

To sort a list of unsigned bytes in descending order, replace the JAE CONT instruction with JBE CONT.

To sort a list of signed bytes, replace the JAE CONT instruction with JGE CONT (ascending) or JLE CONT (descending).

Subroutine Listing

```
; BUBBLEBA - Bubble-sorts a byte list in ascending order
; Inputs: SI = Offset of list
;         CX = Length of list in bytes
; Results: None
; SI and CX are unaffected.
```

```
                PUBLIC  BUBBLEBA
CSEG    SEGMENT  PARA PUBLIC 'CODE'
                ASSUME   CS:CSEG,DS:CSEG,ES:CSEG,SS:CSEG
                JMP      BUBBLEBA          ;Skip past data area
COUNT           DW       ?
OFFL            DW       ?
BUBBLEBA        PROC     NEAR
                CMP      CX,2              ;Exit if count is 1 or 0
                JB       EXIT
                PUSH     CX                ;Save caller's registers
                PUSH     AX
                PUSH     BX
                MOV      OFFL,SI           ;Save starting address in memory
                MOV      COUNT,CX          ;Save element count in memory
                CLD                        ;Move forward through list
INIT:           MOV      BX,1              ;Exchange flag (BX) = 1
                DEC      COUNT             ;Get ready for count-1 compares
                JZ       SORTED            ;COUNT = 0?
                MOV      CX,COUNT          ; No. Load count into CX
                MOV      SI,OFFL           ;   and start address into SI
NEXT:           LODSB                      ;Read next element into AL
                CMP      [SI],AL           ;Is next el. < this el.?
                JAE      CONT              ; No.  Go check next pair
                XCHG     [SI],AL           ; Yes. Exchange these els.
                MOV      [SI-1],AL
                SUB      BX,BX             ; and make exchange flag 0
CONT:           LOOP     NEXT              ;Process entire list
                CMP      BX,0              ;Any exchanges made?
                JE       INIT              ; Yes. Process list again
SORTED:         MOV      SI,OFFL           ; No. Restore registers
                POP      BX
                POP      AX
                POP      CX
EXIT:           RET                        ;  and exit.
BUBBLEBA        ENDP
CSEG    ENDS
                END
```

ASCENDING SORT OF UNSIGNED WORDS (BUBBLEWA)

BUBBLEWA arranges a list of unsigned words in ascending order, using the bubble sort technique.

Operation

The subroutine operates as described under Ascending Sort of Unsigned Bytes (BUBBLEBA) in this chapter, except it reads elements into word register AX instead of byte register AL.

Entry Values

SI = Offset of the list
CX = Length of the list in words

Results

None.
SI and CX are unaffected.

Link Command

```
link callprog+bubblewa;
```

Special Case

If the element count in CX is 1 or 0, the subroutine exits immediately with no sorting.

Comments

To sort a list of unsigned words in descending order, replace the JAE CONT instruction with JBE CONT.

To sort a list of signed words, replace the JAE CONT instruction with JGE CONT (ascending) or JLE CONT (descending).

Subroutine Listing

```
; BUBBLEWA - Bubble-sorts a word list in ascending order
; Inputs: SI = Offset of list
;         CX = Length of list in words
; Results: None
; SI and CX are unaffected.

          PUBLIC   BUBBLEWA
CSEG    SEGMENT  PARA PUBLIC 'CODE'
          ASSUME   CS:CSEG,DS:CSEG,ES:CSEG,SS:CSEG
          JMP      BUBBLEWA       ;Skip past data area
COUNT     DW       ?
OFFL      DW       ?

BUBBLEWA  PROC     NEAR
          CMP      CX,2           ;Exit if count is 1 or 0
          JB       EXIT
```

```
            PUSH    CX              ;Save caller's registers
            PUSH    AX
            PUSH    BX
            MOV     OFFL,SI         ;Save starting address in memory
            MOV     COUNT,CX        ;Save element count in memory
            CLD                     ;Move forward through list
INIT:       MOV     BX,1            ;Exchange flag (BX) = 1
            DEC     COUNT           ;Get ready for count-1 compares
            JZ      SORTED           COUNT = 0?
            MOV     CX,COUNT         No. Load count into CX
            MOV     SI,OFFL         ,, and start address into SI
NEXT:       LODSW                   ,Read next element into AX
            CMP     [SI],AX         ,Is next el. < this el.?
            JAE     CONT            ; No.  Go check next pair
            XCHG    [SI],AX         ; Yes. Exchange these els.
            MOV     [SI-2],AX
            SUB     BX,BX           ; and make exchange flag 0
CONT:       LOOP    NEXT            ;Process entire list
            CMP     BX,0            ;Any exchanges made?
            JE      INIT            ; If so, process list again
SORTED:     MOV     SI,OFFL         ; If not, restore registers
            POP     BX
            POP     AX
            POP     CX
EXIT:       RET                     ;  and exit.
BUBBLEWA    ENDP
CSEG    ENDS
            END
```

Chapter 13

Ordered List Manipulation

Once you have sorted a list in ascending or descending order, you may want to search for a specific element, insert a new element, or delete an old one. The subroutines in this chapter do those tasks on ascending lists of unsigned bytes or words. I also describe how to modify them for use with signed elements.

As I mention in Chapter 11, you can locate a byte or word value in an unordered list by using the FINDBYTE or FINDWORD subroutine from Chapter 5. These subroutines find a value by searching through a list element by element from the beginning; this process can be time-consuming if the list is long. If a list is ordered, however, you can use any of several search techniques to locate a value. For all but very short lists, most of these techniques are faster and more efficient than searching sequentially. One common technique for searching ordered lists is called the *binary search*.

BINARY SEARCH

The word *binary* reflects the fact that this searching technique divides a list into a series of progressively shorter halves (*bi* is Latin for *two*) to eventually close in on one element. A binary search starts in the middle of a list and determines whether the search value lies above or below that point. It then takes *that* half of the list and divides *it* into halves, and so on.

The flowchart in Fig. 13-1 shows how to make a binary search through an ordered list of bytes and produce an address as the result. If the search value is in the list, the address is that of the matching element. Otherwise, if the value is not in the list, the address is that of the last value to be searched. Of course, the program that performs this search must also return an indicator that tells whether the search was successful or unsuccessful.

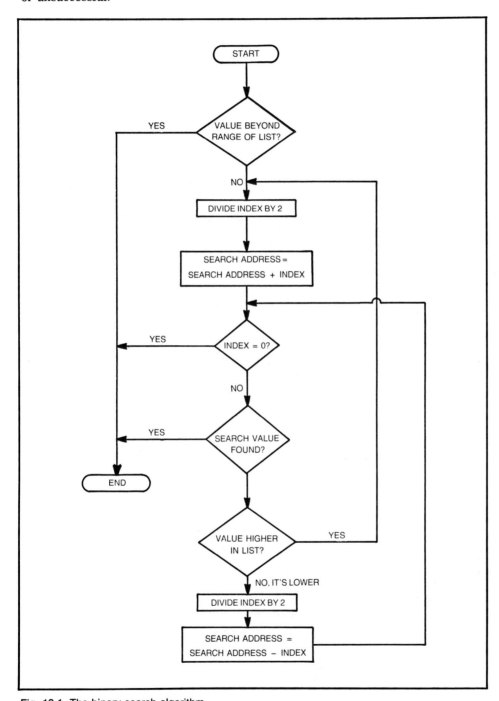

Fig. 13-1. The binary search algorithm.

FIND A BYTE VALUE IN AN ASCENDING LIST (FINDBA)

FINDBA uses the binary search technique to search for a specified unsigned byte value in a list that is arranged in ascending order.

Operation

The subroutine operates according to the binary search algorithm I have just described.

Entry Values

DI = Offset of the list
CX = Length of the list in bytes
AL = Search value

Results

If the value is in the list, ZF = 1 and SI contains its offset.
If the value is not in the list, ZF = 0 and SI contains the offset of the last element to be searched.
The input registers are unaffected.

Link Command

```
link callprog+findba;
```

Special Case

If the element count in CX is zero, the subroutine exits immediately with no searching.

Comments

To search an increasing list of signed bytes, replace the JB NO__MATCH and JA NEXTE instructions with JL NO__MATCH and JG NEXTE, respectively.

To search an increasing list of unsigned words, use the FINDWA subroutine in this chapter.

Subroutine Listing

```
; FINDBA - Searches an ordered list for an unsigned byte
;   value
; Inputs: DI = Offset of the list
;         CX = Length of list in bytes
;         AL = Search value
; Results: If the value is in the list, ZF = 1 and SI =
;             Offset of matching element
;             If the value is not in the list, ZF = 0 and SI =
;             Offset of last element compared
;   DI, CX, and AL are unaffected.

        PUBLIC  FINDBA
CSEG  SEGMENT  PARA PUBLIC 'CODE'
```

```
                ASSUME  CS:CSEG,DS:CSEG,ES:CSEG,SS:CSEG
                JMP     FINDBA      ;Skip past data area
COUNT           DW      ?           ;This holds byte count

FINDBA  PROC  NEAR
                MOV     SI,DI       ;Copy offset to SI
                MOV     COUNT,CX    ; and save byte count in memory
                JCXZ    NO_MATCH    ;If CX = 0, quit

; Find out if AL lies beyond the boundaries of the list.

                CMP     AL,[DI]     ;Search value < or = first el.?
                JE      EXIT        ; Yes. Exit
                JB      NO_MATCH
                ADD     SI,CX       ; No. Point to last element
                DEC     SI
                CMP     AL,[SI]     ;Search value > or = last el.?
                JE      EXIT        ; Yes. Exit
                JA      NO_MATCH

; Search for value within the list.

                MOV     SI,DI       ;Starting at the middle
NEXTE:          SHR     CX,1        ; by dividing index by 2
                ADD     SI,CX       ;Calculate next search address
COMPARE:        JCXZ    NO_MATCH    ;If index = 0, stop searching
                CMP     AL,[SI]     ;Search value found?
                JE      EXIT        ; If so, exit
                JA      NEXTE       ; Otherwise, find correct half

; The search value is lower in the list.

                SHR     CX,1        ;Otherwise, divide index by 2
                SUB     SI,CX       ;Calculate next address
                JMP     COMPARE     ; and go check that element

; Following are exit instructions.

NO_MATCH: OR    CX,1        ;Not found. Clear Zero Flag
EXIT:     MOV   CX,COUNT    ;Retrieve the count
          RET               ; and exit
FINDBA ENDP
CSEG   ENDS
                END
```

FIND A WORD VALUE IN AN ASCENDING LIST (FINDWA)

FINDWA uses the binary search technique to search for a specified unsigned word value in a list that is arranged in ascending order.

Operation

The subroutine operates in a manner similar to that of the subroutine Find Byte Value in an Ascending List (FINDBA) in this chapter. However, because words are two bytes long, FINDWA includes instructions that ensure the index in CX is always a multiple of two; that is, it is an *even* value. For the same reason, FINDWA stops searching when the index has decreased to 2 (instead of 0).

Entry Values

DI = Offset of the list
CX = Length of the list in words
AX = Search value

Results

If the value is in the list, ZF = 1 and SI contains its offset.
If the value is not in the list, ZF = 0 and SI contains the offset of the last element
    to be searched.
Input registers are unaffected.

Link Command

```
link callprog+findwa;
```

Special Case

If the element count in CX is zero, the subroutine exits immediately with no searching.

Comment

To search an increasing list of signed words, replace the JB NO__MATCH and JA NEXTE instructions with JL NO__MATCH and JG NEXTE, respectively.

Subroutine Listing

```
; FINDWA - Searches an ordered list for an unsigned word
;    value
; Inputs: DI = Offset of the list
;         CX = Length of list in words
;         AX = Search value
; Results: If the value is in the list, ZF = 1 and SI =
;              Offset of matching element
;              If the value is not in the list, ZF = 0 and SI =
;              Offset of last element compared
;    DI, CX, and AX are unaffected.
```

```
               PUBLIC   FINDWA
CSEG   SEGMENT  PARA PUBLIC 'CODE'
               ASSUME   CS:CSEG,DS:CSEG,ES:CSEG,SS:CSEG
               JMP      FINDWA    ;Skip past data area
COUNT          DW       ?         ;This holds word count

FINDWA PROC  NEAR
               MOV      SI,DI     ;Copy offset to SI
               MOV      COUNT,CX  ; and save word count in memory
               JCXZ     NO_MATCH  ;If CX = 0, quit

;  Find out if AX lies beyond the boundaries of the list.

               CMP      AX,[DI]   ;Search value < or = first el.?
               JE       EXIT      ; Yes. Exit
               JB       NO_MATCH
               SHL      CX,1      ; No. Point to last element
               ADD      SI,CX
               SUB      SI,2
               CMP      AX,[SI]   ;Search value > or = last el.?
               JE       EXIT      ; Yes. Exit
               JA       NO_MATCH

;  Search for value within the list.

               MOV      SI,DI     ;Start at the middle
NEXTE:         SHR      CX,1      ; by dividing index by 2
               AND      CX,0FFFEH ;Force index to an even value
               ADD      SI,CX     ;Calculate next search address
COMPARE:       CMP      CX,2      ;Index = 2?
               JE       NO_MATCH  ; If so, stop searching
               CMP      AX,[SI]   ;Search value found?
               JE       EXIT      ; If so, exit
               JA       NEXTE     ; Otherwise, find correct half

;  The search value is lower in the list.

               SHR      CX,1      ;Divide index by 2
               AND      CX,0FFFEH ; and force it to an even value
               SUB      SI,CX     ;Calculate next address
               JMP      COMPARE   ; and go check that element

;  Following are exit instructions.

NO_MATCH: OR   CX,1      ;Not found. Clear Zero Flag
EXIT:     MOV  CX,COUNT  ;Retrieve the count
          RET            ; and exit
FINDWA ENDP
CSEG   ENDS
               END
```

INSERT A BYTE VALUE IN AN ASCENDING LIST (INSBA)

INSBA inserts a specified unsigned byte value in a list that is arranged in ascending order, unless the value is already in the list.

Operation

The subroutine begins by calling FINDBA to determine whether or not the value is already in the list. If the value is in the list, the subroutine clears the Zero Flag and exits. Otherwise, if the value is not in the list, the subroutine opens a one-element gap (working from the end of the string backwards) and stores the value in it.

Entry Values

DI = Offset of the list
CX = Length of the list in bytes
AL = Byte value to be inserted

Results

If the value is already in the list, ZF = 0 and SI contains its offset.
If the value is inserted in the list, ZF = 1, SI contains its offset, and CX is increased
  by 1.
DI and AL are unaffected.

Link Command

```
link callprog+insba+findba;
```

Special Case

If the element count in CX is zero, the subroutine stores the new byte in the list and then exits.

Comments

To insert into an increasing list of signed bytes, replace the JB MAKE_GAP instructions with JL MAKE_GAP, and CALL your signed-byte search subroutine instead of FINDBA.

To insert into an increasing list of unsigned words, use the INSWA subroutine in this chapter.

Subroutine Listing

```
; INSBA - Inserts an unsigned byte value in an ascending list
; Inputs: DI = Offset of the list
;         CX = Length of list in bytes
;         AL = Value to be inserted
; Results: If the value is in the list, ZF = 0 and SI =
;              Offset of matching element
;          If the value is inserted, ZF = 1, SI = Offset,
;              and CX is increased
```

```
; DI and AL are unaffected.
; Calls FINDBA.

            EXTRN   FINDBA:NEAR
            PUBLIC  INSBA
CSEG  SEGMENT  PARA PUBLIC 'CODE'
            ASSUME  CS:CSEG,DS:CSEG,ES:CSEG,SS:CSEG


INSBA  PROC  NEAR
            CMP     CX,0        ;If the list is empty,
            JNZ     SEARCH
            MOV     [DI],AL     ; just store the byte
            JZ      EXIT
SEARCH:     PUSH    CX          ;Save count
            CALL    FINDBA      ;Is value already in the list?
            JNZ     COMPARE     ; No. Go insert it
            OR      CX,1        ; Yes. Clear the Zero Flag
            POP     CX
            RET                 ;  and return

; Value was not found.  Determine whether to insert it
; just ahead of or just beyond the final search element.

COMPARE:    CMP     AL,[SI]     ;Is byte > search element?
            JB      MAKE_GAP
            INC     SI          ; Yes. Move search element, too.

; Open a one-element gap for the new byte, then insert it.

MAKE_GAP:   PUSH    DI          ;Save the offset
            PUSH    SI          ; and the element pointer
            ADD     DI,CX       ;Destination is end + 1
            MOV     CX,DI       ;Copy this into CX, too
            SUB     CX,SI       ;Bytes to move = CX - SI
            MOV     SI,DI       ;Source is end
            DEC     SI
            STD                 ;Work from end of string
REP         MOVSB               ;Open the gap
            POP     SI          ; and make the insertion
            MOV     [SI],AL
            POP     DI
            POP     CX          ;Retrieve count
            INC     CX          ; and increase it
            CMP     CX,CX       ;Set the Zero Flag
EXIT:       RET                 ; and return
INSBA ENDP
CSEG  ENDS
            END
```

INSERT A WORD VALUE IN AN ASCENDING LIST (INSWA)

INSWA inserts a specified unsigned word value in a list that is arranged in ascending order, unless the value is already in the list.

Operation

The subroutine begins by calling FINDWA to determine whether or not the value is already in the list. If the value is in the list, the subroutine clears the Zero Flag and exits. Otherwise, if the value is not in the list, the subroutine opens a one-element gap (working from the end of the string backwards) and stores the value in it.

Entry Values

DI = Offset of the list
CX = Length of the list in words
AX = Word value to be inserted

Results

If the value is already in the list, ZF = 0 and SI contains its offset.
If the value is inserted in the list, ZF = 1, SI contains its offset, and CX is increased by 1.
DI and AX are unaffected.

Link Command

```
link callprog+inswa+findwa;
```

Special Case

If the element count in CX is zero, the subroutine stores the new word in the list and then exits.

Comments

To insert into an increasing list of signed words, replace the JB MAKE__GAP instructions with JL MAKE__GAP, and CALL your signed-word search subroutine instead of FINDWA.

To insert into an increasing list of unsigned bytes, use the INSBA subroutine in this chapter.

Subroutine Listing

```
; INSWA - Inserts an unsigned word value in an ascending list
; Inputs: DI = Offset of the list
;         CX = Length of list in words
;         AX = Value to be inserted
; Results: If the value is in the list, ZF = 0 and SI =
;            Offset of matching element
;          If the value is inserted, ZF = 1, SI = Offset,
;            and CX is increased
; DI and AX are unaffected.
```

```
; Calls FINDWA.

          EXTRN   FINDWA:NEAR
          PUBLIC  INSWA
CSEG  SEGMENT  PARA PUBLIC 'CODE'
          ASSUME  CS:CSEG,DS:CSEG,ES:CSEG,SS:CSEG


INSWA  PROC  NEAR
          CMP    CX,0      ;If the list is empty,
          JNZ    SEARCH
          MOV    [DI],AX   ; just store the word
          JZ     EXIT
SEARCH:   PUSH   CX        ;Save count
          CALL   FINDWA    ;Is value already in the list?
          JNZ    COMPARE   ; No. Go insert it
          OR     CX,1      ; Yes. Clear the Zero Flag
          POP    CX
          RET              ;  and return

; Value was not found.  Determine whether to insert it
; just ahead of or just beyond the final search element.

COMPARE:  CMP    AX,[SI]   ;Is word > search element?
          JB     MAKE_GAP
          ADD    SI,2      ; Yes. Move search element, too.

; Open a one-element gap for the new word, then insert it.

MAKE_GAP: PUSH   DI        ;Save the offset
          PUSH   SI        ; and the element pointer
          SHL    CX,1      ;Destination is end + 1
          ADD    DI,CX
          MOV    CX,DI     ;Copy this into CX, too
          SUB    CX,SI     ;Words to move = (CX - SI)/2
          SHR    CX,1
          MOV    SI,DI     ;Source is end
          SUB    SI,2
          STD              ;Work from end of string
REP       MOVSW            ;Open the gap
          POP    SI        ; and make the insertion
          MOV    [SI],AX
          POP    DI
          POP    CX        ;Retrieve count
          INC    CX        ; and increase it
          CMP    CX,CX     ;Set the Zero Flag
EXIT:     RET              ; and return
INSWA ENDP
CSEG  ENDS
          END
```

DELETE A BYTE VALUE FROM AN ASCENDING LIST (DELBA)

DELBA deletes a specified unsigned byte value from a list that is arranged in ascending order.

Operation

The subroutine begins by calling FINDBA to determine whether or not the value is in the list. If the value is not in the list, the subroutine clears the Zero Flag and exits. Otherwise, if the value is in the list, the subroutine deletes it by moving the remaining elements up by one position.

Entry Values

DI = Offset of the list
CX = Length of the list in bytes
AL = Byte value to be deleted

Results

If the value is not in the list, ZF = 0.
If the value is deleted from the list, ZF = 1 and CX is decreased by 1.
DI and AL are unaffected.

Link Command

```
link callprog+delba+findba;
```

Special Case

If the element count in CX is zero, the subroutine exits immediately without searching the list.

Comments

To delete from an increasing list of signed bytes, CALL your signed-byte search subroutine instead of FINDBA.

To delete from an increasing list of unsigned words, use the DELWA subroutine in this chapter.

Subroutine Listing

```
; DELBA - Deletes an unsigned byte value from an ascending
;    list
; Inputs: DI = Offset of the list
;         CX = Length of list in bytes
;         AL = Value to be deleted
; Results: If the value is not in the list, ZF = 0.
;          If the value is deleted, ZF = 1 and CX is
;            decreased.
; DI and AL are unaffected.
; Calls FINDBA.
```

```
                EXTRN   FINDBA:NEAR
                PUBLIC   DELBA
CSEG   SEGMENT  PARA PUBLIC 'CODE'
                ASSUME   CS:CSEG,DS:CSEG,ES:CSEG,SS:CSEG

DELBA   PROC  NEAR
                PUSH    SI          ;Save working register
                PUSH    CX          ; and the count
                JCXZ    NOT_HERE    ;If the list is empty, quit
                CALL    FINDBA      ;Is value in the list?
                JZ      DELETE      ; Yes. Go delete it
NOT_HERE: OR    CX,1        ; No. Clear the Zero Flag
                POP     CX
                JNZ     POPSI       ; and leave

; Value was found.  Delete it by moving the remaining
; elements up one position.

DELETE:   PUSH    DI          ;Save the offset
                MOV     DI,SI       ;Destination is element position
                ADD     CX,DI       ;Bytes to move = DI + CX
                SUB     CX,SI       ; - SI
                DEC     CX          ; - 1
                INC     SI          ;Source is SI + 1
                CLD                 ;Work from beginning of string
REP       MOVSB               ;Overwrite the element
                POP     DI          ;Retrieve the offset
                POP     CX          ; and count
                DEC     CX          ;Decrease the count
                CMP     CX,CX       ;Set the Zero Flag
POPSI:    POP     SI          ;Retrieve SI
                RET                 ; and return
DELBA   ENDP
CSEG   ENDS
                END
```

DELETE A WORD VALUE FROM AN ASCENDING LIST (DELWA)

DELWA deletes a specified unsigned word value from a list that is arranged in ascending order.

Operation

The subroutine begins by calling FINDWA to determine whether or not the value is in the list. If the value is not in the list, the subroutine clears the Zero Flag and exits. Otherwise, if the value is in the list, the subroutine deletes it by moving the remaining elements up by one position.

Entry Values

DI = Offset of the list
CX = Length of the list in words
AX = Word value to be deleted

Results

If the value is not in the list, ZF = 0.
If the value is deleted from the list, ZF = 1 and CX is decreased by 1.
DI and AX are unaffected.

Link Command

```
link callprog+delwa+findwa;
```

Special Case

If the element count in CX is zero, the subroutine exits immediately without searching the list.

Comments

To delete from an increasing list of signed words, CALL your signed-word search subroutine instead of FINDWA.

To delete from an increasing list of unsigned bytes, use the DELBA subroutine in this chapter.

Subroutine Listing

```
; DELWA - Deletes an unsigned word value from an ascending
;   list
; Inputs: DI = Offset of the list
;         CX = Length of list in words
;         AX = Value to be deleted
; Results: If the value is not in the list, ZF = 0.
;          If the value is deleted, ZF = 1 and CX is
;            decreased.
; DI and AX are unaffected.
; Calls FINDWA.
```

```
            EXTRN   FINDWA:NEAR
            PUBLIC  DELWA
CSEG  SEGMENT  PARA PUBLIC 'CODE'
            ASSUME   CS:CSEG,DS:CSEG,ES:CSEG,SS:CSEG

DELWA  PROC  NEAR
            PUSH    SI          ;Save working register
            PUSH    CX          ; and the count
            JCXZ    NOT_HERE    ;If the list is empty, quit
            CALL    FINDWA      ;Is value in the list?
            JZ      DELETE      ; Yes. Go delete it
NOT_HERE:   OR      CX,1        ; No. Clear the Zero Flag
            POP     CX
            JNZ     POPSI       ;  and leave

; Value was found.  Delete it by moving the remaining
; elements up one position.

DELETE:     PUSH  DI          ;Save the offset
            SHL     CX,1        ;Words to move =
            ADD     CX,DI       ; (2*CX + DI - SI)/2 - 1
            SUB     CX,SI
            SHR     CX,1
            DEC     CX
            MOV     DI,SI       ;Destination is element position
            ADD     SI,2        ;Source is SI + 2
            CLD                 ;Work from the beginning
REP         MOVSW               ;Overwrite the element
            POP     DI          ;Retrieve the offset
            POP     CX          ; and count
            DEC     CX          ;Decrease the count
            CMP     CX,CX       ;Set the Zero Flag
POPSI:      POP     SI          ;Retrieve SI
            RET                 ; and return
DELWA ENDP
CSEG  ENDS
            END
```

Chapter 14

General-Purpose
Input and Output

All of the previous subroutines in this book have obtained input values from registers or memory locations. Each one has assumed that these values have been previously set up by instructions in your calling program or that you have entered them manually using DEBUG (for an IBM Macro Assembler) or SYMDEB (for a Microsoft Macro Assembler). Similarly, earlier subroutines have returned results to registers or memory, on the assumption that your calling program will read them and perform any further processing.

While there are certainly some applications in which inputs and results are handled entirely within the computer, most involve some degree of communication with the user. For example, programs often require the user to choose an option from a menu or to enter text or numbers that the program is to use for processing. Likewise, most programs produce some kind of visual result on the screen. This is often a number, a list of numbers, or simply a message such as "Done" or a prompt such as "Press any key to continue."

The point is that at some time or other you will have the need to write programs that obtain information from the keyboard and produce prompts, messages, and results on the screen. The subroutines in this chapter provide the input and output operations you need to communicate with the keyboard, display, and other simple peripheral devices. Some of these subroutines transfer individual characters; others transfer sequences of characters, or *strings*. Chapter 16 provides additional input and output subroutines for readers who have an IBM Personal Computer.

One more comment needs to be made: All of the subroutines in this chapter (and most of those in the remaining chapters) do their work by activating a multipurpose interrupt that DOS has installed in the computer. This interrupt, 21H, provides a variety of options, or *function calls*, that the programmer selects by loading a number into the AH register. The subroutines save you the bother of remembering, numbering, and loading AH; they do it for you.

ASCII

MS-DOS computers use a coding scheme called *ASCII* (for American Standard Code for Information Interchange) to communicate with peripheral devices. For example, when you type a *T*, the keyboard circuitry sends the ASCII number for T into the computer. Likewise, when DOS or any other program displays or prints a T, the computer sends the same numeric code to the screen or printer. In short, any operation that involves text usually involves ASCII—and that applies to the subroutines in this chapter. Specifically, subroutines that read characters from the keyboard or other input device return those characters in ASCII form. Similarly, subroutines that send characters to the screen, printer, or any other output device transmit them in ASCII.

Appendix B provides a summary table of the ASCII character set, in case you ever want to work with the actual numeric codes. However, when you're dealing with a letter, number, or symbol character on the keyboard, you can simply refer to it directly, and let the assembler supply the numeric code that the character represents.

ASSEMBLER NOTATION FOR ASCII CODES

To make the assembler produce the ASCII code for a character, simply enclose it with single or double quotation marks. For example, to display a *T*, first load its ASCII code into the DL register with

```
MOV    DL,'T'
```

Similarly, to determine whether or not the user pressed *Y* in response to a prompt, use

```
CMP    AL,'Y'
```

Again, the character-in-quotes format is sufficient for most ASCII operations, but Appendix B is available if you ever need the numeric form. You *must* use the numeric form when you're working with a noncharacter code. For example, to determine whether or not the user pressed the Return key, use

```
CMP    AL,0DH
```

where 0DH is the numeric code for the Carriage Return character.

STANDARD INPUT AND OUTPUT DEVICES

In describing subroutines in this chapter, I use two MS-DOS terms that I haven't mentioned earlier: *standard input device* and *standard output device*. The standard input device is the peripheral from which DOS obtains information, while the standard output device is the peripheral on which it displays information. When you start DOS, it designates the keyboard as the standard input device and the display as the standard output device.

Since that's the case, you may wonder why I don't just say "keyboard" and "display" instead of "standard device." The reason is that the keyboard and display are only the starting assignments; they are DOS's guesses at what you want. You can make it use some other peripheral (e.g., make it send display material to a printer) by reassigning, or *redirecting*, the standard input or output device.

To redirect input or output, simply append a statement of the form <*device* (for input) or >*device* (for output). Here *device* is one of the following DOS abbreviations for peripheral devices:

- CON (short for Console) is the keyboard and screen.
- AUX or COM1 is the first asynchronous communications adapter port.
- COM2 is the second asynchronous communications adapter port.
- LPT1 or PRN is the first parallel printer.
- LPT2 and LPT3 are the second and third parallel printers.

For example, to send the output of a program called SORT.COM to a parallel printer (instead of the screen), run SORT.COM using the command

```
sort >prn
```

DISPLAY A STRING (LIST$)

LIST$ outputs a string to the standard output device, which is initially the display. This subroutine is convenient for displaying messages and prompts.

Operation

The subroutine uses DOS function call 9H to transmit a string in memory to the standard output device.

Entry Value

DX = Offset of string
The string must end with a $ character.

Results

String is displayed.
DX is unaffected.

Link Command

```
link callprog+list$;
```

Comments

To print a string instead of displaying it, redirect output to the printer by following your run command with >prn. For example, if WARNING.COM displays a message, print the message by entering

warning >prn

To read a string from the keyboard, use the GET$ subroutine in this chapter.

Example

Display the message "List is being sorted." Then move the cursor to the next line:

```
            EXTRN   LIST$:NEAR
CR          EQU     0DH             ;Carriage Return character
LF          EQU     0AH             ;Line Feed character
ENTRY:      JMP     START           ;Skip past message string
MESSAGE     DB      'List is being sorted.',CR,LF,'$'
START       PROC    NEAR
            LEA     DX,MESSAGE      ;Load string offset into DX
            CALL    LIST$           ;Display the message
```

Note the equate (EQU) directives that assign names to 0DH and 0AH, the ASCII codes for the Carriage Return and Line Feed characters. While the equates are not required, they make the program easier to understand. Without them, the MESSAGE string would read

```
'List is being sorted.',0DH,0AH,'$'
```

Subroutine Listing

```
;  LIST$ - Display a string
;  Input: DX = Offset of string
;  Results: None
;           DX is unaffected.

        PUBLIC  LIST$
CSEG    SEGMENT  PARA PUBLIC 'CODE'
        ASSUME  CS:CSEG,DS:CSEG,ES:CSEG,SS:CSEG

LIST$   PROC  NEAR
        PUSH  AX
        MOV   AH,9H        ;Call DOS function 9H
        INT   21H
        POP   AX
        RET                ;Return to calling program
LIST$   ENDP
CSEG    ENDS
        END
```

READ A STRING (GET$)

GET$ reads a string from the standard input device, which is initially the keyboard. As each character is entered, the subroutine displays it on the standard output device.

Operation

The subroutine uses DOS function call 0AH to read a string from the standard input device and store it in a buffer in memory. The user-provided memory buffer must be two bytes longer than the maximum number of keystrokes, and must have this format:

- A one-byte count of the maximum number of characters (excluding the Return key), plus one.
- An uninitialized byte into which the subroutine will return the count of characters received.
- One uninitialized byte for each character.

For example, to set up a buffer for up to 30 keystrokes, enter a statement of the form

```
BUFFER   DB   31,31 DUP(?)
```

After reading the string, the subroutine copies the start-of-buffer offset (DX) into the BX register. It then clears CH and reads the second buffer byte (the character count) into CL. Finally, it adds 2 to BX to make it point to the first character, which is in the third byte of the buffer.

Entry Value

DX = Offset of input buffer

Results

String is available in buffer.
BX = Offset of first character.
CX = Number of characters received.
DX is unaffected.

Link Command

```
link callprog+get$;
```

Special Case

Pressing Ctrl-C (or Ctrl-Break for IBM compatibles) makes DOS issue Interrupt 23H, "Ctrl-C Handler Address."

Comment

To display a string, use the preceding LIST$ subroutine.

Example

Display the prompt "What is your name? " Then read the user's response of up to 30 keystrokes:

```
            EXTRN   LIST$:NEAR,GET$:NEAR
ENTRY       JUMP    START             ;Skip the string area
PROMPT      DB      'What is your name? $'
RESPONSE    DB      31,31 DUP(?)

START       PROC    NEAR
            LEA     DX,PROMPT         ;Display the prompt
            CALL    LIST$
            LEA     DX,RESPONSE       ;Get the user's response
            CALL    GET$
```

Subroutine Listing

```
; GET$ - Read a string from the standard input device
; Input: DX = Offset of user-defined buffer for string
; Results: BX = Offset of first character
;          CX = Character count
;          DX is unaffected

            PUBLIC  GET$
CSEG    SEGMENT  PARA PUBLIC 'CODE'
            ASSUME  CS:CSEG,DS:CSEG,ES:CSEG,SS:CSEG

GET$    PROC  NEAR
            PUSH    AX
            MOV     AH,0AH        ;Call DOS function 0AH
            INT     21H
            MOV     BX,DX         ;Copy string address into BX
            MOV     CX,[BX]+1     ;Move character count into CX
            ADD     BX,2          ;Make BX point to first character
            POP     AX
            RET                   ;Return to calling program
GET$        ENDP
CSEG    ENDS
            END
```

DISPLAY A CHARACTER (LISTCHR)

LISTCHR outputs a specified character to the standard output device, which is initially the display.

Operation

The subroutine uses DOS function call 2 to transmit an ASCII character in DL to the standard output device.

Entry Value

DL = ASCII character

Results

Character is displayed.
DL is unaffected.

Link Command

```
link callprog+listchr;
```

Comments

To print a character instead of displaying it, use the PRINTCHR subroutine in this chapter.

To read a character from the keyboard, use the GETCHR or GETCHRE subroutine in this chapter.

Example

Display five asterisks at the current cursor position:

```
          EXTRN   LISTCHR:NEAR
START     PROC    NEAR
          MOV     CX,5          ;Set loop counter to five
          MOV     DL,'*'        ;Character is *
NEXTCHR:  CALL    LISTCHR       ;Display the character
          LOOP    NEXTCHR       ;Repeat until done
```

Subroutine Listing

```
; LISTCHR - Display a character
; Input: DL = Character
; Results: None
;          DL is unaffected.

          PUBLIC  LISTCHR
CSEG  SEGMENT  PARA PUBLIC 'CODE'
          ASSUME  CS:CSEG,DS:CSEG,ES:CSEG,SS:CSEG

LISTCHR PROC  NEAR
```

211

```
        PUSH    AX
        MOV     AH,2        ;Call DOS function 2H
        INT     21H
        POP     AX
        RET                 ;Return to calling program
LISTCHR ENDP
CSEG  ENDS
        END
```

PRINT A CHARACTER (PRINTCHR)

PRINTCHR outputs a specified character to the standard printer device.

Operation

The subroutine uses DOS function call 5 to transmit an ASCII character in DL to the standard printer device.

Entry Value

DL = ASCII character

Results

Character is printed.
DL is unaffected.

Link Command

```
link callprog+printchr;
```

Comments

To display a character rather than print it, use the LISTCHR subroutine in this chapter.

To read a character from the keyboard, use the GETCHR or GETCHRE subroutine in this chapter.

Subroutine Listing

```
; PRINT - Print a character
; Input: DL = Character
; Results: None
;          DL is unaffected.

        PUBLIC  PRINTCHR
CSEG   SEGMENT  PARA PUBLIC 'CODE'
        ASSUME  CS:CSEG,DS:CSEG,ES:CSEG,SS:CSEG

PRINTCHR  PROC   NEAR
          PUSH   AX
          MOV    AH,2      ;Call DOS function 2H
          INT    21H
          POP    AX
          RET              ;Return to calling program
PRINTCHR  ENDP
CSEG   ENDS
          END
```

READ A CHARACTER (GETCHR)

GETCHR reads a character from the standard input device, but does not display it. The fact that the user's response is invisible makes this subroutine useful for obtaining passwords and other sensitive information.

Operation

The subroutine uses DOS function call 8, which waits for a character to be entered from the standard input device and loads it into AL in ASCII form.

Entry Value

None

Result

AL = Character entered (ASCII)

Link Command

```
link callprog+getchr;
```

Special Case

Pressing Ctrl-C (or Ctrl-Break for IBM compatibles) makes DOS issue Interrupt 23H, "Ctrl-C Handler Address." To make the GETCHR subroutine ignore Ctrl-C, use function call 7 rather than 8, by preceding the INT 21H instruction with MOV AH,7.

Comments

To read a character and display it, use the GETCHRE subroutine that follows. To display a character, use the LISTCHR subroutine in this chapter.

Example 1

Prompt for a password of up to eight characters and read the characters into memory, but don't display the password. Return the password's starting address in BX:

```
            EXTRN   LIST$:NEAR,GETCHR:NEAR
ENTRY       JUMP    START           ;Skip the string area
PROMPT      DB      'Please enter your password: $'
PASSWORD    DB      8 DUP(?)

START       PROC    NEAR
            LEA     DX,PROMPT        ;Ask for the password
            CALL    LIST$
            MOV     CX,8             ;Store up to eight keystrokes
            LEA     BX,PASSWORD      ; starting at PASSWORD
NEXTKEY:    CALL    GETCHR           ;Read the next key
            CMP     AL,0DH           ;Is it a Carriage Return?
            JE      EXIT             ; Yes. Done.
            MOV     [BX],AL          ; No. Put character in string
            INC     BX               ;  and point to next location
```

```
        LOOP   NEXTKEY            ;Get another key
EXIT:   LEA    BX,PASSWORD        ;Put string address back in BX
        RET                       ; and leave
```

Example 2

Some programs require the user to press a specific key or any of several keys within a given range (say, a number between 1 and 5). For example, suppose you are developing a program that displays some text and instructs the user to "Press Return to continue." To wait for the Return key (and ignore all others), use a sequence such as:

```
WAIT_HERE: CALL   GETCHR       ;Read a key
           CMP    AL,0DH        ;Is it Return?
           JNE    WAIT_HERE     ; No. Wait for another key
             . .                ; Yes. Continue here
             . .
```

Of course, you could also make the JNE transfer to instructions that display a message such as "Wrong key. Please press Return" before returning to CALL GETCHR.

Subroutine Listing

```
; GETCHR - Read a character, but don't display it
; Input: None
; Result: AL = Character

        PUBLIC  GETCHR
CSEG    SEGMENT PARA PUBLIC 'CODE'
        ASSUME  CS:CSEG,DS:CSEG,ES:CSEG,SS:CSEG

GETCHR  PROC   NEAR
        JMP    SAVEAH             ;Skip data area
AHLOC   DB     ?
SAVEAH: MOV    AHLOC,AH           ;Save AH
        MOV    AH,8               ;Call DOS function 8
        INT    21H
        MOV    AH,AHLOC           ;Restore AH
        RET                       ; and exit
GETCHR  ENDP
CSEG    ENDS
        END
```

READ A CHARACTER AND ECHO (GETCHRE)

GETCHRE reads a character from the standard input device and displays it on the standard output device.

Operation

The subroutine uses DOS function call 1, which waits for a character to be entered from the standard input device, loads it into AL in ASCII form, and displays it.

Entry Value

None

Result

AL = Character entered (ASCII)

Link Command

```
link callprog+getchre;
```

Special Case

Pressing Ctrl-C (or Ctrl-Break for IBM compatibles) makes DOS issue Interrupt 23H, "Ctrl-C Handler Address." To make the GETCHRE subroutine ignore Ctrl-C, use function call 6 rather than 1, by replacing MOV AH,1 with two instructions: MOV AH,6 and MOV DL,0FFH.

Comments

To read a character without displaying it, use the preceding GETCHR subroutine.
To display a character, use the LISTCHR subroutine in this chapter.

Example

Display the prompt "Do you want to continue? (Y/N) " and read the user's response. A "Y" makes the program skip to CONTINUE; any other key makes it exit.

```
            EXTRN   LIST$:NEAR,GETCHRE:NEAR
ENTRY       JUMP    START           ;Skip the string area
PROMPT      DB      'Do you want to continue? (Y/N)$'

START       PROC    NEAR
            LEA     DX,PROMPT       ;Display the prompt
            CALL    LIST$
            CALL    GETCHRE         ;Read the response
            CMP     AL,'Y'          ;Is it a Y?
            JE      CONTINUE
            RET                     ; No. Exit.
CONTINUE:   ..                      ; Yes. Continue here.
            ..
```

Note that this program only checks for a "Y" (uppercase). To make it accept "y" as well, precede the CONTINUE line with

```
CMP    AL,'y'            ;Is it a y?
JE     CONTINUE
RET                      ; No. Exit.
```

Subroutine Listing

```
; GETCHRE - Read a character and display it
; Input: None
; Result: AL = Character

            PUBLIC  GETCHRE
CSEG  SEGMENT  PARA PUBLIC 'CODE'
            ASSUME  CS:CSEG,DS:CSEG,ES:CSEG,SS:CSEG

GETCHRE    PROC   NEAR
           JMP    SAVEAH         ;Skip data area
AHLOC      DB     ?
SAVEAH:    MOV    AHLOC,AH       ;Save AH
           MOV    AH,1           ;Call DOS function 1
           INT    21H
           MOV    AH,AHLOC       ;Restore AH
           RET                   ; and exit
GETCHRE    ENDP
CSEG  ENDS
           END
```

SEND A CHARACTER TO THE SERIAL PORT (SENDCSER)

SENDCSER sends a specified character to the standard auxiliary device, which is initially the RS-232 serial port. This subroutine is convenient for communicating with modems and serial printers.

Operation

The subroutine uses DOS function call 4 to transmit an ASCII character in DL to the standard auxiliary device.

Entry Value

DL = ASCII character

Results

None.
DL is unaffected.

Link Command

```
link callprog+sendcser;
```

Comments

If the output device is busy, the subroutine will wait until it is ready to accept a character.

To send a character to a parallel port, use the LISTCHR or PRINTCHR subroutine in this chapter.

Example

Get characters from the keyboard (using the previous GETCHRE subroutine) and send them to the auxiliary device. Stop when the user presses Return.

```
            EXTRN   SENDCSER:NEAR,GETCHRE:NEAR
START       PROC    NEAR
NEXTKEY:    CALL    GETCHRE         ;Read next keystroke
            CMP     AL,0DH          ;Return key?
            JE      DONE            ; Yes. Exit.
            MOV     DL,AL           ; No. Send character to aux.
            CALL    SENDCSER
            JMP     NEXTKEY:        ; and go read next key
DONE:       . .                     ;End of output operation
```

Subroutine Listing

```
; SENDCSER - Send a character to auxiliary device
; Input: DL = Character
; Results: None
;          DL is unaffected.
```

```
          PUBLIC   SENDCSER
CSEG   SEGMENT  PARA PUBLIC 'CODE'
          ASSUME   CS:CSEG,DS:CSEG,ES:CSEG,SS:CSEG

SENDCSER   PROC   NEAR
           PUSH   AX
           MOV    AH,4      ;Call DOS function 4
           INT    21H
           POP    AX
           RET              ;Return to calling program
SENDCSER   ENDP
CSEG   ENDS
           END
```

READ A CHARACTER FROM THE SERIAL PORT (GETCSER)

GETCSER reads a character from the standard auxiliary device, which is usually a modem.

Operation

The subroutine uses DOS function call 3, which waits for a character to be entered from the standard auxiliary device and loads it into AL in ASCII form.

Entry Value

None

Result

AL = Character entered (ASCII)

Link Command

```
link callprog+getcser;
```

Special Case

Pressing Ctrl-C (or Ctrl-Break for IBM compatibles) makes DOS issue Interrupt 23H, "Ctrl-C Handler Address."

Comments

In most MS-DOS systems, the auxiliary device is unbuffered and is not interrupt driven. Hence, you may lose characters if the auxiliary device sends data faster than your program can process it.

At startup on the IBM PC, PC-DOS initializes the first auxiliary port to 2400 baud, no parity, one stop bit, and 8-bit words.

To read a character from the standard input device (normally the keyboard), use the GETCHR or GETCHRE subroutine in this chapter.

Example

Print characters from the auxiliary device until an end-of-file character (ASCII 1AH, or Ctrl-Z) is received:

```
          EXTRN   GETCSER:NEAR,PRINTCHR:NEAR
START     PROC    NEAR
NXTCHAR:  CALL    GETCSER         ;Get next auxiliary character
          CMP     AL,1AH          ;End of file?
          JE      DONE            ; Yes. Exit.
          MOV     DL,AL           ; No. Print the character
          CALL    PRINTCHR
          JMP     NXTCHAR         ;  and go get next character
DONE:     . .                     ;No more characters
          . .
```

Subroutine Listing

```
; GETCSER - Read a character from the auxiliary device
; Input: None
; Result: AL = Character

          PUBLIC  GETCSER
CSEG  SEGMENT  PARA PUBLIC 'CODE'
          ASSUME  CS:CSEG,DS:CSEG,ES:CSEG,SS:CSEG

GETCSER  PROC  NEAR
          JMP    SAVEAH           ;Skip data area
AHLOC     DB     ?
SAVEAH:   MOV    AHLOC,AH         ;Save AH
          MOV    AH,3             ;Call DOS function
          INT    21H
          MOV    AH,AHLOC         ;Restore AH
          RET                     ; and exit
GETCSER  ENDP
CSEG  ENDS
          END
```

BEEP THE SPEAKER (BEEP)

BEEP issues a "beep" through the computer's speaker. The beep is convenient for indicating the end of an operation, informing the user of an error, or any other application where an audible signal is helpful.

Operation

The subroutine uses DOS function call 2 to transmit an ASCII "Bell" (07H) character in DL to the standard output device.

Entry Value

None

Result

Speaker emits a "beep."

Comments

Note that BEEP is simply a character-specific version of the LISTCHR subroutine.

Chapter 16 contains a more versatile sound-emitting subroutine, SOUND, which lets you specify the frequency and duration of the tone.

Subroutine Listing

```
; BEEP - Beep the speaker
; Inputs: None
; Results: None

        PUBLIC  BEEP
CSEG    SEGMENT  PARA PUBLIC 'CODE'
        ASSUME  CS:CSEG,DS:CSEG,ES:CSEG,SS:CSEG

BEEP    PROC  NEAR
        PUSH    AX
        PUSH    DX
        MOV     DL,7        ;Load beep character into D
        MOV     AH,2        ; and call DOS function 2
        INT     21H
        POP     DX
        POP     AX
        RET                 ;Return to calling program
BEEP    ENDP
CSEG    ENDS
        END
```

Chapter 15

Time and Date Operations

MS-DOS computers keep track of the time and date based on values the user enters in response to the starting Time and Date prompts. The IBM PC AT and some compatibles also include a battery-powered clock/calendar that maintains these values while the computer is off. Most so-called multifunction cards also provide a built-in clock and calendar.

The subroutines in this chapter use the same function calls that DOS uses to perform any command that involves the computer's time or date values. In addition to the Time and Date commands, DOS uses these function calls to *stamp* the current time and date on disk files during COPY, DIR, FORMAT, and MKDIR operations. Some of DOS's auxiliary programs, such as EDLIN and DEBUG, also use the time and date values when they create a new file or copy an existing one.

GET THE TIME (GETTIME)

GETTIME reads the computer's time values into registers.

Operation

The subroutine uses DOS function call 2CH to read the binary values of the computer's time parameters. It loads the hour into CH, the minutes into CL, the seconds into DH, and the hundredths into DL.

Entry Values

None.

Results

CH = Hour in binary (0-23)
CL = Minutes in binary (0-59)
DH = Seconds in binary (0-59)
DL = Hundredths in binary (0-99)

Link Command

```
link callprog+gettime;
```

Comments

Some computers and multifunction cards cannot report time more accurate than the seconds value.

To set the time, use the SETTIME subroutine in this chapter.

Subroutine Listing

```
; GETTIME - Read the current time
; Inputs. None
; Results: CH = Hour (0-59)
;          CL = Minutes (0-59)
;          DH = Seconds (0-59)
;          DL = Hundredths (0-99)


        PUBLIC  GETTIME
CSEG  SEGMENT  PARA PUBLIC 'CODE'
        ASSUME  CS:CSEG,DS:CSEG,ES:CSEG,SS:CSEG

GETTIME  PROC  NEAR
        PUSH  AX        ;Save AX on the stack
        MOV   AH,2CH    ;Call DOS function 2CH
        INT   21H
        POP   AX        ;Retrieve original AX
        RET             ;Return to calling program
GETTIME  ENDP
CSEG  ENDS
        END
```

SET THE TIME (SETTIME)

SETTIME changes the computer's time values.

Operation

The subroutine uses DOS function call 2DH to set the computer's time parameters. It obtains the hour from CH, the minutes from CL, the seconds from DH, and the hundredths from DL. All parameters are BCD values, but the subroutine uses BCDW2B in Chapter 7 to convert them to binary.

Entry Values

CH = Hour in BCD (0-23)
CL = Minutes in BCD (0-59)
DH = Seconds in BCD (0-59)
DL = Hundredths in BCD (0-99)

Results

If AL = 0, the time was valid.
If AL = 0FFH, the time was invalid and the time is unchanged.
CH, CL, DH, and DL are unchanged.

Link Command

```
link callprog+settime+bcdw2b;
```

Comments

Generally, you should follow CALL SETTIME with instructions of the form

```
CMP    AL,0FFH
JE     INVALID
```

where INVALID is a set of instructions that process an invalid time entry.

To read the time, use the GETTIME subroutine in this chapter.

Example

Set the time from the keyboard:

```
GETUSER   MACRO   message,maxval,savereg
          LOCAL   NEXTTIME,RANGE,OKAY,CLRCH
          JMP     NEXTTIME
savereg   DB      ?
NEXTTIME: LEA     DX,message  ;;Get the time value
          CALL    LIST$
          LEA     DX,INPUT
          CALL    GET$
          LEA     DX,CRLF
          CALL    LIST$
          MOV     CL,INPUT+1
```

```
                CMP     CL,0        ;;If the user pressed Return,
                JNE     CLRCH
                MOV     AL,0        ;; make the input 0
                JMP     OKAY
CLRCH:          SUB     CH,CH
                LEA     DX,INPUT+2
                CALL    $2UBIN
                JNC     RANGE       ;;Make sure the input is decimal
                LEA     DX,NOTDEC
                CALL    LIST$
RANGE:          CMP     AX,maxval ;; and less than the maximum
                JBE     OKAY
                LEA     DX,TOOBIG
                CALL    LIST$
                JMP     NEXTTIME
OKAY:           CALL    BIN2BCD
                MOV     savereg,AL
              ENDM


                EXTRN   LIST$:NEAR,GET$:NEAR,$2UBIN:NEAR
                EXTRN   SETTIME:NEAR,BIN2BCD:NEAR
CSEG    SEGMENT PARA PUBLIC 'CODE'
                ASSUME  CS:CSEG,DS:CSEG,ES:CSEG,SS:CSEG
                ORG     100H
ENTRY:          JMP     START       ;Skip the data area
HRMSG           DB      'Hours: $'
MINMSG          DB      'Minutes: $'
SECMSG          DB      'Seconds: $'
HUNMSG          DB      'Hundreths: $'
INPUT           DB      3,3 DUP(?)
NOTDEC          DB      'This entry is not a valid decimal number.'
                DB      0DH,0AH,'$'
TOOBIG          DB      'This entry is out of range.',0DH,0AH,'$'
CRLF            DB      0DH,0AH,'$'

START   PROC  NEAR
                GETUSER HRMSG,23,SAVECH    ;Get the hours
                GETUSER MINMSG,59,SAVECL   ;Get the minutes
                GETUSER SECMSG,59,SAVEDH   ;Get the seconds
                GETUSER HUNMSG,99,SAVEDL   ;Get the hundredths
                MOV     CH,SAVECH       ;Read the final values
                MOV     CL,SAVECL
                MOV     DH,SAVEDH
                MOV     DL,SAVEDL
                CALL    SETTIME         ; and set the time
                RET
```

Subroutine Listing

```
; SETTIME - Set the time
; Inputs: CH = Hour in BCD (0-59)
```

```
;               CL = Minutes in BCD (0-59)
;               DH = Seconds in BCD (0-59)
;               DL = Hundredths in BCD (0-99)
; Results: None

            EXTRN   BCDW2B:NEAR
            PUBLIC  SETTIME
CSEG  SEGMENT  PARA PUBLIC 'CODE'
            ASSUME  CS:CSEG,DS:CSEG,ES:CSEG,SS:CSEG
SETTIME  PROC  NEAR
            PUSH    CX              ;Save input registers on the stack
            PUSH    DX
            MOV     AL,CH           ;Convert hours to binary
            SUB     AH,AH
            CALL    BCDW2B
            MOV     CH,AL
            MOV     AL,CL           ;Convert minutes to binary
            SUB     AH,AH
            CALL    BCDW2B
            MOV     CL,AL
            MOV     AL,DH           ;Convert seconds to binary
            SUB     AH,AH
            CALL    BCDW2B
            MOV     DH,AL
            MOV     AL,DL           ;Convert hundredths to binary
            SUB     AH,AH
            CALL    BCDW2B
            MOV     DL,AL
            MOV     AH,2DH          ;Call DOS function 2DH
            INT     21H
            POP     DX              ;Restore registers
            POP     CX
            RET                     ;Return to calling program
SETTIME  ENDP
CSEG  ENDS
            END
```

GENERATE A DELAY (DELAY)

DELAY waits for a specified amount of time.

Operation

The subroutine calculates a target time by adding the intervals specified in CL (minutes), DH (seconds), and DL (hundredths) to the current time. After that, it continually reads the time and compares it with the target time. When the times match, the subroutine returns to the calling program.

Entry Values

CL = Minutes interval (0-59)
DH = Seconds interval (0-59)
DL = Hundredths interval (0-99)

Results

If AL = 0, the intervals were valid.
If AL = 0FFH, one or more intervals are invalid and no delay occurs.
CL, DH, and DL are unchanged.

Link Command

```
link callprog+delay+gettime;
```

Comment

Generally, you should follow CALL DELAY with instructions of the form

```
CMP    AL,0FFH
JE     INVALID
```

where INVALID is a set of instructions that process an invalid time entry.

Subroutine Listing

```
; DELAY - Wait for the specified amount of time
; Inputs: CL = Minutes interval (0-59)
;         DH = Seconds interval (0-59)
;         DL = Hundredths interval (0-99)
; Results: AL = 0 indicates no error.
;          AL = 0FFH indicates invalid input.

        EXTRN   GETTIME:NEAR
        PUBLIC  DELAY
CSEG    SEGMENT PARA PUBLIC 'CODE'
        ASSUME  CS:CSEG,DS:CSEG,ES:CSEG,SS:CSEG
        JMP     DELAY       ;Skip the data area
SAVEAH  DB      ?           ;Save AH here

DELAY   PROC    NEAR
        PUSH    BX          ;Save affected registers
```

```
            PUSH    CX
            PUSH    DX
            MOV     SAVEAH,AH
            CMP     CL,59       ;Make sure inputs are valid
            JA      TOOHIGH
            CMP     DH,59
            JA      TOOHIGH
            CMP     DL,99
            JBE     SAVEINS
TOOHIGH:    MOV     AL,0FFH     ;An input was too large, so exit
            JMP     LEAVE
SAVEINS:    MOV     AL,CL       ;Move input mins to AL,
            MOV     BX,DX       ; secs and hunds to BX
            SUB     AH,AH       ;Set the hours count to 0
            CALL    GETTIME     ;Read the time
            ADD     BL,DL       ;Calculate the target time
            CMP     BL,100
            JB      SECT
            SUB     BL,100
            INC     BH
SECT:       ADD     BH,DH
            CMP     BH,60
            JB      MINT
            SUB     BH,60
            INC     AL
MINT:       ADD     AL,CL
            CMP     AL,60
            JB      HRT
            SUB     AL,60
            INC     AH
HRT:        ADD     AH,CH
            CMP     AH,24
            JB      WAIT
            SUB     AH,24
WAIT:       CALL    GETTIME     ;Read the time again
            CMP     CH,AH       ;Compare hours,
            JNE     WAIT
            CMP     CL,AL       ; minutes,
            JB      WAIT
            JA      CLRAL
            CMP     DX,BX       ; seconds and hundredths
            JB      WAIT
CLRAL:      MOV     AL,0        ;The times match, set AL = 0
LEAVE:      POP     DX          ;Restore registers
            POP     CX
            POP     BX
            MOV     AH,SAVEAH
            RET                 ; and exit
DELAY       ENDP
CSEG  ENDS
            END
```

GET THE DATE (GETDATE)

GETDATE reads the computer's date values into registers.

Operation

The subroutine uses DOS function call 2AH to read the binary values of the current year, month, day, and day of the week into CX, DH, DL, and AL, respectively.

Entry Values

None.

Results

CX = Year in binary (1980-2099)
DH = Month in binary (1-12)
DL = Day in binary (1-31)
AL = Day of the week (0 = Sunday, 6 = Saturday)

Link Command

```
link callprog+getdate;
```

Comment

To set the date, use the SETDATE subroutine in this chapter.

Subroutine Listing

```
; GETDATE - Read the current date
; Inputs: None
; Results: CX = Year (1980-2099)
;          DH = Month (1-12)
;          DL = Day (1-31)
;          AL = Day of the week (0=Sun., 6=Sat.)

          PUBLIC  GETDATE
CSEG    SEGMENT  PARA PUBLIC 'CODE'
          ASSUME   CS:CSEG,DS:CSEG,ES:CSEG,SS:CSEG
          JMP     GETDATE   ;Skip the data area
SAVEAH    DB      ?

GETDATE   PROC   NEAR
          MOV     SAVEAH,AH     ;Save the value of AH
          MOV     AH,2AH        ;Call DOS function 2AH
          INT     21H
          MOV     AH,SAVEAH     ;Restore AH
          RET                   ; and exit
GETDATE   ENDP
CSEG    ENDS
          END
```

SET THE DATE (SETDATE)

SETDATE changes the computer's date.

Operation

The subroutine uses DOS function call 2BH to set the computer's date. It obtains the year from CX, the month from DH, and the day from DL. All parameters are BCD values, but the subroutine uses BCDW2B (Chapter 7) to convert CX to binary and BCD2BIN (Chapter 9) to convert DH and DL to binary.

Entry Values

CX = Year in BCD (1980-2099)
DH = Month in BCD (1-12)
DL = Day in BCD (1-31)

Results

If AL = 0, the date was valid.
If AL = 0FFH, the date was invalid and the date is unchanged.
CX, DH, and DL are unchanged.

Link Command

```
link callprog+setdate+bcdw2b+bcd2bin;
```

Comments

Generally, you should follow CALL SETDATE with instructions of the form

```
CMP     AL,0FFH
JE      INVALID
```

where INVALID is a set of instructions that process an invalid date entry.

To read the date, use the GETDATE subroutine in this chapter.

Subroutine Listing

```
; SETDATE - Set the date
; Inputs: CX = Year in BCD (1980-2099)
;         DH = Month in BCD (1-12)
;         DL = Day in BCD (1-31)
; Results: None

        EXTRN BCDW2B:NEAR,BCD2BIN:NEAR
        PUBLIC  SETDATE
CSEG    SEGMENT  PARA PUBLIC 'CODE'
        ASSUME   CS:CSEG,DS:CSEG,ES:CSEG,SS:CSEG
        JMP     SETDATE  ;Skip the data area
SAVEAH  DB      ?

SETDATE PROC  NEAR
```

```
        PUSH    CX              ;Save the input values
        PUSH    DX
        MOV     SAVEAH          ; and AH
        MOV     AX,CX           ;Convert the year to binary
        CALL    BCDW2B
        MOV     CX,AX
        MOV     AL,DH           ;Convert the month to binary
        CALL    BCD2BIN
        MOV     DH,AL
        MOV     AL,DL           ;Convert the year to binary
        CALL    BCD2BIN
        MOV     DL,AL
        MOV     AH,2BH          ;Call DOS function 2BH
        INT     21H
        MOV     AH,SAVEAH       ;Restore AH
        POP     DX              ; and the input values
        POP     CX
        RET
SETDATE ENDP
CSEG    ENDS
        END
```

Chapter 16

IBM PC-Specific Input and Output

In the preceding chapters, I have presented some subroutines that can run on any computer that has an 8088, 8086, or 80286 microprocessor (regardless of the operating system) and others that can run on any computer that operates under MS-DOS or its IBM PC version, PC-DOS. This chapter contains six subroutines that IBM PC owners can use to access the resources of their own computer. (Owners of some PC compatibles may also be able to use these subroutines, depending on how "compatible" their computer actually is.)

The first subroutine returns a code that indicates the model number of the PC being used. IBM has stored this code in the next-to-last byte in regular memory, at location F000:FFFE. The next three subroutines perform display-related functions: reading the cursor position, moving the cursor, and clearing the screen. The last two subroutines manipulate the PC's built-in speaker to produce tones and play tunes.

The display-related subroutines here access the ROM that governs the PC's operation, its so-called Basic Input/Output System, or *BIOS*. Like DOS, the BIOS uses some of the processor's internal interrupts for its own purposes, and you can access them to perform tasks that DOS doesn't provide.

GET IBM PC MODEL (GETPCMOD)

GETPCMOD returns a code that indicates which model IBM PC is being used. This is convenient for time-critical applications that require that you know whether the processor is running at 4.77 MHz (8088) or 6 MHz (80286).

Operation

IBM PCs identify themselves via a one-byte code in location F000:FFFE, the next-to-last location in regular memory. The subroutine reads this code into AL.

Entry Values

None.

Result

AL = Code for PC model, as follows:
FF - Original PC
FE - PC XT, Portable PC, or PC with revised System Board
FD - PCjr
FC - PC AT

Link Command

```
link callprog+getpcmod;
```

Comment

The GETDOSV subroutine in Chapter 21 returns numbers that indicate the DOS version number (e.g., 2.10) under which the computer is running.

Subroutine Listing

```
; GETPCMOD - Reads a code that identifies the IBM PC model
; Inputs: None
; Result: AL = Code for PC model, as follows:
;               FF - Original PC
;               FE - PC XT, Portable PC, or PC with revised
;                    System Board
;               FD - PCjr
;               FC - PC AT

        PUBLIC  GETPCMOD
CSEG    SEGMENT PARA PUBLIC 'CODE'
        ASSUME  CS:CSEG,DS:CSEG,ES:CSEG,SS:CSEG

GETPCMOD PROC   NEAR
        PUSH    DS              ;Save working registers
        PUSH    BX
        MOV     BX,0F000H       ;Point to location F000:FFFE
        MOV     DS,BX
        MOV     BX,0FFFEH
```

```
        MOV    AL,[BX]      ; and read this location
        POP    BX           ;Restore working registers
        POP    DS
        RET
GETPCMOD  ENDP
CSEG  ENDS
        END
```

READ THE CURSOR POSITION (READCURS)

READCURS reads the cursor's row and column positions.

Operation

The subroutine uses option 3 of interrupt 10H to read the cursor's row and column positions into DH and DL. It also returns the cursor's range (its starting and ending line numbers) into CH and CL.

Entry Value

BH = Page number (0 for graphics)

Results

DH = Row in binary
DL = Column in binary
CH = Start line for cursor
CL = End line for cursor
BH is unaffected.

Link Command

```
link callprog+readcurs;
```

Comment

To move the cursor, use the MOVECURS subroutine in this chapter.

Subroutine Listing

```
; READCURS - Reads the cursor position
; Input: BH = Page number
; Results: DH = Row
;          DL = Column
;          CH = Start line
;          CL = End line
;          BH is unaffected

          PUBLIC  READCURS
CSEG   SEGMENT  PARA PUBLIC 'CODE'
          ASSUME  CS:CSEG,DS:CSEG,ES:CSEG,SS:CSEG
          JMP     READCURS   ;Skip the data area
SAVEAH    DB      ?

READCURS  PROC    NEAR
          MOV     SAVEAH,AH  ;Save AH in memory
          MOV     AH,3       ;Use option 3
          INT     10H        ; of interrupt 10H
          MOV     AH,SAVEAH  ;Retrieve AH
          RET
READCURS  ENDP
CSEG   ENDS
          END
```

MOVE THE CURSOR (MOVECURS)

MOVECURS moves the cursor to the specified row and column positions.

Operation

The subroutine uses option 2 of interrupt 10H to move the cursor to the row and column positions specified in DH and DL.

Entry Values

DH = Row in binary
DL = Column in binary
BH = Page number (0 for graphics)

Results

None.
DH, DL, and BH are unaffected.

Link Command

```
link callprog+movecurs;
```

Comments

On an 80-column screen, rows range from 0 to 24 and columns range from 0 to 79.
To read the current cursor position, use the READCURS subroutine in this chapter.

Examples

Move the cursor to the upper left-hand corner of the screen (the *home* position):

```
MOV    DX,0      ;Select the home position
CALL   MOVECURS  ; and move the cursor there
```

Move the cursor two rows down and three columns to the right:

```
CALL   READCURS  ;Read the cursor position
ADD    DH,2      ;Increase row by 2
ADD    DL,3      ; and column by 3
CALL   MOVECURS  ;Move the cursor
```

Subroutine Listing

```
; MOVECURS - Moves the cursor to the specified row and column
; Inputs: DH = Row
;         DL = Column
;         BH = Page number
; Results: None
;          DH, DL, and BH are unaffected

        PUBLIC  MOVECURS
CSEG  SEGMENT  PARA PUBLIC 'CODE'
```

```
            ASSUME   CS:CSEG,DS:CSEG,ES:CSEG,SS:CSEG
            JMP      MOVECURS      ;Skip the data area
SAVEAH      DB       ?

MOVECURS    PROC     NEAR
            MOV      SAVEAH,AH     ;Save AH in memory
            MOV      AH,2          ;Use option 2
            INT      10H           ; of interrupt 10H
            MOV      AH,SAVEAH     ;Retrieve AH
            RET
MOVECURS    ENDP
CSEG   ENDS
            END
```

CLEAR THE SCREEN (CLEARS)

CLEARS erases the screen and moves the cursor to the top left-hand corner, the *home* position.

Operation

The subroutine uses two options of interrupt 10H. It first uses option 15 to read the video mode; then it uses option 0 to set the display to this same mode.

Entry Values

None.

Results

The screen is cleared and the cursor is at the home position.
The registers are unaffected.

Link Command

```
link callprog+clears;
```

Subroutine Listing

```
; CLEARS - Clears the screen and homes the cursor
; Inputs: None.
; Results: None.
;          Registers are unaffected.

           PUBLIC  CLEARS
CSEG    SEGMENT  PARA PUBLIC 'CODE'
           ASSUME  CS:CSEG,DS:CSEG,ES:CSEG,SS:CSEG
CLEARS     PROC  NEAR
           PUSH  AX          ;Save affected registers
           PUSH  BX
           MOV   AH,15       ;Read the video mode
           INT   10H
           MOV   AH,0        ;Set the video mode
           INT   10H
           POP   BX          ;Restore the registers
           POP   AX
           RET
CLEARS     ENDP
CSEG    ENDS
           END
```

EMIT A TONE THROUGH THE SPEAKER (SOUND)

SOUND produces a tone of a specified frequency and duration.

Operation

The subroutine obtains the frequency from DI and the duration from CL (minutes), DH (seconds), and DL (hundredths of a second). To begin, it calls GETPCMOD in this chapter to determine whether the computer on which the program is being run has an 8088 or 80286 microprocessor. Based on the model code, it executes one of two instruction sequences that set up the PC's timer 2 for either 4.77 MHz or 6 MHz. It then turns the speaker on and calls the DELAY subroutine from Chapter 15 to keep the speaker on for the specified interval.

Entry Values

DI = Frequency in Hertz (21 to 65535)
CL = Duration in minutes (0 to 59)
DH = Duration in seconds (0 to 59)
DL = Duration in hundredths of a second (0 to 99)

Results

The tone sounds through the speaker.
Registers are unaffected.

Link Command

```
link callprog+sound+getpcmod+delay+gettime;
```

Comment

SOUND can be used as the basis for a program that plays music. To create such

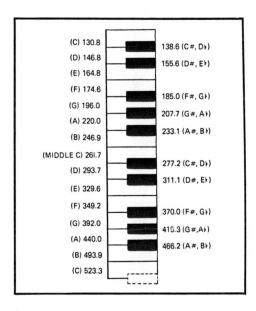

Fig. 16-1. Two octaves on a piano keyboard.

a program, however, you must know how frequencies relate to musical notes. Figure 16-1 shows a portion of a piano keyboard spanning two octaves (an octave is eight notes) and the frequency of each key in hertz. The lower octave runs from low C to middle C, while the upper octave runs from middle C to high C.

In this drawing, each key is marked with its standard note name. The white keys (A through G) produce the *natural* notes. The black keys produce the *accidentals,* the tones one-half note higher (sharp) or one-half note lower (flat) than the white keys beside them.

Subroutine Listing

```
; SOUND - Produces a tone through the speaker
; Inputs: DI = Frequency in Hertz (21 to 65535)
;         CL = Duration in minutes (0 to 59)
;         DH = Duration in seconds (0 to 59)
;         DL = Duration in hundredths (0 to 99)
; Results: None.
;          Registers are unaffected.

            EXTRN   GETPCMOD:NEAR,DELAY:NEAR
            PUBLIC  SOUND
CSEG    SEGMENT PARA PUBLIC 'CODE'
            ASSUME  CS:CSEG,DS:CSEG,ES:CSEG,SS:CSEG
SOUND       PROC  NEAR
            PUSH  AX         ;Save affected registers
            PUSH  CX
            PUSH  DX
            MOV   AL,0B6H    ;Write timer mode register
            OUT   43H,AL
            CALL  GETPCMOD ;Get PC model code
            CMP   AL,0FDH
            JB    SIXMEG

; Set up Timer 2 for a 4.77-MHz microprocessor.

            MOV   DX,14H     ;Timer/divisor =
            MOV   AX,4F38H ; 1331000/Frequency
            JMP   DIVDI

; Set up Timer 2 for a 6-MHz microprocessor.

SIXMEG:     MOV   DX,14H        ;Timer/divisor =
            MOV   AX,533H*896 ; 533H*896/Frequency

; The instructions are identical from this point.

DIVDI:      DIV   DI
            POP   DX           ;Restore DX
            OUT   42H,AL       ;Write Timer 2 count low byte
            MOV   AL,AH
```

```
        OUT    42H,AL      ;Write Timer 2 count high byte
        IN     AL,61H      ;Get Port B setting
        MOV    AH,AL       ; and save it in AH
        OR     AL,3        ;Turn the speaker on
        OUT    61H,AL
        SUB    CH,CH       ;Set the hours value to zero
        CALL   DELAY       ;Wait for the specified interval
        MOV    AL,AH       ;Recover value of port
        OUT    61H,AL
        POP    CX          ;Restore registers
        POP    AX
        RET
SOUND   ENDP
CSEG  ENDS
        END
```

PLAY MUSIC THROUGH THE SPEAKER (PLAY)

PLAY plays a tune through the speaker, based on tables of frequency and time in memory.

Operation

The subroutine obtains the offsets of the frequency and duration tables from SI and BP, respectively. (The frequency table is word-size, while the duration table is byte-size. The duration table contains time values in hundredths of a second.) It then reads a frequency value and compares it to 0FFFFH, the end-of-tune marker. If the value is a valid frequency, the subroutine obtains the corresponding duration and uses it to call SOUND. Finally, it updates SI and BP and goes to get the next frequency.

Entry Values

SI = Offset of frequency table
BP = Offset of duration table
The frequency table must end with 0FFFFH.

Results

The tune plays through the speaker.
The registers are unaffected.

Link Command

```
link callprog+play+sound+getpcmod+delay+gettime;
```

Comments

See Fig. 16-1 under the SOUND description for a drawing of a piano keyboard, with note frequencies.

Values in the duration table depend on what tempo you want and how many beats the note should be sustained. In 4/4 time, which has four beats to the measure, a whole note is sustained for four beats, a half note for two beats, a quarter note for one beat, and so on. Thus, if the duration table contains the value 80 (i.e., eight-tenths of a second) for a whole note, it would contain 40 for a half note.

Example

Figure 16-2 shows the music for "Mary Had a Little Lamb." The calling program that plays it follows. (Note that I arbitrarily gave the whole note a duration of one second, but I had to enter 99 for its duration because that is the largest value DELAY accepts for the hundredths parameter.)

```
            EXTRN   PLAY:NEAR
CSEG    SEGMENT PARA PUBLIC 'CODE'
            ASSUME  CS:CSEG,DS:CSEG,ES:CSEG,SS:CSEG
            ORG     100H            ;Skip to end of the PSP
ENTRY:      JMP     START           ;Skip data
MARY_FREQ DW 330,294,262,294,3 DUP(330)   ;Bars 1&2
```

```
              DW  3 DUP(294),330,392,392      ;Bars 3&4
              DW  330,294,262,294,4 DUP(330)  ;Bars 5&6
              DW  294,294,330,294,262,0FFFFH  ;Bars 7&8
MARY_TIME DB  6 DUP(25),50                 ;Bars 1&2
              DB  2 DUP(25,25,50)             ;Bars 3&4
              DB  12 DUP(25),99               ;Bars 5-8


START     PROC  NEAR
          LEA   SI,MARY_FREQ   ;Initialize SI and BP
          LEA   BP,MARY_TIME
          CALL  PLAY           ;Play the tune
          RET                  ;Return to DOS or DEBUG
START     ENDP
CSEG      ENDS
          END   ENTRY
```

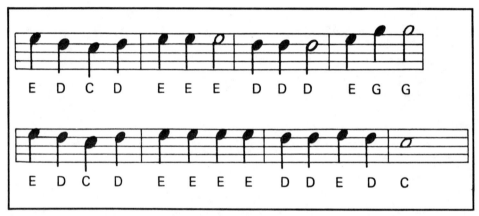

E D C D E E E D D D E G G

E D C D E E E D D E D C

Fig. 16-2. Music for "Mary Had a Little Lamb."

Subroutine Listing

```
; PLAY - Plays a tune through the speaker
; Inputs: SI = Offset of frequency table
;         BP = Offset of duration table
; Results: None.
;          Registers are unaffected.

          EXTRN  SOUND:NEAR
          PUBLIC  PLAY
CSEG   SEGMENT  PARA PUBLIC 'CODE'
          ASSUME  CS:CSEG,DS:CSEG,ES:CSEG,SS:CSEG
PLAY      PROC  NEAR
          PUSH  CX          ;Save affected registers
          PUSH  DX
          PUSH  SI
          PUSH  BP
FREQ:     MOV   DI,[SI]   ;Read next frequency
```

```
              CMP     DI,0FFFFH  ;End of tune?
              JE      END_PLAY   ; If so, exit
              MOV     DL,[BP]    ; Otherwise, get the duration
              SUB     CL,CL
              SUB     DH,DH
              CALL    SOUND      ;Play the note
              ADD     SI,2       ;Update the table pointers
              INC     BP
              JMP     FREQ
END_PLAY:     POP     BP         ;Restore the registers
              POP     SI
              POP     DX
              POP     CX
              RET                ; and exit
PLAY          ENDP
CSEG  ENDS
              END
```

Chapter 17

Disk Drive Operations

The subroutines in this chapter let you control the active, or *default*, disk drive.

GET THE DEFAULT DISK DRIVE (GETDRIVE)

GETDRIVE returns data about the default disk drive.

Operation

See Results below.

Entry Values

None.

Results

AL = Sectors per cluster (8 for a 10-megabyte fixed disk, 4 for a fixed disk with more than 10 megabytes, 2 for a double-sided floppy disk)

DS:BX = Offset of the first byte of the file allocation table (FAT). This byte identifies the disk type as follows:

FF = Double-sided diskette, 8 sectors/track
FE = Single-sided diskette, 8 sectors/track
FD = Double-sided diskette, 9 sectors/track
FC = Single-sided diskette, 9 sectors/track
F9 = Double-sided diskette, 15 sectors/track
F8 = Fixed disk

CX = Bytes per sector (200H or 512 for DOS 2 and 3)

DX = Number of clusters on the disk

Link Command

```
link callprog+getdrive;
```

Comments

To read the disk type into a register, follow CALL GETDRIVE with a MOV instruction of the form MOV reg,DS:[BX]. For example, to read it into BL, follow the CALL with MOV BL,DS:[BX].

To select the default drive, use the SETDRIVE subroutine in this chapter.

The DSKSPACE subroutine presented later in this chapter returns the number of available bytes on any drive in the computer.

Subroutine Listing

```
; GETDRIVE - Obtain data about the default disk drive
; Input: None
; Result: AL = Sectors per cluster
;         DS:BX = Offset of first byte of FAT (drive type)
;         CX = Bytes per sector
;         DX = Number of clusters on the disk

        PUBLIC  GETDRIVE
CSEG    SEGMENT  PARA PUBLIC 'CODE'
        ASSUME  CS:CSEG,DS:CSEG,ES:CSEG,SS:CSEG
```

```
             JMP     GETDRIVE    ;Skip past the data area
SAVEAH       DB      ?
GETDRIVE     PROC    NEAR
             MOV     SAVEAH,AH   ;Save AH in memory
             MOV     AH,1BH      ;Call DOS function 1BH
             INT     21H
             MOV     AH,SAVEAH   ;Restore AH
             RET                 ;Return to calling program

GETDRIVE     ENDP
CSEG   ENDS
             END
```

SET THE DEFAULT DISK DRIVE (SETDRIVE)

SETDRIVE sets the default disk drive.

Operation

The subroutine changes the default disk drive to the number in DL.

Entry Value

DL = Disk drive number (0 = A, 1 = B, etc.)

Result

AL = Number of drives (2 minimum).

Link Command

```
link callprog+setdrive;
```

Comments

Note that the subroutine always returns a value of at least 2 in AL (with DOS 3, the minimum value is 5). This is consistent with the MS-DOS philosophy of treating a single floppy disk as two drives, "A" and "B."

To read information about the default drive, use the preceding GETDRIVE subroutine.

Special Case

If the drive number in DL is invalid, the subroutine uses the highest available drive number. For example, entering DL = 5 for a computer that has one floppy disk and one fixed disk causes the hard disk drive (C) to be selected.

Subroutine Listing

```
; SETDRIVE - Select the default disk drive
; Input: DL = Drive number (0 = A, 1 = B, etc.)
; Result: AL = Number of drives (2 = One floppy disk;
;            3 = One floppy disk, one hard disk)
          PUBLIC   SETDRIVE
CSEG   SEGMENT   PARA PUBLIC 'CODE'
          ASSUME   CS:CSEG,DS:CSEG,ES:CSEG,SS:CSEG
          JMP      SETDRIVE   ;Skip past the data area
SAVEAH    DB       ?

SETDRIVE  PROC     NEAR
          MOV      SAVEAH,AH  ;Save AH in memory
          MOV      AH,0EH     ;Call DOS function 0EH
          INT      21H
          MOV      AH,SAVEAH  ;Restore AH
          RET                 ;Return to calling program

SETDRIVE  ENDP
CSEG   ENDS
          END
```

GET THE VERIFY SWITCH STATE (GETVERIF)

GETVERIF reads the state of the verify switch. When the verify switch is *on*, the computer compares files as it copies them.

Operation

The subroutine reads the state of the verify switch into AL.

Entry Values

None.

Result

AL = 0 if verify is off or 1 if it is on.

Link Command

```
link callprog+getverif;
```

Comment

To set or reset the verify switch, use the SETVERIF subroutine in this chapter.

Subroutine Listing

```
; GETVERIF - Obtain the state of the verify switch
; Input: None
; Result: AL = 1 if verify is on or 0 if it is off

          PUBLIC  GETVERIF
CSEG   SEGMENT  PARA PUBLIC 'CODE'
          ASSUME  CS:CSEG,DS:CSEG,ES:CSEG,SS:CSEG
          JMP     GETVERIF  ;Skip past the data area
SAVEAH    DB      ?

GETVERIF  PROC  NEAR
          MOV     SAVEAH,AH ;Save AH in memory
          MOV     AH,54H    ;Call DOS function 54H
          INT     21H
          MOV     AH,SAVEAH ;Restore AH
          RET               ;Return to calling program

GETVERIF  ENDP
CSEG   ENDS
          END
```

SET/RESET THE VERIFY SWITCH (SETVERIF)

SETVERIF turns the verify switch on or off.

Operation

The subroutine turns the verify switch on or off, depending on the value in AL.

Entry Value

AL = 1 to turn verify on or 0 to turn it off.

Result

The verify switch is turned on or off.

Link Command

```
link callprog+setverif;
```

Comments

The subroutine uses only the lowest bit of AL to set or reset verify. Thus, if you set AL to some value other than 1 or 0, the state of bit 0 determines whether verify is turned on or off; no error indicator is produced.

To read the current state of the verify switch, use the preceding GETVERIF subroutine.

Subroutine Listing

```
; SETVERIF - Set or reset the verify switch
; Input: AL = 1 to turn verify on or 0 to turn it off
; Result: None

          PUBLIC   SETVERIF
CSEG   SEGMENT  PARA PUBLIC 'CODE'
          ASSUME   CS:CSEG,DS:CSEG,ES:CSEG,SS:CSEG
          JMP      SETVERIF  ;Skip past the data area
SAVEAH    DB       ?

SETVERIF  PROC   NEAR
          PUSH   DX            ;Save DX
          MOV    SAVEAH,AH  ; and AH
          MOV    AH,2EH      ;Call DOS function 2EH
          INT    21H
          MOV    AH,SAVEAH ;Restore AH
          POP    DX          ; and DX
          RET                ;Return to calling program

SETVERIF  ENDP
CSEG   ENDS
          END
```

GET DISK FREE SPACE (DSKSPACE)

DSKSPACE reports the number of available bytes on a disk. This is handy for determining whether or not the disk is too full to accept a subsequent save or copy operation.

Operation

The subroutine begins by calling DOS function 36H. If the drive number is valid, this function returns the sectors per cluster in AX, the number of available clusters in BX, the bytes per cluster in CX, and the number of clusters on the disk in DX. If the drive number is invalid, it returns FFFF in AX. A 10-megabyte fixed disk has eight sectors per cluster, while a fixed disk with more than 10 megabytes has four and a double-sided floppy disk has two. Both DOS 2 and 3 provide 512 bytes per sector.

To obtain the number of available bytes on the disk, the subroutine multiplies the sectors per cluster by the bytes per sector, and then multiplies the result by the number of available clusters.

Entry Value

DL = Drive number (0 = default, 1 = A, etc.)

Results

The Carry Flag indicates the success or failure of the operation. If the drive number was invalid, CF = 1 and DX:AX = 0. Otherwise, CF = 0 and DX:AX = Number of available bytes.

Link Command

```
link callprog+dskspace;
```

Comments

The GETDRIVE subroutine presented earlier in this chapter returns data about the default disk drive.

Generally, you should follow CALL DSKSPACE with instructions of the form JC INVALID_DRIVE, where INVALID_DRIVE is a set of instructions that display a message if the drive number is invalid.

Subroutine Listing

```
; DSKSPACE - Obtain available space on a disk
; Input: DL = Drive number (0 = Default, 1 = A, etc.)
; Results: If the drive number was invalid, CF = 1 and DX:AX =
;          If the drive number was valid, CF = 0 and DX:AX =
;             Number of available bytes
; DL is unaffected.

        PUBLIC  DSKSPACE
CSEG    SEGMENT  PARA PUBLIC 'CODE'
        ASSUME  CS:CSEG,DS:CSEG,ES:CSEG,SS:CSEG
```

```
DSKSPACE    PROC    NEAR
            PUSH    BX          ;Save affected registers
            PUSH    CX
            MOV     AH,36H      ;Call DOS function 36H
            INT     21H
            CMP     AX,0FFFFH   ;Drive invalid?
            JNE     GET_BYTES
            SUB     AX,AX       ; Yes. Make AX and DX zero
            SUB     DX,DX
            STC                 ;  and set the Carry Flag
            JMP     QUIT
GET_BYTES:  MUL     CX          ;Calculate available bytes
            MUL     BX
            CLC                 ; and clear the Carry Flag
QUIT:       POP     CX          ;Restore the registers
            POP     BX
            RET                 ;Return to calling program
DSKSPACE    ENDP
CSEG    ENDS
            END
```

Chapter 18

Subdirectory Operations

The subroutines in this chapter and the remaining chapters use DOS function calls that Microsoft introduced with DOS 2.0. These later function calls are somewhat sophisticated in that they not only indicate errors, but they also specify what caused the error. Specifically, they indicate errors by setting the Carry Flag (CF) to either 0 or 1. Here, CF = 1 means that an error has occurred and signals the user to check AX for an error code; CF = 0 indicates no error.

The first subroutine in this chapter uses a function call error code to look up an appropriate message in a table and display it on the screen. The remaining subroutines operate on disk subdirectories. The first reads the current subdirectory *pathname* on a specified drive into memory; the last three provide assembly language equivalents of the DOS commands Make Directory (MKDIR), Remove Directory (RMDIR), and Change Directory (CHDIR).

For the last three subroutines, you must specify subdirectory pathnames as *AS-CIIZ* strings. An ASCIIZ string is simply a regular ASCII text string that is followed by a 0. For example, *'c:\progs',0* is an ASCIIZ string that specifies a subdirectory called PROGS on drive C. The last three subroutines obtain the offset of the ASCII string from DX. I have, however, also included a subroutine that reads a string in from the keyboard and initializes DX, because that's how most people want to set up strings.

DISPLAY AN ERROR MESSAGE (SHOWERR)

SHOWERR displays a message based on an error code.

Operation

The subroutine treats the contents of AX as an error code, and uses it to display a message from one of two look-up tables. The ERTAB1 table covers messages for codes between 1 and 35, while ERTAB2 covers messages for codes between 80 and 83.

Entry Value

AX = Error code.

Results

The message is displayed on the screen.
AX is unaffected.

Link Command

```
link callprog+subr+showerr;
```

(SUBR is a subroutine that returns an error indicator in CF.)

Comment

DOS 2 uses only the first 18 codes, the remaining codes were added with DOS 3.0.

Subroutine Listing

```
; SHOWERR - Display DOS function call error messages
; Input: AX = Error code.
; Result: Error message is displayed.
;         AX is unaffected.

          PUBLIC  SHOWERR
CSEG   SEGMENT  PARA PUBLIC 'CODE'
          ASSUME  CS:CSEG,DS:CSEG,ES:CSEG,SS:CSEG
          JMP     SHOWERR    ;Skip past the data area
SAVEAH    DB      ?
CR        EQU     13
LF        EQU     10
EOM       EQU     '$'

OUT_OF_RANGE DB 'Error code is not between 1 and 83',CR,LF,EOM
RESERVED DB      'Error code is reserved (36-79)',CR,LF,EOM

ER1       DB      'Invalid function number',CR,LF,EOM
ER2       DB      'File not found',CR,LF,EOM
ER3       DB      'Path not found',CR,LF,EOM
ER4       DB      'Too many open files (No handles left)',CR,LF,EOM
ER5       DB      'Access denied',CR,LF,EOM
ER6       DB      'Invalid handle',CR,LF,EOM
ER7       DB      'Memory control blocks destroyed',CR,LF,EOM
```

255

```
ER8         DB      'Insufficient memory',CR,LF,EOM
ER9         DB      'Invalid memory block address',CR,LF,EOM
ER10        DB      'Invalid environment',CR,LF,EOM
ER11        DB      'Invalid format',CR,LF,EOM
ER12        DB      'Invalid access code',CR,LF,EOM
ER13        DB      'Invalid data',CR,LF,EOM
ER14        DB      'No such message',CR,LF,EOM
ER15        DB      'Invalid drive was specified',CR,LF,EOM
ER16        DB      'Attempted to remove current directory',CR,LF,EOM
ER17        DB      'Not same device',CR,LF,EOM
ER18        DB      'No more files',CR,LF,EOM
ER19        DB      'Disk is write-protected',CR,LF,EOM
ER20        DB      'Unknown unit',CR,LF,EOM
ER21        DB      'Drive not ready',CR,LF,EOM
ER22        DB      'Unknown command',CR,LF,EOM
ER23        DB      'Data error (CRC)',CR,LF,EOM
ER24        DB      'Bad request structure length',CR,LF,EOM
ER25        DB      'Seek error',CR,LF,EOM
ER26        DB      'Unknown media type',CR,LF,EOM
ER27        DB      'Sector not found',CR,LF,EOM
ER28        DB      'Printer out of paper',CR,LF,EOM
ER29        DB      'Write fault',CR,LF,EOM
ER30        DB      'Read fault',CR,LF,EOM
ER31        DB      'General failure',CR,LF,EOM
ER32        DB      'Sharing violation',CR,LF,EOM
ER33        DB      'Lock violation',CR,LF,EOM
ER34        DB      'Invalid disk change',CR,LF,EOM
ER35        DB      'FCB unavailable',CR,LF,EOM
ER80        DB      'File exists',CR,LF,EOM
ER81        DB      'Reserved',CR,LF,EOM
ER82        DB      'Cannot make',CR,LF,EOM
ER83        DB      'Fail on INT 24',CR,LF,EOM

ERTAB1      DW      ER1,ER2,ER3,ER4,ER5,ER6,ER7,ER8,ER9
            DW      ER10,ER11,ER12,ER13,ER14,ER15,ER16,ER17,ER18
            DW      ER19,ER20,ER21,ER22,ER23,ER24,ER25,ER26,ER27
            DW      ER28,ER29,ER30,ER31,ER32,ER33,ER34,ER35
ERTAB2      DW      ER80,ER81,ER82,ER83

SHOWERR     PROC    NEAR
            PUSH    AX              ;Save input error number
            PUSH    BX              ;Save other working registers
            PUSH    DX
            CMP     AX,0            ;Check for error code in range
            JE      O_O_R
            CMP     AX,83
            JBE     IN_RANGE
O_O_R:      LEA     DX,OUT_OF_RANGE
            JMP     SHORT DISP_MSG

;   Error code is valid.  Determine which table to use.
```

```
IN_RANGE:   CMP     AX,35           ;Error code 1-35?
            JG      TRY79
            LEA     BX,ERTAB1-2     ; Yes. Point to ERTAB1
            JMP     FORM_ADDR
TRY79:      CMP     AX,79           ;Error code 36-79?
            JG      LAST_4
            LEA     DX,RESERVED     ; Yes. Display "reserved" message
            JMP     DISP_MSG
LAST_4:     LEA     BX,ERTAB2       ;Error code 80-83
            AND     AX,3
FORM_ADDR:  SHL     AX,1            ;Point to correct offset
            ADD     BX,AX
            MOV     DX,[BX]         ;Put message address into DX
DISP_MSG:   MOV     AH,9            ;Display message
            INT     21H
            POP     DX              ;Restore registers
            POP     BX
            POP     AX
            RET                     ;Return to calling program
SHOWERR     ENDP
CSEG  ENDS
            END
```

GET THE CURRENT DIRECTORY (GETDIR)

GETDIR returns the pathname of the current directory on a specified drive.

Operation

The subroutine uses DOS function call 47H to read the pathname into a 64-byte buffer in memory.

Entry Values

SI = Offset of a 64-byte buffer
DL = Drive number (0 = default, 1 = A, etc.)

Results

The buffer contains the pathname, followed by zeroes. The pathname does not begin with a backslash and does not include the drive letter.
If Carry is set, AX = Error code.
If Carry is not set (no error), AX is undefined.
SI and DL are unaffected.

Link Command

```
link callprog+getdir+showerr;
```

(SHOWERR displays a message based on an error code.)

Special Case

Reading the root directory pathname returns an empty buffer.

Example

Read the directory pathname on drive C into a buffer called PATHNAME:

```
             EXTRN   GETDIR:NEAR,SHOWERR:NEAR
   ENTRY:    JMP     START           ;Skip past buffer
   PATHNAME  DB      64 DUP(?)
   START     PROC    NEAR

             LEA     SI,PATHNAME     ;Load buffer offset into SI
             MOV     DL,3            ; and specify drive C in DL
             CALL    GETDIR          ;Read the pathname
             JNC     CONTINUE        ;Error?
             CALL    SHOWERR         ; Yes. Display error message
             RET                     ;  and exit
   CONTINUE: ..                      ; No. Continue here
             . .
```

If the pathname is *C:\PROGS\SUBS*, the buffer will contain *progs\subs*.

Subroutine Listing

```
; GETDIR - Read the pathname of the current directory
; Inputs: SI = Offset of 64-byte buffer
;         DL = Drive number
; Results: If Carry is set, AX = Error code
;          If Carry is not set (no error), AX is undefined
;          SI and DL are unaffected

        PUBLIC  GETDIR
CSEG  SEGMENT  PARA PUBLIC 'CODE'
        ASSUME  CS:CSEG,DS:CSEG,ES:CSEG,SS:CSEG

GETDIR  PROC  NEAR
        MOV   AH,47H    ;Call DOS function 47H
        INT   21H
        RET             ;Return to calling program
GETDIR  ENDP
    CSEG  ENDS
            END
```

READ THE PATHNAME (GETPATH)

GETPATH reads a string of up to 64 characters from the standard input device (initially the keyboard), stores it in memory in ASCIIZ format, and then advances to the next line. As each character is entered, the subroutine displays it on the standard output device.

Operation

The subroutine uses DOS function call 0AH to read a string from the standard input device and store it in a 65-byte memory buffer called PATH$. It then makes DX point to the first character (third byte) and stores a zero just past the final character. Finally, it uses DOS function call 2 to send a Carriage Return and Line Feed to the standard output device.

Entry Values

None.

Result

DX = Offset of an ASCIIZ string that contains the pathname.

Link Command

```
link callprog+getpath;
```

Special Case

Pressing Ctrl-C (or Ctrl-Break for IBM compatibles) makes DOS issue Interrupt 23H, "Ctrl-C Handler Address."

Subroutine Listing

```
; GETPATH - Read a pathname from the standard input device
; Inputs: None.
; Result: DX = Offset of ASCIIZ string

          PUBLIC  GETPATH
CSEG   SEGMENT  PARA PUBLIC 'CODE'
          ASSUME  CS:CSEG,DS:CSEG,ES:CSEG,SS:CSEG
          JMP     GETPATH  ;Skip the pathname buffer
PATH$     DB      65,65 DUP(?)

GETPATH PROC  NEAR
          PUSH   AX          ;Save affected registers
          PUSH   BX
          PUSH   SI
          LEA    DX,PATH$    ;Make DX point to the buffer
          MOV    AH,0AH      ;Call DOS function 0AH
          INT    21H
          ADD    DX,2        ;Make DX point to first char.,
          MOV    SI,DX       ; copy this offset into SI,
```

```
            PUSH    DX              ; and save it on the stack
            MOV     BL,PATH$+1  ;Read character count into BX
            SUB     BH,BH
            MOV     BYTE PTR [BX][SI],0   ;Store the ending zero
            MOV     DL,0DH      ;Do a carriage return
            MOV     AH,2
            INT     21H
            MOV     DL,0AH      ; and line feed
            MOV     AH,2
            INT     21H
            POP     DX              ;Retrieve the offset
            POP     SI              ;Restore registers
            POP     BX
            POP     AX
            RET                     ;Return to calling program
GETPATH     ENDP
CSEG   ENDS
            END
```

MAKE A SUBDIRECTORY (MAKEDIR)

MAKEDIR creates a new subdirectory based on a specified path and filename.

Operation

The subroutine creates a new subdirectory using DOS function call 39H.

Entry Value

DX = Offset of an ASCIIZ string that contains the pathname of the new subdirectory.

Results

If Carry is set, AX = Error code
If Carry is not set (no error), AX is undefined.
DX is unaffected.

Link Command

```
link callprog+makedir+showerr;
```

(SHOWERR displays a message based on an error code.)

Example

Create a new subdirectory using a pathname entered from the keyboard:

```
            EXTRN   MAKEDIR:NEAR,SHOWERR:NEAR,GETPATH:NEAR
            EXTRN   LIST$:NEAR
ENTRY:      JMP     START       ;Skip past string buffer
PROMPT      DB      'Enter the pathname of the new subdirectory: $'

START       PROC    NEAR
            LEA     DX,PROMPT        ;Issue the prompt
            CALL    LIST$
            CALL    GETPATH          ; and get user's response
            CALL    MAKEDIR          ;Create the directory
            JNC     LEAVE            ;Error?
            CALL    SHOWERR          ; Yes. Display error message
LEAVE:      RET                      ; and exit
```

Subroutine Listing

```
; MAKEDIR - Create a new subdirectory
; Input: DX = Offset of pathname
; Results: If Carry is set, AX = Error code
;          If Carry is not set, no error
;          DX is unaffected

        PUBLIC  MAKEDIR
CSEG  SEGMENT  PARA PUBLIC 'CODE'
```

262

```
          ASSUME   CS:CSEG,DS:CSEG,ES:CSEG,SS:CSEG
MAKEDIR   PROC   NEAR
          MOV    AH,39H    ;Call DOS function 39H
          INT    21H
          RET              ;Return to calling program
MAKEDIR   ENDP
CSEG   ENDS
          END
```

REMOVE A SUBDIRECTORY (REMDIR)

REMDIR remove a specified subdirectory.

Operation

The subroutine deletes the specified subdirectory using the DOS function call 3AH.

Entry Value

DX = Offset of an ASCIIZ string that contains the pathname of the subdirectory.

Results

If Carry is set, AX = Error code.
If Carry is not set (no error), AX is undefined.
DX is unaffected.

Link Command

```
link callprog+remdir+showerr;
```

(SHOWERR displays a message based on an error code.)

Example

Delete a subdirectory by entering its pathname from the keyboard:

```
EXTRN   REMDIR:NEAR,SHOWERR:NEAR,GETPATH:NEAR
EXTRN   LIST$:NEAR
ENTRY:  JMP     START       ;Skip past string buffer
PROMPT  DB      'Enter the pathname of the subdirectory: $'

START   PROC    NEAR
        LEA     DX,PROMPT      ;Issue the prompt
        CALL    LIST$
        CALL    GETPATH        ; and get user's response
        CALL    REMDIR         ;Remove the directory
        JNC     LEAVE          ;Error?
        CALL    SHOWERR        ; Yes. Display error message
LEAVE:  RET                    ;  and exit
```

Subroutine Listing

```
; REMDIR - Remove a subdirectory
; Input: DX = Offset of pathname
; Results: If Carry is set, AX = Error code
;          If Carry is not set, no error
;          DX is unaffected

        PUBLIC  REMDIR
CSEG    SEGMENT PARA PUBLIC 'CODE'
        ASSUME  CS:CSEG,DS:CSEG,ES:CSEG,SS:CSEG
```

```
REMDIR   PROC   NEAR
         MOV    AH,3AH     ;Call DOS function 3AH
         INT    21H
         RET               ;Return to calling program
REMDIR   ENDP
CSEG  ENDS
         END
```

CHANGE THE CURRENT DIRECTORY (CHGDIR)

CHGDIR changes to a specified directory.

Operation

The subroutine changes directories using DOS function call 3BH.

Entry Value

DX = Offset of an ASCIIZ string that contains the pathname of the new directory.

Results

If Carry is set, AX = Error code.
If Carry is not set (no error), AX is undefined.
DX is unaffected.

Link Command

```
link callprog+chgdir+showerr;
```

(SHOWERR displays a message based on an error code.)

Example

Change to a subdirectory entered from the keyboard:

```
            EXTRN   CHGDIR:NEAR,SHOWERR:NEAR,GETPATH:NEAR
            EXTRN   LIST$:NEAR
ENTRY:      JMP     START       ;Skip past string buffer
PROMPT      DB      'Enter the pathname of the subdirectory: $'
START       PROC    NEAR
            LEA     DX,PROMPT       ;Issue the prompt
            CALL    LIST$
            CALL    GETPATH         ; and get user's response
            CALL    CHGDIR          ;Change directories
            JNC     LEAVE           ;Error?
            CALL    SHOWERR         ; Yes. Display error message
LEAVE:      RET                     ;  and exit
```

Subroutine Listing

```
; CHGDIR - Change the current directory
; Input: DX = Offset of pathname
; Results: If Carry is set, AX = Error code
;          If Carry is not set, no error
;          DX is unaffected

        PUBLIC  CHGDIR
CSEG    SEGMENT PARA PUBLIC 'CODE'
        ASSUME  CS:CSEG,DS:CSEG,ES:CSEG,SS:CSEG
```

```
CHGDIR   PROC  NEAR
         MOV   AH,3BH    ;Call DOS function 3BH
         INT   21H
         RET             ;Return to calling program
CHGDIR   ENDP
CSEG  ENDS
         END
```

Chapter 19

Disk File Operations

The subroutines in this chapter manipulate disk files. The first two provide assembly language equivalents of the DOS RENAME (or REN) and ERASE (or DEL) commands. The remaining subroutines work with file *attributes*. The attributes tell DOS whether a file is write-protected (read-only), hidden, and so on.

ATTRIBUTES

MS-DOS keeps track of the information on a disk in an internal directory and produces a summary of this directory when you give a DIR command. In the directory, DOS records the volume label and the names of the files and subdirectories. It also maintains an *attribute byte* for each entry, to distinguish them.

The bits in the attribute byte tell whether the entry is read-only (bit 0 = 1), a hidden file (bit 1 = 1), a system file (bit 2 = 1), a volume label (bit 3 = 1), or a subdirectory name (bit 4 = 1). Bit 5 is the *archive* bit for fixed disk files. DOS sets it to 1 when you change the file and clears it to 0 when you use the BACKUP command to copy the file to a floppy disk. For floppy disk files, bit 5 is always 1. Figure 19-1 shows the format of an attribute byte.

Note that the attribute byte for the volume label or a subdirectory name on a hard disk usually has only a single "1" bit (bit 3 or 4, respectively), while the attribute byte for a regular file may have several "1" bits. For example, the attribute byte for a read-only hidden file would contain 3H on a hard disk or 23H on a floppy disk. A normal read/write file would contain 0 on a hard disk.

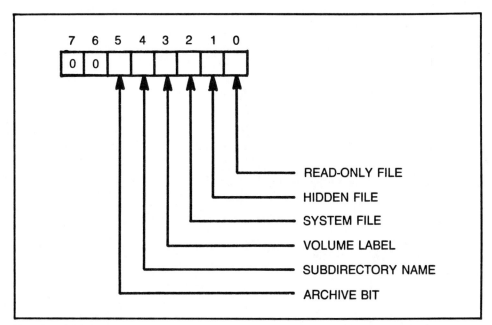

Fig. 19-1. Attribute byte.

RENAME A FILE (RENFILE)

RENFILE renames a file by changing its directory entry.

Operation

The subroutine creates a new subdirectory using DOS function call 56H.

Entry Value

DX = Offset of an ASCIIZ string that contains the pathname of the file to be renamed.

DI = Offset of an ASCIIZ string that contains the new pathname.

Results

If Carry is set, AX = Error code.
If Carry is not set (no error), AX is undefined.
DX and DI are unaffected.

Link Command

```
link callprog+renfile+showerr;
```

(SHOWERR displays a message based on an error code.)

Comments

This subroutine cannot be used to rename a hidden file, system file, or subdirectory.

If the second pathname specifies a drive, the first pathname must specify or default to the same drive.

You may not use the DOS wildcard characters (* and ?) in the second pathname. If you do, RENFILE will replace them with question marks.

You can also use RENFILE to move a file to another directory. To do this, enter the same filename, but a different directory path, in the second pathname. For example, to move the file BILLING.LET from subdirectory LETTERS1 to subdirectory LETTERS2 on drive C, enter c:\letters1\billing.let for the first pathname and c:\letters2\billing.let for the second pathname.

Example

Rename a file using a pathname entered from the keyboard:

```
          EXTRN   RENFILE:NEAR,SHOWERR:NEAR,GETPATH:NEAR
          EXTRN   LIST$:NEAR
ENTRY:    JMP     START     ;Skip past string buffer
OLD       DB      'Enter the pathname of the file to be renamed: $'
NEW       DB      'Enter the new pathname for the file: $'
OLDNAME   DB      65 DUP(?)   ;Save old pathname string here

START     PROC    NEAR
          LEA     DX,OLD    ;Issue the first prompt
          CALL    LIST$
```

```
            CALL    GETPATH   ; and get user's response
            MOV     SI,DX     ;Copy this string to OLDNAME
            LEA     DI,OLDNAME
NEXTCHAR:   MOVSB
            CMP     BYTE PTR [DI]-1,0  ;Done?
            JNZ     NEXTCHAR  ; No.  Get next character
            LEA     DX,NEW    ; Yes.  Issue the second prompt
            CALL    LIST$
            CALL    GETPATH   ; and get user's response
            MOV     DI,DX     ;Move this offset to DI
            LEA     DX,OLDNAME  ; and first offset to DX
            CALL    RENFILE   ;Rename the file directory
            JNC     LEAVE     ;Error?
            CALL    SHOWERR   ; Yes. Display error message
LEAVE:      RET               ;  and exit
```

Note that after calling GETPATH the first time, I saved the response string in OLDNAME. If I had not done this, the user's second string would have overwritten the first one.

Subroutine Listing

```
; RENFILE - Rename a file
; Inputs: DX = Pointer to ASCIIZ string containing pathname
;              of the file to be renamed
;         DI = Pointer to ASCIIZ string containing new
;              pathname
; Results: If Carry is set, AX = Error code
;          If Carry is not set, file is renamed
;          DX and DI are unaffected

            PUBLIC  RENFILE
CSEG    SEGMENT  PARA PUBLIC 'CODE'
            ASSUME  CS:CSEG,DS:CSEG,ES:CSEG,SS:CSEG

RENFILE   PROC   NEAR
            MOV     AH,56H    ;Call DOS function 56H
            INT     21H
            RET               ;Return to calling program
RENFILE   ENDP
CSEG    ENDS
            END
```

DELETE A FILE (DELFILE)

DELFILE erases or deletes a specified file by deleting its directory entry.

Operation

The subroutine deletes the file using DOS function call 41H.

Entry Value

DX = Offset of an ASCIIZ string that contains the pathname of the file.

Results

If Carry is set, AX = Error code.
If Carry is not set (no error), AX is undefined.
DX is unaffected.

Link Command

```
link callprog+delfile+showerr;
```

(SHOWERR displays a message based on an error code.)

Example

Delete a file by entering its pathname from the keyboard:

```
            EXTRN   DELFILE:NEAR,SHOWERR:NEAR,GETPATH:NEAR
            EXTRN   LIST$:NEAR
ENTRY:      JMP     START        ;Skip past string buffer
PROMPT      DB      'Enter the pathname of the file: $'

START       PROC    NEAR
            LEA     DX,PROMPT        ;Issue the prompt
            CALL    LIST$
            CALL    GETPATH          ; and get user's response
            CALL    DELFILE          ;Delete the file
            JNC     LEAVE            ;Error?
            CALL    SHOWERR          ; Yes. Display error message
LEAVE:      RET                      ;  and exit
```

Subroutine Listing

```
; DELFILE - Delete a file
; Input: DX = Offset of pathname
; Results: If Carry is set, AX = Error code
;          If Carry is not set, no error
;          DX is unaffected

            PUBLIC  DELFILE
CSEG   SEGMENT  PARA PUBLIC 'CODE'
            ASSUME  CS:CSEG,DS:CSEG,ES:CSEG,SS:CSEG
```

```
DELFILE   PROC   NEAR
          MOV    AH,41H    ;Call DOS function 41H
          INT    21H
          RET              ;Return to calling program
DELFILE   ENDP
CSEG   ENDS
          END
```

READ THE FILE MODE (GETMODE)

GETMODE reads the attribute byte of a specified file into a register.

Operation

The subroutine reads the attribute byte into CL using the AL = 0 option of DOS function call 43H. If the pathname was invalid or the file doesn't exist, it sets the Carry Flag to 1 and returns an error code in AX; otherwise, it sets CF to 0 and returns the attribute byte in CL.

Entry Value

DX = Offset of an ASCIIZ string that contains the pathname of the file.

Results

If Carry is set, AX = Error code.
If Carry is not set (no error), CL = Attribute byte.
DX is unaffected.

Link Command

```
link callprog+getmode+showerr;
```

(SHOWERR displays a message based on an error code.)

Example

Read the attribute byte of a file whose pathname is entered from the keyboard:

```
              EXTRN   GETMODE:NEAR,SHOWERR:NEAR,GETPATH:NEAR
              EXTRN   LIST$:NEAR
ENTRY:        JMP     START       ;Skip past string buffer
PROMPT        DB      'Enter the pathname of the file: $'

START         PROC    NEAR
              LEA     DX,PROMPT         ;Issue the prompt
              CALL    LIST$
              CALL    GETPATH           ; and get user's response
              CALL    GETMODE           ;Read the attribute byte
              JNC     LEAVE             ;Error?
              CALL    SHOWERR           ; Yes. Display error message
LEAVE:        RET                       ;  and exit
```

Subroutine Listing

```
; GETMODE - Read a file's attribute byte
; Input: DX = Offset of pathname
; Results: If Carry is set, AX = Error code
;          If Carry is not set, CL = Attribute byte
;          DX is unaffected
```

```
        PUBLIC   GETMODE
CSEG   SEGMENT  PARA PUBLIC 'CODE'
        ASSUME   CS:CSEG,DS:CSEG,ES:CSEG,SS:CSEG

GETMODE   PROC   NEAR
          MOV    AL,0      ;Select a read operation
          MOV    AH,43H    ;Call DOS function 43H
          INT    21H
          RET              ;Return to calling program
GETMODE   ENDP
CSEG   ENDS
          END
```

CHANGE THE FILE MODE (CHMODE)

CHMODE sets the attributes of a file. This is convenient for changing a regular read/write file to read-only or hidden, or vice versa.

Operation

The subroutine begins by using the preceding GETMODE subroutine to read the current attributes into CX. If the pathname was invalid or the file doesn't exist, it sets the Carry Flag to 1 and returns an error code in AX; otherwise, it sets CF to 0 and returns AX with undefined contents. If no error occurred, the subroutine changes the low byte of CX (i.e., the attribute byte) to the specified value and writes it to the file using the AL = 1 option of DOS function call 43H.

Entry Values

DX = Offset of an ASCIIZ string that contains the pathname of the file.
CL = Attribute byte.

Results

If Carry is set, AX = Error code.
If Carry is not set (no error), AX is undefined.
DX and CL are unaffected.

Link Command

```
link callprog+chmode+getmode+showerr;
```

(SHOWERR displays a message based on an error code.)

Comment

You cannot change the volume label bit (3) or the subdirectory bit (4) with this subroutine.

Example

Make a file read-only using a pathname entered from the keyboard:

```
             EXTRN   GETMODE:NEAR,CHMODE:NEAR,SHOWERR:NEAR
             EXTRN   GETPATH:NEAR,LIST$:NEAR
ENTRY:       JMP     START      ;Skip past string buffer
PROMPT       DB      'Enter the pathname of the file: $'

START        PROC    NEAR
             LEA     DX,PROMPT  ;Issue the prompt
             CALL    LIST$
             CALL    GETPATH    ; and get user's response
             CALL    GETMODE    ;Read the attribute byte
             JNC     CHBYTE     ;Error?
DISPMSG:     CALL    SHOWERR    ; Yes. Display error message
             RET                ;  and exit
CHBYTE:      OR      CL,1       ; No. Set the read-only bit
```

```
            CALL    CHMODE      ;  and change the attribute byte
            JC      DISPMSG     ;Error?
            RET                 ;  No. Exit
```

Note that with one change, you can use this program to change a read-only file to a read/write file: simply replace the OR instruction at label CHBYTE with *AND CL,0FEH*. Similarly, to hide a file or unhide a hidden file, replace the OR at CHBYTE with *OR CL,2* or *AND CL,0FDH*.

Subroutine Listing

```
; CHMODE - Change a file's attributes
; Inputs: DX = Offset of pathname
;         CL = Attribute byte
; Results: If Carry is set, AX = Error code
;          If Carry is not set, AX is undefined
;          DX and CL are unaffected.
; Note: Calls GETMODE, an external subroutine.

            EXTRN   GETMODE:NEAR
            PUBLIC  CHMODE
CSEG    SEGMENT  PARA PUBLIC 'CODE'
            ASSUME  CS:CSEG,DS:CSEG,ES:CSEG,SS:CSEG
            JMP     CHMODE      ;Skip data area
SAVECL      DB      ?

CHMODE  PROC   NEAR
            MOV     SAVECL,CL   ;Save attribute byte
            CALL    GETMODE     ;Get the current attributes
            JC      EXIT        ;Error?
            MOV     CL,SAVECL   ; No. Load the attribute byte
            MOV     AL,1        ;Select a write operation
            MOV     AH,43H      ;Call DOS function 43H
            INT     21H
EXIT:       RET                 ;Return to calling program
CHMODE      ENDP
CSEG    ENDS
            END
```

FIND THE FIRST MATCHING FILE (FINDF)

FINDF searches a specified subdirectory for the first entry that matches a specified pathname. If it finds a match, it returns the file's attribute byte, time, date, size, name, and extension in memory.

Operation

The subroutine searches using DOS function call 4EH. This function call returns file information in a block of memory called the *Disk Transfer Area (DTA)*. The DTA is 43 bytes long. DOS uses the first 21 bytes as a work area and records the actual file information in the remaining 22 bytes. Thus, before searching the disk, the subroutine uses DOS function call 1AH (Set Disk Transfer Address) to establish a buffer called MYDTA as the Disk Transfer Area. If the pathname is invalid or the file cannot be found, the subroutine sets the Carry Flag to 1 and returns an error code in AX; otherwise, it sets CF to 0 and returns the offset of the file information (the 22nd byte of MYDTA) in BX.

Entry Values

DX = Offset of an ASCIIZ string that contains the pathname of the file. The pathname may include wildcard characters.

CL = Attributes to match

Results

If Carry is set, AX = Error code.

If Carry is not set (no error), BX = Offset of file information. File information consists of 22 bytes, as follows:

Byte(s)	Contents
0	Attribute byte
1-2	Time in binary (see Fig. 19-2)
3-4	Date in binary (see Fig. 19-2)
5-6	Low word of file size in binary
7-8	High word of file size in binary
9-20	Name and extension of the file, separated by a period (e.g., MY-FILE.ASM)
21	Zero byte

DX and CL are unaffected.

Link Command

```
link callprog+findf;
```

Comments

If the attribute byte specifies searching for hidden files, system files, or subdirec-

278

tory entries (bit 1, 2, or 4 is set to 1), the subroutine also detects regular read/write files.

To search all entries except the volume label, set the attribute byte to 16H.

If you omit the path and give only a filename, the subroutine searches the current subdirectory.

To search the root directory, precede the filename with a backslash (\).

To search for the next occurrence of a pathname, use the FINDNXTF subroutine in this chapter.

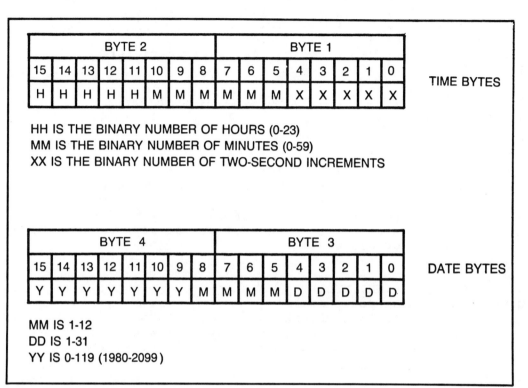

HH IS THE BINARY NUMBER OF HOURS (0-23)
MM IS THE BINARY NUMBER OF MINUTES (0-59)
XX IS THE BINARY NUMBER OF TWO-SECOND INCREMENTS

MM IS 1-12
DD IS 1-31
YY IS 0-119 (1980-2099)

Fig. 19-2. The format of time and date bytes.

Example

Find the first file that matches a pathname entered from the keyboard, and display its name:

```
                EXTRN   FINDF:NEAR,SHOWERR:NEAR,LISTCHR:NEAR
                EXTRN   GETPATH:NEAR,LIST$:NEAR
ENTRY:          JMP     START      ;Skip past string buffer
PROMPT          DB      'Enter the pathname of the file: $'

START           PROC    NEAR
                LEA     DX,PROMPT  ;Issue the prompt
                CALL    LIST$
                CALL    GETPATH    ; and get user's response
                MOV     CL,16H     ;Accept any file
```

```
            CALL    FINDF        ;Do the search
            JNC     SHOWNAME     ;Error?
            CALL    SHOWERR      ; Yes. Display error message
            RET
SHOWNAME:   ADD     BX,8         ; No. Point to byte preceding name
            MOV     CX,12        ;Display up to 12 characters
NEXTCHAR:   INC     BX           ;Point to next character
            MOV     DL,[BX]      ; and read it
            CMP     DL,0         ;Is it zero?
            JZ      QUIT         ; Yes. Exit
            CALL    LISTCHR      ; No. Display it
            LOOP    NEXTCHAR     ; and go get next character
QUIT:       RET
```

Note that the value 16H for the attribute byte makes the program search for any file,
including read-only and hidden files.

Subroutine Listing

```
; FINDF - Find first matching file
; Inputs: DX = Offset of pathname (may include wildcards)
;         CL = Attribute byte
; Results: If Carry is set, AX = Error code
;          If Carry is not set, BX = Offset of file data
;          DX and CL are unaffected.


            PUBLIC  FINDF,MYDTA
CSEG    SEGMENT  PARA PUBLIC 'CODE'
            ASSUME  CS:CSEG,DS:CSEG,ES:CSEG,SS:CSEG
            JMP     FINDF        ;Skip past the data area
MYDTA       DB      43 DUP(?)    ;This will hold the file data

FINDF   PROC  NEAR
            PUSH    DX
            LEA     DX,MYDTA ;Make MYDTA the DTA
            MOV     AH,1AH       ; using function call 1AH
            INT     21H
            POP     DX
            MOV     CH,0         ;Search for the file
            MOV     AH,4EH       ; using function call 4EH
            INT     21H
            LEA     BX,MYDTA+21 ;Make BX point to file data
            RET                  ;Return to calling program
FINDF       ENDP
CSEG    ENDS
            END
```

FIND THE NEXT MATCHING FILE (FINDNXTF)

FINDNXTF searches for the next entry that matches the pathname and attributes specified in a previous call to subroutine FINDF (Find First Matching File). If it finds a match, it returns the file's attribute byte, time, date, size, name, and extension in memory.

Operation

The subroutine searches using DOS function call 4FH, and returns file information in the last 22 bytes of the MYDTA buffer set up by the FINDF subroutine. If the pathname was invalid or the file cannot be found, the subroutine sets the Carry Flag to 1 and returns an error code value of 18 in AX; otherwise, it sets CF to 0 and returns the offset of the file information in BX.

Entry Values

None.

Results

If Carry is set (no more matching files), AX = 18.
If Carry is not set (file found), BX = Offset of file information. File information is described for the preceding FINDF subroutine.

Link Command

```
link callprog+findf+findnxtf;
```

Example

Display the names of all hidden files in the root directory:

```
    EXTRN   FINDF:NEAR,FINDNXTF:NEAR,LISTCHR:NEAR,LIST$:NEAR
ENTRY:      JMP     START       ;Skip past strings
PATH        DB      '\*.*',0 ;Pathname for root directory
NOMORE      DB      'No more hidden files.$'
CRLF        DB      0AH,0DH '$' ;Carriage Return, Line Feed

START       PROC    NEAR
            LEA     DX,PATH     ;Put offset of pathname in DX
            MOV     CL,16H      ;Accept any file
            CALL    FINDF       ;Search for the first file
            JC      DONE        ;File found?
CHKHIDE:    TEST    BYTE PTR [BX],2 ; Yes, but is it hidden?
            JZ      NEXTFILE
            ADD     BX,8        ; Yes. Point to byte preceding name
            MOV     CX,12       ;Display up to 12 characters
NEXTCHAR:   INC     BX          ;Point to next character
            MOV     DL,[BX]     ; and read it
            CMP     DL,0        ;Is it zero?
            JZ      NEWLINE     ; Yes. Search again
```

```
                CALL    LISTCHR   ; No. Display it
                LOOP    NEXTCHAR  ;  and go get next character
NEWLINE:        LEA     DX,CRLF   ;Advance to next line
                CALL    LIST$
NEXTFILE:       CALL    FINDNXTF  ;Search for the next file
                JNC     CHKHIDE   ;Found. Go see if it's hidden
DONE:           LEA     DX,NOMORE ;Not found. Display ending message
                CALL    LIST$
                RET               ; and leave
```

MS-DOS stores two hidden files, IO.SYS and MSDOS.SYS, in the root directory of bootable disks. (On an IBM PC, these files are named IBMBIO.COM and IBMDOS.COM.) Besides being hidden, they are also marked as read-only and system files.

Subroutine Listing

```
; FINDNXTF - Find next matching file
; Inputs: None.
; Results: If Carry is set, AX = 18
;          If Carry is not set, BX = Offset of file data

            EXTRN   MYDTA:BYTE
            PUBLIC  FINDNXTF
CSEG    SEGMENT  PARA PUBLIC 'CODE'
            ASSUME  CS:CSEG,DS:CSEG,ES:CSEG,SS:CSEG

FINDNXTF    PROC    NEAR
            MOV     AH,4FH     ;Search for the file
            INT     21H        ; using function call 4FH
            LEA     BX,MYDTA+21 ;Make BX point to file data
            RET                ;Return to calling program
FINDNXTF    ENDP
CSEG    ENDS
            END
```

WRITE-PROTECT A FILE (PROTF)

PROTF changes the attributes of a read/write file to write-protect it. That is, PROTF makes the file read-only.

Operation

The subroutine reads the attributes into CX using the AL = 0 option of DOS function call 43H; then it forces the read-only bit (0) to 1. Finally, it stores the new attributes in the directory using the AL = 1 option of function call 43H. If the pathname was invalid or the file doesn't exist, it sets the Carry Flag to 1 and returns an error code in AX; otherwise, it sets CF to 0 and returns AX undefined.

Entry Value

DX = Offset of an ASCIIZ string that contains the pathname of the file.

Results

If Carry is set, AX = Error code.
If Carry is not set (no error), AX is undefined.
DX is unaffected.

Link Command

```
link callprog+protf+showerr;
```

(SHOWERR displays a message based on an error code.)

Comment

To unprotect a file, use the UNPROTF subroutine in this chapter.

Example 1

Write-protect a file whose pathname is entered from the keyboard:

```
            EXTRN   PROTF:NEAR,SHOWERR:NEAR,GETPATH:NEAR
            EXTRN   LIST$:NEAR
ENTRY:      JMP     START        ;Skip past string buffer
PROMPT      DB      'Enter the pathname of the file: $'

START       PROC    NEAR
            LEA     DX,PROMPT        ;Issue the prompt
            CALL    LIST$
            CALL    GETPATH          ; and get user's response
            CALL    PROTF            ;Protect the file
            JNC     QUIT             ;Error?
            CALL    SHOWERR          ; Yes. Display error message
QUIT:       RET                      ;   and exit
```

Example 2

Display the name of each read/write file that matches a user-entered pathname and allow the user to write-protect it by typing Y in response to a prompt:

```
                EXTRN   FINDF:NEAR,FINDNXTF:NEAR,LISTCHR:NEAR
                EXTRN   LIST$:NEAR,PROTF:NEAR,GETCHRE:NEAR
                EXTRN   GETPATH:NEAR
ENTRY:          JMP     START       ;Skip past strings
PROMPT1         DB      'Enter the pathname name: $'
NOMORE          DB      'No more files.$'
CRLF            DB      0AH,0DH,'$' ;Carriage Return, Line Feed
MSG             DB      'As each filename is displayed, press...',
                DB      0AH,0DH,0AH,0DH,
                DB      '   Y to protect it,',0AH,0DH,
                DB      '   N leave it read/write, or',0AH,0DH,
                DB      '   Return to exit.',0AH,0DH,'$'
PROMPT2         DB      '? (Y/N/CR) $'
NAMEOFF         DW      ?           ;For offset of a filename

START           PROC    NEAR
                LEA     DX,PROMPT1 ;Prompt user for subdirectory
                CALL    LIST$
                CALL    GETPATH     ; and get the response
                PUSH    DX
                LEA     DX,CRLF     ;Advance to next line
                CALL    LIST$
                LEA     DX,MSG      ; and display the instructions
                CALL    LIST$
                POP     DX
                MOV     CL,6        ;Accept any file
                CALL    FINDF       ;Search for the first file
                JC      DONE        ;File found?
                MOV     NAMEOFF,BX  ;Save the offset of the name
                ADD     NAMEOFF,9
CHKRW:          TEST    BYTE PTR [BX],1 ; Yes, but is it read/write?
                JNZ     NEXTFILE
                ADD     BX,8        ; Yes. Point to byte preceding name
                MOV     CX,12       ;Display up to 12 characters
NEXTCHAR:       INC     BX          ;Point to next character
                MOV     DL,[BX]     ; and read it
                CMP     DL,0        ;Is it zero?
                JZ      FINISH      ; Yes Go display second prompt
                CALL    LISTCHR     ; No. Display it
                LOOP    NEXTCHAR    ; and go get next character
FINISH:         LEA     DX,PROMPT2 ;Issue protect prompt
                CALL    LIST$
                CALL    GETCHRE     ; and get user's answer
                LEA     DX,CRLF     ;Advance to next line
                CALL    LIST$
                CMP     AL,0DH      ;Do what the user said
                JE      LEAVE
                CMP     AL,'Y'
                JE      PROTECT
```

```
               CMP     AL,'y'
               JNE     NEXTFILE
PROTECT:       MOV     DX,NAMEOFF  ;Make the file read-only
               CALL    PROTF
NEXTFILE:      CALL    FINDNXTF    ;Search for the next file
               JNC     CHKRW       ;Found. Go see if it's read/write
DONE:          LEA     DX,NOMORE   ;Not found. Display ending message
               CALL    LIST$
LEAVE:         RET                 ; and leave
```

Subroutine Listing

```
; PROTF - Write-protect a file
; Input: DX = Offset of pathname
; Results: If Carry is set, AX = Error code
;          If Carry is not set, AX is undefined
;          DX is unaffected.

               PUBLIC  PROTF
CSEG    SEGMENT  PARA PUBLIC 'CODE'
               ASSUME  CS:CSEG,DS:CSEG,ES:CSEG,SS:CSEG

PROTF   PROC  NEAR
               PUSH    CX          ;Save CX
               MOV     AL,0        ;Read the file's attributes
               MOV     AH,43H      ; using option AL = 0
               INT     21H         ; of DOS function call 43H
               JC      LEAVE       ;Error?
               OR      CX,1        ;No. Set the read-only bit (0)
               MOV     AL,1        ;Change the file's attributes
               MOV     AH,43H      ; using option AL = 1
               INT     21H         ; of DOS function call 43H
LEAVE:         POP     CX          ;Retrieve CX
               RET                 ; and return to calling program
PROTF   ENDP
CSEG    ENDS
               END
```

UNPROTECT A FILE (UNPROTF)

UNPROTF changes the attributes of a read-only file to unprotect it. That is, UN-PROTF makes the file read/write.

Operation

The subroutine reads the attributes into CX using the AL = 0 option of DOS function call 43H; then it forces the read-only bit (0) to 0. Finally, it stores the new attributes in the directory using the AL = 1 option of function call 43H. If the pathname is invalid or the file doesn't exist, it sets the Carry Flag to 1 and returns an error code in AX; otherwise, it sets CF to 0 and returns AX undefined.

Entry Value

DX = Offset of an ASCIIZ string that contains the pathname of the file.

Results

If Carry is set, AX = Error code.
If Carry is not set (no error), AX is undefined.
DX is unaffected.

Link Command

```
link callprog+unprotf+showerr;
```

(SHOWERR displays a message based on an error code.)

Comment

To write-protect a file, use the PROTF subroutine in this chapter.

Example

Unprotect a file whose pathname is entered from the keyboard:

```
        EXTRN   UNPROTF:NEAR,SHOWERR:NEAR,GETPATH:NEAR
        EXTRN   LIST$:NEAR
ENTRY:  JMP     START       ;Skip past string buffer
PROMPT  DB      'Enter the pathname of the file: $'

START   PROC NEAR
        LEA     DX,PROMPT       ;Issue the prompt
        CALL    LIST$
        CALL    GETPATH         ; and get user's response
        CALL    UNPROTF         ;Unprotect the file
        JNC     QUIT            ;Error?
        CALL    SHOWERR         ; Yes. Display error message
QUIT:   RET                     ; and exit
```

Subroutine Listing

```
; UNPROTF - Remove write protection from a file
; Input: DX = Offset of pathname
; Results: If Carry is set, AX = Error code
;          If Carry is not set, AX is undefined
;          DX is unaffected.

        PUBLIC  UNPROTF
CSEG  SEGMENT  PARA PUBLIC 'CODE'
        ASSUME  CS:CSEG,DS:CSEG,ES:CSEG,SS:CSEG

UNPROTF  PROC  NEAR
         PUSH  CX        ;Save CX
         MOV   AL,0      ;Read the file's attributes
         MOV   AH,43H    ; using option AL = 0
         INT   21H       ; of DOS function call 43H
         JC    LEAVE     ;Error?
         AND   CL,0FEH   ;No. Clear the read-only bit (0)
         MOV   AL,1      ;Change the file's attributes
         MOV   AH,43H    ; using option AL = 1
         INT   21H       ; of DOS function call 43H
LEAVE:   POP   CX        ;Retrieve CX
         RET             ; and return to calling program
UNPROTF  ENDP
CSEG  ENDS
         END
```

HIDE A FILE (HIDEF)

HIDEF hides a file, so it doesn't appear in normal DOS directory operations.

Operation

The subroutine reads the attributes into CX using the AL = 0 option of DOS function call 43H; it then forces the hidden bit (1) to 1. Finally, it stores the new attributes in the directory using the AL = 1 option of function call 43H. If the pathname was invalid or the file doesn't exist, it sets the Carry Flag to 1 and returns an error code in AX; otherwise, it sets CF to 0 and returns AX undefined.

Entry Value

DX = Offset of an ASCIIZ string that contains the pathname of the file.

Results

If Carry is set, AX = Error code.
If Carry is not set (no error), AX is undefined.
DX is unaffected.

Link Command

```
link callprog+hidef+showerr;
```

(SHOWERR displays a message based on an error code.)

Comment

To unhide a file, use the UNHIDE subroutine in this chapter.

Example 1

Hide a file whose pathname is entered from the keyboard:

```
            EXTRN   HIDEF:NEAR,SHOWERR:NEAR,GETPATH:NEAR
            EXTRN   LIST$:NEAR
ENTRY:      JMP     START       ;Skip past string buffer
PROMPT      DB      'Enter the pathname of the file: $'

START       PROC    NEAR
            LEA     DX,PROMPT       ;Issue the prompt
            CALL    LIST$
            CALL    GETPATH         ; and get user's response
            CALL    HIDEF           ;Hide the file
            JNC     QUIT            ;Error?
            CALL    SHOWERR         ; Yes. Display error message
QUIT:       RET                     ;  and exit
```

Example 2

Display the name of each file that matches a user-entered pathname, and allow the user to hide it by typing Y in response to a prompt:

```
                EXTRN   FINDF:NEAR,FINDNXTF:NEAR,LISTCHR:NEAR
                EXTRN   LIST$:NEAR,HIDE:NEAR,GETCHRE:NEAR
                EXTRN   GETPATH:NEAR
ENTRY:          JMP     START       ;Skip past strings
PROMPT1         DB      'Enter the pathname name: $'
NOMORE          DB      'No more files.$'
CRLF            DB      0AH,0DH,'$' ;Carriage Return, Line Feed
MSG             DB      'As each filename is displayed, press...',
                DB      0AH,0DH,0AH,0DH,
                DB      '  Y to hide it,',0AH,0DH,
                DB      '  N leave it as is, or',0AH,0DH,
                DB      '  Return to exit.',0AH,0DH,'$'
PROMPT2         DB      '? (Y/N/CR) $'
NAMEOFF         DW      ?           ;For offset of a filename

START           PROC    NEAR
                LEA     DX,PROMPT1 ;Prompt user for subdirectory
                CALL    LIST$
                CALL    GETPATH    ; and get the response
                PUSH    DX
                LEA     DX,CRLF    ;Advance to next line
                CALL    LIST$
                LEA     DX,MSG     ; and display the instructions
                CALL    LIST$
                POP     DX
                MOV     CL,6       ;Accept any file
                CALL    FINDF      ;Search for the first file
                JC      DONE       ;File found?
                MOV     NAMEOFF,BX ;Save the offset of the name
                ADD     NAMEOFF,9
CHKH:           TEST    BYTE PTR [BX],2 ; Yes, but is it hidden?
                JNZ     NEXTFILE
                ADD     BX,8       ; Yes. Point to byte preceding name
                MOV     CX,12      ;Display up to 12 characters
NEXTCHAR:       INC     BX         ;Point to next character
                MOV     DL,[BX]    ; and read it
                CMP     DL,0       ;Is it zero?
                JZ      FINISH     ; Yes. Go display second prompt
                CALL    LISTCHR    ; No. Display it
                LOOP    NEXTCHAR   ; and go get next character
FINISH:         LEA     DX,PROMPT2 ;Issue hide prompt
                CALL    LIST$
                CALL    GETCHRE    ; and get user's answer
                LEA     DX,CRLF    ;Advance to next line
                CALL    LIST$
                CMP     AL,0DH     ;Do what the user said
                JE      LEAVE
                CMP     AL,'Y'
                JE      HIDE
```

```
            CMP     AL,'y'
            JNE     NEXTFILE
HIDE:       MOV     DX,NAMEOFF   ;Make the file hidden
            CALL    HIDEF
NEXTFILE:   CALL    FINDNXTF     ;Search for the next file
            JNC     CHKH         ;Found. Go see if it's hidden
DONE:       LEA     DX,NOMORE    ;Not found. Display ending message
            CALL    LIST$
LEAVE:      RET                  ; and leave
```

Subroutine Listing

```
; HIDEF - Hide a file
; Input: DX = Offset of pathname
; Results: If Carry is set, AX = Error code
;          If Carry is not set, AX is undefined
;          DX is unaffected.

            PUBLIC  HIDEF
CSEG    SEGMENT  PARA PUBLIC 'CODE'
            ASSUME  CS:CSEG,DS:CSEG,ES:CSEG,SS:CSEG

HIDEF   PROC  NEAR
            PUSH    CX           ;Save CX
            MOV     AL,0         ;Read the file's attributes
            MOV     AH,43H       ; using option AL = 0
            INT     21H          ; of DOS function call 43H
            JC      LEAVE        ;Error?
            OR      CX,2         ;No. Set the hidden bit (1)
            MOV     AL,1         ;Change the file's attributes
            MOV     AH,43H       ; using option AL = 1
            INT     21H          ; of DOS function call 43H
LEAVE:      POP     CX           ;Retrieve CX
            RET                  ; and return to calling program
HIDEF       ENDP
CSEG    ENDS
            END
```

UNHIDE A FILE (UNHIDEF)

UNHIDEF changes the attributes of a hidden file to unhide it.

Operation

The subroutine reads the attributes into CX using the AL = 0 option of DOS function call 43H; then it forces the hidden bit (1) to 0. Finally, it stores the new attributes in the directory using the AL = 1 option of function call 43H. If the pathname is invalid or the file doesn't exist, it sets the Carry Flag to 1 and returns an error code in AX; otherwise, it sets CF to 0 and returns AX undefined.

Entry Value

DX = Offset of an ASCIIZ string that contains the pathname of the file.

Results

If Carry is set, AX = Error code.
If Carry is not set (no error), AX is undefined.
DX is unaffected.

Link Command

```
link callprog+unhidef+showerr;
```

(SHOWERR displays a message based on an error code.)

Comments

To hide a file, use the HIDEF subroutine in this chapter.
The Find Next Matching File (FINDNXTF) section of this chapter lists an example program that displays the names of hidden files.

Example

Unhide a file whose pathname is entered from the keyboard:

```
        EXTRN   UNHIDEF:NEAR,SHOWERR:NEAR,GETPATH:NEAR
        EXTRN   LIST$:NEAR
ENTRY:  JMP     START       ;Skip past string buffer
PROMPT  DB      'Enter the pathname of the file: $'

START   PROC    NEAR
        LEA     DX,PROMPT       ;Issue the prompt
        CALL    LIST$
        CALL    GETPATH         ; and get user's response
        CALL    UNHIDEF         ;Unhide the file
        JNC     QUIT            ;Error?
        CALL    SHOWERR         ; Yes. Display error message
QUIT:   RET                     ;  and exit
```

Subroutine Listing

```
; UNHIDEF - Unhide a file
; Input: DX = Offset of pathname
; Results: If Carry is set, AX = Error code
;          If Carry is not set, AX is undefined
;          DX is unaffected.

          PUBLIC   UNHIDEF
CSEG   SEGMENT   PARA PUBLIC 'CODE'
          ASSUME   CS:CSEG,DS:CSEG,ES:CSEG,SS:CSEG

UNHIDEF   PROC   NEAR
          PUSH   CX          ;Save CX
          MOV    AL,0        ;Read the file's attributes
          MOV    AH,43H      ; using option AL = 0
          INT    21H         ; of DOS function call 43H
          JC     LEAVE       ;Error?
          AND    CL,0FDH     ;No. Clear the hidden bit (1)
          MOV    AL,1        ;Change the file's attributes
          MOV    AH,43H      ; using option AL = 1
          INT    21H         ; of DOS function call 43H
LEAVE:    POP    CX          ;Retrieve CX
          RET                ; and return to calling program
UNHIDEF   ENDP
CSEG   ENDS
          END
```

Chapter 20

Disk Input and Output

Sometimes you want to work with the contents of a disk file, to add data to it or to read data from it. Disk data files are the computerized equivalent of an office filing system. The disk is like a file cabinet, and the data files on it are like electronic file folders. Just as with a file folder, you must first open a data file and then add new information to it, read the information that's already there, or remove old information from it. Finally, when you finish working with the file, you must close it.

Data file operations in assembly language are similar to those in BASIC. Thus, by way of introduction, I will now review how BASIC works with data files.

DATA FILE OPERATIONS IN BASIC

In BASIC, you open a data file with an OPEN statement. An OPEN statement must include the file's name (and, if it is on a different drive or in a different subdirectory, the drive and/or directory names) and a number by which you want to identify the file. The number must be 1, 2, or 3; you can have only three open files at a time.

A BASIC data file can be either sequential or random. A sequential file is like information on a cassette tape; to read a particular item, the computer must pass through all preceding items. A random file acts like a book; that is, you can flip to any page (access any record) without passing through all previous pages.

To open a sequential file, your OPEN statement must specify what you plan to do with the file. Your plans may include creating a new file (specify *FOR OUTPUT*), reading data from a file (specify *FOR INPUT*) or adding data to the end of a file (specify *FOR APPEND*). A typical OPEN statement is

The statement that adds data to a file is PRINT # for sequential files or PUT for random files. The statement that reads data from a file is INPUT # for sequential files or GET for random files.

CLOSE is the BASIC statement that closes a file after you are finished with it. You can close file 2 with the statement

```
CLOSE 2
```

or you can close all opened files at once with

```
CLOSE
```

DATA FILE OPERATIONS IN ASSEMBLY LANGUAGE

MS-DOS includes Interrupt 21 function calls that provide the same kinds of data file services that I just described for BASIC. DOS 1.υ only allowed you to operate on sequential files; DOS 2.0 added calls for random files. Sequential file operations are too complex for everyday use, so I will concentrate on random file operations.

DOS provides function calls that do the same tasks as BASIC's data file statements. That is, it provides function calls that create, open, and close files, as well as function calls that write data to files and read data from them. For random files, DOS also maintains a so-called *file pointer* that keeps track of where you are working in a file.

When you open a file, DOS assumes that you want to start reading or writing from the beginning, so it makes the file pointer point at the first byte. As you read or write data from there, DOS advances the pointer automatically. You can also start reading or writing at a different place in a file by using a function call to move the file pointer.

In summary, these are the tasks your assembly language program must perform for data file operations:

1. Create or open the file you want to use.
2. Move the file pointer to where you want to start reading or writing.
3. Read or write the data.
4. Close the file.

Like BASIC, DOS refers to open files by a number rather than a name. However, DOS assigns the number; you don't do it yourself, as you do in BASIC. In DOS terminology, the number that identifies an open file is called a *handle*.

FILE HANDLES

To understand handles, think of DOS as the central office for a small telephone system. When you start a program, the office has five lines connected to it, and each line has its own number, called a *handle*. DOS assigns these first five handles to so-called "standard" devices, as follows:

0 Standard input device (initially the keyboard)

1   Standard output device (initially the display)
2   Standard error output device
3   Standard auxiliary device
4   Standard printer

When you create a file, DOS adds it to the system by connecting, or *opening*, it and assigning the next available handle to it. Thus, if your program begins by creating a file called MYDATA, DOS connects, or opens a spot in the system for it, and calls it handle 5. Thereafter, whenever you want to write data to MYDATA or read data from it, you simply tell DOS to write or read handle 5. Once opened, a file remains connected to the system until you explicitly close it or return to DOS.

You can also connect an existing file to the system by explicitly opening it. Opening a file makes DOS assign a handle to it just as it does when you create a new file. (The devices assigned to the first five handles are always open; you don't need to open them to use them.) DOS can work with 20 open handles (as opposed to three in BASIC), including the five standard ones, so a program can maintain up to 15 open files at a time.

When you're through using a file, you must *close* it. Closing a file makes DOS put the file's handle number back on the "available" list.

CREATE A FILE (NEWFILE)

NEWFILE creates a new file and opens it for both reading and writing. If the file already exits, NEWFILE discards its contents, giving it a length of zero.

Operation

The subroutine begins by using DOS function call 43H to find out whether the file already exists. If the file *does* exist, the subroutine selects the "File exists" error code, sets the Carry Flag, and exits. Otherwise, it creates the file using DOS function call 3CH. This call obtains the attributes from CX, so the subroutine makes CX zero, to open the file for both reading and writing. If the pathname is invalid, the subroutine sets the Carry Flag to 1 and returns an error code in AX; otherwise, it sets CF to 0 and returns the handle in AX.

Entry Value

DX = Offset of an ASCIIZ string that contains the pathname of the file

Results

If Carry is set, AX = Error code.
If Carry is not set (no error), AX = Handle.
DX is unaffected.

Link Command

```
link callprog+newfile+showerr;
```

(SHOWERR displays a message based on an error code)

Comments

If your ASCIIZ string contains a filename but no path, the subroutine will create the file in the current directory.

To write data to a new file, use the WRITFILE subroutine in this chapter.

To close a file, use the CLOSFILE subroutine in this chapter.

DOS 3.0 and later provides a "Create New File" function call (5BH) that creates a file only if it doesn't already exist. Using call 5BH instead of call 3CH in your subroutine eliminates the need for the attribute-reading instructions.

Example

Create a file by entering its pathname from the keyboard:

```
            EXTRN   NEWFILE:NEAR,SHOWERR:NEAR,GETPATH:NEAR
            EXTRN   LIST$:NEAR
ENTRY:      JMP     START      ;Skip past string buffer
PROMPT      DB      'Enter the pathname of the file: $'

START       PROC    NEAR
            LEA     DX,PROMPT      ;Issue the prompt
```

```
        CALL    LIST$
        CALL    GETPATH         ; and get user's response
        CALL    NEWFILE         ;Create the file
        JNC     LEAVE           ;Error?
        CALL    SHOWERR         ; Yes. Display error message
LEAVE:  RET                     ;  and exit
```

Subroutine Listing

```
; NEWFILE - Create a file
; Inputs: DX = Offset of pathname
; Results: If Carry is set, AX = Error code
;          If Carry is not set, AX = Handle
;          DX is unaffected

        PUBLIC  NEWFILE
CSEG    SEGMENT  PARA PUBLIC 'CODE'
        ASSUME  CS:CSEG,DS:CSEG,ES:CSEG,SS:CSEG

NEWFILE PROC    NEAR
        PUSH    CX
        MOV     AL,0            ;See if file exists
        MOV     AH,43H          ; by trying to read its attributes
        INT     21H
        JC      CREATE          ;Does file already exist?
        MOV     AX,80           ; Yes. Select "File exists" error,
        STC                     ;  set Carry,
        JC      QUIT            ;  and leave
CREATE: SUB     CX,CX           ; No. Set attributes for read/write
        MOV     AH,3CH          ;Call DOS function 3CH
        INT     21H
QUIT:   POP     CX
        RET                     ;Return to calling program
NEWFILE ENDP
CSEG    ENDS
        END
```

OPEN A FILE (OPENFILE)

OPENFILE opens any file, including read-only and hidden files, for reading, writing, or both.

Operation

The subroutine opens the file using DOS function call 3DH. This call obtains an access code from AL that tells DOS what kind of operation to allow on the file. AL must contain 0 for reading, 1 for writing, or 2 for both reading and writing. If the pathname is invalid, the subroutine sets the Carry Flag to 1 and returns an error code in AX; otherwise, it sets CF to 0 and returns the handle in AX.

Entry Values

DX = Offset of an ASCIIZ string that contains the pathname of the file.
AL = Access code (0 = reading, 1 = writing, 2 = both).

Results

If Carry is set, AX = Error code.
If Carry is not set (no error), AX = Handle.
DX is unaffected.

Link Command

```
link callprog+openfile+showerr;
```

(SHOWERR displays a message based on an error code)

Special Case

If the value in AL is greater than 2, the subroutine exits with Carry set to 1 and an error code of 1 in AX.

Comments

To close a file, use the CLOSFILE subroutine in this chapter.

If your ASCIIZ string contains a filename but no path, the subroutine assumes that the file is in the current directory.

Example

Open a file for reading or writing by entering its pathname from the keyboard:

```
            EXTRN   OPENFILE:NEAR,SHOWERR:NEAR,GETPATH:NEAR
            EXTRN   LIST$:NEAR
ENTRY:      JMP     START      ;Skip past string buffer
PROMPT      DB      'Enter the pathname of the file: $'

START       PROC  NEAR
            LEA     DX,PROMPT       ;Issue the prompt
            CALL    LIST$
            CALL    GETPATH         ; and get user's response
```

```
            MOV     AL,2            ;Allow both read and write
            CALL    OPENFILE        ;Open the file
            JNC     LEAVE           ;Error?
            CALL    SHOWERR         ; Yes. Display error message
LEAVE:      RET                     ;  and exit
```

Subroutine Listing

```
; OPENFILE - Open a file
; Inputs: DX = Offset of pathname
;         AL = Access code (0=read, 1=write, 2=both)
; Results: If Carry is set, AX = Error code
;          If Carry is not set, AX = Handle
;          DX is unaffected

            PUBLIC  OPENFILE
CSEG   SEGMENT  PARA PUBLIC 'CODE'
            ASSUME  CS:CSEG,DS:CSEG,ES:CSEG,SS:CSEG

OPENFILE    PROC    NEAR
            CMP     AL,2            ;Valid access code?
            JBE     OKAY
            STC                     ; No.  Set Carry,
            MOV     AX,1            ;  put error code 1 in AX,
            JMP     QUIT            ;  and leave
OKAY:       MOV     AH,3DH          ;Call DOS function 3DH
            INT     21H
QUIT:       RET                     ;Return to calling program
OPENFILE    ENDP
CSEG   ENDS
            END
```

CLOSE A FILE (CLOSFILE)

CLOSFILE closes a file opened with subroutine NEWFILE (Create File) or OPEN-FILE (Open File).

Operation

The subroutine closes the file using DOS function call 3EH. If the handle is invalid, the subroutine sets the Carry Flag to 1 and returns an error code in AX; otherwise, it sets CF to 0 and AX is undefined.

Entry Value

BX = Handle

Results

If Carry is set, AX = Error code.
If Carry is not set (no error), AX is undefined.
BX is unaffected.

Link Command

```
link callprog+closfile+showerr;
```

(SHOWERR displays a message based on an error code)

Subroutine Listing

```
; CLOSFILE - Close a file
; Inputs: BX = Handle
; Results: If Carry is set, AX = Error code
;          If Carry is not set, no error
;          DX is unaffected

        PUBLIC  CLOSFILE
CSEG   SEGMENT  PARA PUBLIC 'CODE'
        ASSUME  CS:CSEG,DS:CSEG,ES:CSEG,SS:CSEG

CLOSFILE  PROC  NEAR
        MOV   AH,3EH    ;Call DOS function 3EH
        INT   21H
        RET             ;Return to calling program
CLOSFILE  ENDP
CSEG   ENDS
        END
```

MOVE FILE POINTER (MOVEPTR)

MOVEPTR moves the file pointer in preparation for a read or write operation.

Operation

The subroutine uses DOS function call 42H to move the file pointer. Using the handle specified in BX, the subroutine moves the pointer according to the moving technique in AL and then moves it the additional number of bytes contained in the 32-bit register combination CX:DX. If the handle or moving code is invalid, the subroutine sets the Carry Flag to 1 and returns an error code in AX; otherwise, it sets CF to 0 and returns the new file pointer location in CX:DX.

Entry Values

    AL = Method of moving:
    AL = 0 moves the pointer to the beginning of the file plus the offset.
    AL = 1 adds the offset to move the Pointer from its current location.
    AL = 2 moves the Pointer to the end of the file plus the offset.
    BX = Handle.
 CX:DX = Distance in bytes (offset).

Results

If Carry is set, AX = Error code.
If Carry is not set (no error), DX:AX = New Pointer location.
BX is unaffected.

Link Command

```
link callprog+moveptr+showerr;
```

(SHOWERR displays a message based on an error code)

Example

To determine the length of a file, you can call MOVEPTR with zero in CX:DX and 2 in AL. The following program does this, using a pathname entered from the keyboard:

```
            EXTRN   OPENFILE:NEAR,SHOWERR:NEAR,GETPATH:NEAR
            EXTRN   LIST$:NEAR,MOVEPTR:NEAR,CLOSFILE:NEAR
ENTRY:      JMP     START      ;Skip past string buffer
PROMPT      DB      'Enter the pathname of the file: $'

START       PROC    NEAR
            LEA     DX,PROMPT       ;Issue the prompt
            CALL    LIST$
            CALL    GETPATH         ; and get user's response
            SUB     AL,AL           ;Open the file
            CALL    OPENFILE
```

```
                  JNC    GOTOEND          ;Open error?
                  CALL   SHOWERR          ; Yes. Display error message
                  RET                     ;   and exit
       GOTOEND:   MOV    BX,AX            ; No. Copy handle to BX
                  MOV    AL,2             ;Move Pointer to end of file
                  SUB    CX,CX            ; and use offset of zero
                  SUB    DX,DX
                  CALL   MOVEPTR
                  JNC    CLOSE            ;Move error?
                  CALL   SHOWERR          ; Yes. Display error message
       CLOSE:     CALL   CLOSFILE         ;Close the file
                  RET                     ; and exit
```

If no error occurred, the size of the file in bytes is returned in DX:AX.

Subroutine Listing

```
; MOVEPTR - Move the File Pointer
; Inputs: AL = Method of moving
;            0 = Beginning of file plus offset
;            1 = Current position plus offset
;            2 = End of file plus offset
;         BX = Handle
;         CX:DX = Distance in bytes (offset)
; Results: If Carry is set, AX = Error code
;          If Carry is not set, DX:AX = New Pointer location
;          BX is unaffected.

          PUBLIC  MOVEPTR
CSEG   SEGMENT  PARA PUBLIC 'CODE'
          ASSUME   CS:CSEG,DS:CSEG,ES:CSEG,SS:CSEG

MOVEPTR  PROC  NEAR
          MOV    AH,42H        ;Call DOS function 42H
          INT    21H
          RET                  ;Return to calling program
MOVEPTR  ENDP
CSEG   ENDS
          END
```

WRITE TO A FILE (WRITFILE)

WRITFILE writes the contents of a memory buffer to the file that has a specified handle.

Operation

The subroutine writes to the file using DOS function call 40H. It obtains the handle from BX, the byte count from CX, and the offset of the data from DX. If the handle is invalid or the file is not open for writing, the subroutine sets the Carry Flag to 1 and returns an error code in AX; otherwise, it sets CF to 0 and AX reports the number of bytes written.

Entry Values

BX = Handle
CX = Number of bytes to write
DX = Offset of data buffer

Results

If Carry is set, AX = Error code.
If Carry is not set (no error), AX = Bytes written.
BX, CX, and DX are unaffected.

Link Command

```
link callprog+writfile+showerr;
```

(SHOWERR displays a message based on an error code)

Special Case

If the byte count in CX is zero, the subroutine exits without writing to the file.

Comments

Read and write operations always start at the current file pointer location. When you open a file, the pointer points to the beginning of it. To start writing somewhere else, use the MOVEPTR subroutine in this chapter to move there. For example, to append data to a file, move the pointer to the end by calling MOVEPTR with zero in CX and DX and 2 in AL.

Always check the value in AX after writing to a file. If it is 0, the disk is full; if it is less than the number of bytes you specified, some other error occurred.

Example 1

Create a file by entering its pathname from the keyboard; then write the string in PHONE to it and close the file:

```
        EXTRN   NEWFILE:NEAR,SHOWERR:NEAR,GETPATH:NEAR
        EXTRN   LIST$:NEAR,WRITFILE:NEAR,CLOSFILE:NEAR
ENTRY:  JMP     START     ;Skip past string buffer
PROMPT  DB      'Enter the pathname of the file: $'
```

```
DISKFULL    DB      'Disk full or other error!$'
PHONE       DB      'Joe Cooper 344-7865'

START       PROC    NEAR
            LEA     DX,PROMPT       ;Issue the prompt
            CALL    LIST$
            CALL    GETPATH         ; and get user's response
            CALL    NEWFILE         ;Create the file
            JNC     WRITE$          ;Error?
            CALL    SHOWERR         ; Yes. Display error message
            RET                     ;  and exit
WRITE$:     MOV     BX,AX           ; No. Copy handle to BX
            MOV     CX,START-PHONE  ; and write the string
            LEA     DX,PHONE
            CALL    WRITFILE
            JNC     CHECKAX         ;Write error?
SHOWMSG:    CALL    SHOWERR         ; Yes. Display error message
            JMP     CLOSE
CHECKAX:    CMP     AX,CX           ; No, but check for an error
            JE      CLOSE
            LEA     DX,DISKFULL     ;Disk full or other error
            CALL    LIST$
CLOSE:      CALL    CLOSFILE        ;Close the file
            RET                     ; and exit
```

Note how I made the computer calculate the byte count for use by WRITFILE by subtracting the offset of the start of the string (PHONE) from the offset of the START label.

Example 2

Write the string in PHONE to the end of a specified file:

```
            EXTRN   OPENFILE:NEAR,SHOWERR:NEAR,GETPATH:NEAR
            EXTRN   LIST$:NEAR,WRITFILE:NEAR,CLOSFILE:NEAR
            EXTRN   MOVEPTR:NEAR
ENTRY:      JMP     START           ;Skip past string buffer
PROMPT      DB      'Enter the pathname of the file: $'
DISKFULL    DB      'Disk full or other error!$'
PHONE       DB      'Joe Cooper 344-7865'

START       PROC    NEAR
            LEA     DX,PROMPT       ;Issue the prompt
            CALL    LIST$
            CALL    GETPATH         ; and get user's response
            MOV     AL,1            ;Allow only writing
            CALL    OPENFILE        ;Open the file
            JNC     GO2END          ;Open error?
            CALL    SHOWERR         ; Yes. Display error message
            RET                     ;  and exit
GO2END:     MOV     BX,AX           ; No. Copy handle to BX
            MOV     AL,2            ;Move Pointer to end of file
```

```
                SUB     CX,CX
                SUB     DX,DX
                CALL    MOVEPTR
                JC      SHOWMSG         ;If error, close the file
                MOV     BX,AX           ; Otherwise, write the string
                MOV     CX,START-PHONE
                LEA     DX,PHONE
                CALL    WRITFILE
                JNC     CHECKAX         ;Write error?
SHOWMSG:        CALL    SHOWERR         ; Yes. Display error message
                JMP     CLOSE
CHECKAX:        CMP     AX,CX           ; No, but check for an error
                JE      CLOSE
                LEA     DX,DISKFULL     ;Disk full or other error
                CALL    LIST$
CLOSE:          CALL    CLOSFILE        ;Close the file
                RET                     ; and exit
```

Subroutine Listing

```
; WRITFILE - Write bytes to a file
; Inputs: BX = Handle
;         CX = Number of bytes to write
;         DX = Offset of data buffer
; Results: If Carry is set, AX = Error code
;          If Carry is not set, AX = Bytes written
;          BX, CX, and DX are unaffected

        PUBLIC  WRITFILE
CSEG    SEGMENT  PARA PUBLIC 'CODE'
        ASSUME  CS:CSEG,DS:CSEG,ES:CSEG,SS:CSEG

WRITFILE  PROC  NEAR
          CMP   CX,0      ;If byte count is 0, leave
          JZ    EXIT
          MOV   AH,40H    ;Call DOS function 40H
          INT   21H
EXIT:     RET             ;Return to calling program
WRITFILE  ENDP
CSEG    ENDS
        END
```

READ FROM A FILE (READFILE)

READFILE reads a specified number of bytes from a disk file to a memory buffer.

Operation

The subroutine reads the file using DOS function call 3FH. It obtains the handle from BX, the byte count from CX, and the offset of the data buffer from DX. If the handle is invalid or the file is not open for reading, the subroutine sets the Carry Flag to 1 and returns an error code in AX; otherwise, it sets CF to 0 and AX reports the number of bytes read.

Entry Values

    BX = Handle
    CX = Number of bytes to read
    DX = Offset of data buffer

Results

    If Carry is set, AX = Error code.
    If Carry is not set (no error), AX = Bytes read
    BX, CX, and DX are unaffected.

Link Command

```
link callprog+readfile+showerr;
```

(SHOWERR displays a message based on an error code)

Special Cases

If the byte count in CX is zero, the subroutine exits without reading from the file.

If you attempt to read starting at the end of a file, the subroutine returns with zero in AX.

Comments

Read and write operations always start at the current file pointer location. When you open a file, the pointer points to the beginning of it. To start writing somewhere else, use the MOVEPTR subroutine in this chapter to move there. For example, to append data to a file, move the pointer to the end by calling MOVEPTR with zero in CX and DX and 2 in AL.

You can also use READFILE to read from the keyboard, by specifying handle 0. In that case, the subroutine reads keystrokes only until the operator presses Return.

Example

Read the first 25 bytes from a file by entering its pathname from the keyboard, and store the bytes in a buffer called FILEDATA:

```
EXTRN   OPENFILE:NEAR,SHOWERR:NEAR,GETPATH:NEAR
EXTRN   LIST$:NEAR,READFILE:NEAR,CLOSFILE:NEAR
```

```
ENTRY:      JMP     START       ;Skip past string buffer
PROMPT      DB      'Enter the pathname of the file: $'
FILEDATA    DB      25 DUP(?) ;The data will be stored here
START       PROC    NEAR
            LEA     DX,PROMPT       ;Issue the prompt
            CALL    LIST$
            CALL    GETPATH         ; and get user's response
            CALL    OPENFILE        ;Open the file
            JNC     READ$           ;Open error?
            CALL    SHOWERR         ; Yes. Display error message
            RET                     ;   and exit
READ$:      MOV     BX,AX           ; No. Copy handle to BX
            MOV     CX,25           ; and read the data
            LEA     DX,FILEDATA
            CALL    READFILE
            JNC     CLOSE           ;Read error?
SHOWMSG:    CALL    SHOWERR         ; Yes. Display error message
CLOSE:      CALL    CLOSFILE        ;Close the file
            RET                     ; and exit
```

Subroutine Listing

```
; READFILE - Read bytes from a file
; Inputs: BX = Handle
;         CX = Number of bytes to read
;         DX = Offset of data buffer
; Results: If Carry is set, AX = Error code
;          If Carry is not set, AX = Bytes read
;          BX, CX, and DX are unaffected.

            PUBLIC  READFILE
CSEG    SEGMENT PARA PUBLIC 'CODE'
            ASSUME  CS:CSEG,DS:CSEG,ES:CSEG,SS:CSEG

READFILE    PROC    NEAR
            CMP     CX,0        ;If byte count is 0, leave
            JZ      EXIT
            MOV     AH,3FH      ;Call DOS function 3FH
            INT     21H
EXIT:       RET                 ;Return to calling program
READFILE    ENDP
CSEG    ENDS
            END
```

EMPTY A FILE (EMPTYF)

EMPTYF erases a file's data, or truncates it. The file then still exits, but has a length of zero.

Operation

The subroutine begins by using DOS function call 43H to find out whether or not the file exists. If not, the subroutine exits immediately. Otherwise, it empties, or truncates, the file using DOS function call 3CH. Call 3CH is the function I used in the Create File (NEWFILE) section earlier in this chapter. Call 3CH also empties a file if it already exists. If the pathname was invalid or the file is nonexistent, the subroutine sets the Carry Flag to 1 and returns an error code in AX; otherwise, it sets CF to 0 and returns AX undefined.

Entry Value

DX = Offset of an ASCIIZ string that contains the pathname of the file.

Results

If Carry is set, AX = Error code.
If Carry is not set (no error), AX is undefined.
DX is unaffected.

Link Command

```
link callprog+emptyf+showerr;
```

(SHOWERR displays a message based on an error code)

Comment

If your ASCIIZ string contains a filename but no path, the subroutine assumes that the file is in the current directory.

Example

Empty a file by obtaining its pathname from the keyboard, but make the user verify the action before proceeding:

```
            EXTRN   EMPTYF:NEAR,SHOWERR:NEAR,GETPATH:NEAR
            EXTRN   LIST$:NEAR,GETCHRE:NEAR
ENTRY:      JMP     START       ;Skip past string buffer
PROMPT1     DB      'Enter the pathname of the file: $'
PROMPT2     DB      'Are you sure? (Y/N)$'

START       PROC    NEAR
            LEA     DX,PROMPT1   ;Issue the first prompt
            CALL    LIST$
            CALL    GETPATH      ; and get user's response
            PUSH    DX
            LEA     DX,PROMPT2   ;Issue the second prompt
```

```
            CALL    LIST$
            POP     DX
            CALL    GETCHRE         ; and get the response
            CMP     AL,'Y'
            JE      DOIT
            CMP     AL,'y'
            JNE     LEAVE
DOIT:       CALL    EMPTYF          ;Empty the file
            JNC     LEAVE           ;Error?
            CALL    SHOWERR         ; Yes. Display error message
LEAVE:      RET                     ;  and exit
```

Subroutine Listing

```
; EMPTYF - Empty a file (erase its contents)
; Inputs: DX = Offset of pathname
; Results: If Carry is set, AX = Error code
;          If Carry is not set, AX is undefined
;          DX is unaffected

            PUBLIC  EMPTYF
CSEG   SEGMENT  PARA PUBLIC 'CODE'
            ASSUME  CS:CSEG,DS:CSEG,ES:CSEG,SS:CSEG

EMPTYF  PROC  NEAR
            PUSH    CX
            MOV     AL,0        ;See if file exists
            MOV     AH,43H      ; by trying to read its attributes
            INT     21H
            JC      QUIT        ;Does file exist?
EMPTY:      MOV     AH,3CH      ; Yes. Call DOS function 3CH
            INT     21H
QUIT:       POP     CX
            RET                 ;Return to calling program
EMPTYF      ENDP
CSEG   ENDS
            END
```

Chapter 21

Miscellaneous Routines

This chapter provides four miscellaneous subroutines that may be useful to you. The first reports the version of DOS being used (2.10, 3.00, etc.), the next two let you read or change the contents of an interrupt vector, the last reports whether the computer is equipped with an 8087 or an 80287 Math Coprocessor chip.

The microprocessor provides 255 interrupt vectors (0-0FFH), most of which are used by the computer's Basic Input/Output System (BIOS), DOS, and BASIC. For example, the BIOS reserves the first 32 vectors (0-1FH) for its own use, and DOS reserves the next 32 vectors (20H-3FH). A few vectors, however, are unreserved (60H-67H in IBM PCs), and these are the ones that the so-called "pop-up" programs and other memory-resident programs employ. Of course, *you* can also use an unreserved vector, by making it point to the interrupt handler you want to execute.

GET THE DOS VERSION (GETDOSV)

GETDOSV returns MS-DOS's major and minor version numbers under which the computer is running. For example, for DOS 2.10, the major version number is 2 and the minor version number is 10 (0AH).

Operation

The subroutine uses DOS function call 30H to obtain the version numbers.

Entry Values

None.

Results

AL = Major version number
AH = Minor version number
BH = OEM serial number; PC-DOS returns zero
BL:CX = 24-bit user (serial) number; PC-DOS returns zero

Link Command

```
link callprog+getdosv;
```

Comment

The GETPCMOD subroutine in Chapter 16 returns a number that indicates the IBM PC model being used (XT, AT, etc.).

Subroutine Listing

```
; GETDOSV - Get DOS version number
; Inputs: None
; Results: AL = Major version number
.          AH = Minor version number
;          BH = OEM serial number
;          BL:CX = 24-bit user (serial) number

        PUBLIC  GETDOSV
CSEG    SEGMENT PARA PUBLIC 'CODE'
        ASSUME  CS:CSEG,DS:CSEG,ES:CSEG,SS:CSEG

GETDOSV PROC  NEAR
        MOV   AH,30H   ;Use DOS function call 30H
        INT   21H
        RET            ;Return to calling program
GETDOSV ENDP
CSEG  ENDS
        END
```

READ THE INTERRUPT VECTOR (GETINTV)

GETINTV reads the contents of a specified interrupt vector into a pair of registers. This is useful for saving the vector before you change it, so you can restore it later.

Operation

The subroutine uses DOS function call 35H to read the pointer into ES (segment number) and BX (offset).

Entry Value

AL = Interrupt number (0-255)

Results

ES:BX =   Pointer to interrupt handler.
AL is unaffected.

Link Command

```
link callprog+getintv;
```

Comment

The SETINV subroutine in this chapter changes the contents of an interrupt vector.

Subroutine Listing

```
; GETINTV - Read interrupt vector
; Input: AL = Interrupt number (0-255)
; Results: ES:BX = Pointer to interrupt handler
;          AL is unaffected

        PUBLIC  GETINTV
CSEG    SEGMENT PARA PUBLIC 'CODE'
        ASSUME  CS:CSEG,DS:CSEG,ES:CSEG,SS:CSEG
        JMP     GETINTV   ;Skip past data area
SAVEAH  DB      ?         ;Save AH here

GETINTV PROC    NEAR
        MOV     SAVEAH,AH ;Save current AH in memory
        MOV     AH,35H    ;Use DOS function call 35H
        INT     21H
        MOV     AH,SAVEAH ;Retrieve AH
        RET               ;Return to calling program
GETINTV ENDP
CSEG    ENDS
        END
```

CHANGE THE INTERRUPT VECTOR (SETINTV)

SETINTV makes a specified interrupt vector point to a selected interrupt handler in memory.

Operation

The subroutine uses DOS function call 25H to store the pointer in DS (segment number) and DX (offset) at the interrupt vector whose number is in AL.

Entry Values

AL	=	Interrupt number (0-255)
DS:DX	=	Pointer to interrupt handler

Results

None.
AL, DS, and DX are unaffected.

Link Command

```
link callprog+setintv;
```

Comment

In general, before changing an interrupt vector, you should read its current contents and save them in memory, so you can restore them later. The GETINV subroutine in this chapter reads the current contents of an interrupt vector.

Example

Read the contents of interrupt 60H into two word locations in memory; then make it point to an interrupt handler called MYINT:

```
            EXTRN   GETINTV:NEAR,SETINTV:NEAR
            PUBLIC   OLDSEG,OLDOFF
ENTRY:      JMP     START      ;Skip past data area
OLDSEG      DW      ?          ;Save segment number here
OLDOFF      DW      ?          ;Save offset here

START       PROC    NEAR
            PUSH    ES         ;Save this program's ES
            MOV     AL,60H     ;Read interrupt 60H
            CALL    GETINTV
            MOV     OLDSEG,ES  ; and save it in memory
            MOV     OLDOFF,BX
            POP     ES         ;Restore ES
            LEA     DX,MYINT   ;Make DS:DX point to MYINT
            CALL    SETINTV    ;Change the vector
            RET                ; and exit
START       ENDP
```

```
MYINT      PROC  NEAR      ;Interrupt handler
            . .
            . .
           IRET
MYINT      ENDP
```

After executing this program, the computer will activate MYINT whenever it encounters an INT 60H instruction.

To restore the interrupt 60H vector to its original contents, run a program having these instructions:

```
EXTRN   OLDSEG:WORD,OLDOFF:WORD,SETINTV:NEAR
PUSH    DS                ;Save this program's DS
MOV     DS,OLDSEG         ;DS:DX = Original vector
MOV     DX,OLDOFF
CALL    SETINTV           ;Change the vector
POP     DS                ;Restore DS
```

Subroutine Listing

```
; SETINTV - Change interrupt vector
; Inputs: AL = Interrupt number (0-255)
;         DS:DX = Pointer to interrupt handler
; Results: None.
;          Inputs are unaffected.

          PUBLIC  SETINTV
CSEG   SEGMENT  PARA PUBLIC 'CODE'
          ASSUME  CS:CSEG,DS:CSEG,ES:CSEG,SS:CSEG
          JMP    SETINTV  ;Skip past data area
SAVEAH    DB     ?        ;Save AH here

SETINTV  PROC   NEAR
          MOV    SAVEAH,AH ;Save current AH in memory
          MOV    AH,25H    ;Use DOS function call 25H
          INT    21H
          MOV    AH,SAVEAH ;Retrieve AH
          RET              ;Return to calling program
SETINTV   ENDP
CSEG   ENDS
          END
```

CHECK FOR A MATH COPROCESSOR (MATHCHIP)

MATHCHIP displays a message that indicates whether or not the computer is equipped with an 8087 or an 80287 math coprocessor chip.

Operation

The subroutine attempts to initialize the math coprocessor with an FNINIT instruction, and then uses FNSTCW to read the chip's control word into location CWORD in memory. If the coprocessor is installed, the control word has a value of 3; any other value means the socket is empty. Either way, the subroutine displays a message on the screen.

Entry Values

None.

Result

Message is displayed on the screen.

Link Command

```
link callprog+mathchip;
```

Comment

The .287 directive at the beginning of the subroutine tells the assembler to accept 8087 or 80287 instructions.

Subroutine Listing

```
; MATHCHIP - Check for 8087 or 80287 Math Copressor
; Inputs: None
; Result: Message on screen
.287

          PUBLIC  MATHCHIP
CSEG   SEGMENT  PARA PUBLIC 'CODE'
          ASSUME  CS:CSEG,DS:CSEG,ES:CSEG,SS:CSEG
          JMP      MATHCHIP ;Skip the data area
CWORD     DW       ?         ;Control word will go here
HERE      DB       'Computer has an 8087 or 80287.$'
NOT_HERE  DB       'Computer has no 8087 nor 80287.$'

MATHCHIP  PROC   NEAR
          PUSH   AX          ;Save working registers
          PUSH   DX
          FNINIT             ;Initialize the math chip
          MOV    CWORD,0     ;Clear memory word
          FNSTCW CWORD       ;Read chip's control word
          CMP    BYTE PTR CWORD+1,3 ;If high byte is 3,
                             ; chip is present
          JNE    NO_CHIP
          LEA    DX,HERE
```

315

```
          JE     SHOW
NO_CHIP:  LEA    DX,NOT_HERE
SHOW:     MOV    AH,9      ;Display the appropriate message
          INT    21H
          RET              ;Return to calling program
MATHCHIP  ENDP
CSEG  ENDS
          END
```

Hexadecimal/ Decimal Conversion

HEXADECIMAL COLUMNS											
6		**5**		**4**		**3**		**2**		**1**	
HEX	DEC	HEX	DEC	HEX	DEC	HEX	DEC	HEX	DEC	HEX	DEC
0	0	0	0	0	0	0	0	0	0	0	0
1	1,048,576	1	65,536	1	4,096	1	256	1	16	1	1
2	2,097,152	2	131,072	2	8,192	2	512	2	32	2	2
3	3,145,728	3	196,608	3	12,288	3	768	3	48	3	3
4	4,194,304	4	262,144	4	16,384	4	1,024	4	64	4	4
5	5,242,880	5	327,680	5	20,480	5	1,280	5	80	5	5
6	6,291,456	6	393,216	6	24,576	6	1,536	6	96	6	6
7	7,340,032	7	458,752	7	28,672	7	1,792	7	112	7	7
8	8,388,608	8	524,288	8	32,768	8	2,048	8	128	8	8
9	9,437,184	9	589,824	9	36,864	9	2,304	9	144	9	9
A	10,485,760	A	655,360	A	40,960	A	2,560	A	160	A	10
B	11,534,336	B	720,896	B	45,056	B	2,816	B	176	B	11
C	12,582,912	C	786,432	C	49,152	C	3,072	C	192	C	12
D	13,631,488	D	851,968	D	53,248	D	3,328	D	208	D	13
E	14,680,064	E	917,504	E	57,344	E	3,584	E	224	E	14
F	15,728,640	F	983,040	F	61,440	F	3,840	F	240	F	15
7654		3210		7654		3210		7654		3210	
Byte				Byte				Byte			

POWERS OF 2

2^n	n
256	8
512	9
1 024	10
2 048	11
4 096	12
8 192	13
16 384	14
32 768	15
65 536	16
131 072	17
262 144	18
524 288	19
1 048 576	20
2 097 152	21
4 194 304	22
8 388 608	23
16 777 216	24

$$2^0 = 16^0$$
$$2^4 = 16^1$$
$$2^8 = 16^2$$
$$2^{12} = 16^3$$
$$2^{16} = 16^4$$
$$2^{20} = 16^5$$
$$2^{24} = 16^6$$
$$2^{28} = 16^7$$
$$2^{32} = 16^8$$
$$2^{36} = 16^9$$
$$2^{40} = 16^{10}$$
$$2^{44} = 16^{11}$$
$$2^{48} = 16^{12}$$
$$2^{52} = 16^{13}$$
$$2^{56} = 16^{14}$$
$$2^{60} = 16^{15}$$

POWERS OF 16

16^n	n
1	0
16	1
256	2
4 096	3
65 536	4
1 048 576	5
16 777 216	6
268 435 456	7
4 294 967 296	8
68 719 476 736	9
1 099 511 627 776	10
17 592 186 044 416	11
281 474 976 710 656	12
4 503 599 627 370 496	13
72 057 594 037 927 936	14
1 152 921 504 606 846 976	15

ASCII Character Set

LSD \ MSD		0 000	1 001	2 010	3 011	4 100	5 101	6 110	7 111
0	0000	NUL	DLE	SP	0	@	P		p
1	0001	SOH	DC1	!	1	A	Q	a	q
2	0010	STX	DC2	"	2	B	R	b	r
3	0011	ETX	DC3	#	3	C	S	c	s
4	0100	EOT	DC4	$	4	D	T	d	t
5	0101	ENQ	NAK	%	5	E	U	e	u
6	0110	ACK	SYN	&	6	F	V	f	v
7	0111	BEL	ETB	'	7	G	W	g	w
8	1000	BS	CAN	(	8	H	X	h	x
9	1001	HT	EM	)	9	I	Y	i	y
A	1010	LF	SUB	*	:	J	Z	j	z
B	1011	VT	ESC	+	;	K	[	k	{
C	1100	FF	FS	,	<	L	\	l	|
D	1101	CR	GS	–	=	M	]	m	}
E	1110	SO	RS	•	>	N	↑	n	~
F	1111	SI	US	/	?	O	←	o	DEL

NUL — Null	DLE — Data Link Escape
SOH — Start of Heading	DC — Device Control
STX — Start of Text	NAK — Negative Acknowledge
ETX — End of Text	SYN — Synchronous Idle
EOT — End of Transmission	ETB — End of Transmission Block
ENQ — Enquiry	CAN — Cancel
ACK — Acknowledge	EM — End of Medium
BEL — Bell	SUB — Substitute
BS — Backspace	ESC — Escape
HT — Horizontal Tabulation	FS — File Separator
LF — Line Feed	GS — Group Separator
VT — Vertical Tabulation	RS — Record Separator
FF — Form Feed	US — Unit Separator
CR — Carriage Return	SP — Space (Blank)
SO — Shift Out	DEL — Delete
SI — Shift In	

Instruction Set Summary

Table C-1 is an alphabetical summary of the instruction set for the 8086, 8088, 80186, and 80286 microprocessors. (Shaded entries are new with the 80186 and 80286; they are unavailable on the 8086 and 8088.) For each instruction, the table shows the valid assembler formats and the effect on the status flags.

Table C-1. The Instruction Set.

Assembler Format	OF	DF	IF	TF	SF	ZF	AF	PF	CF
				Flags					
AAA	?	–	–	–	?	?	*	?	*
AAD	?	–	–	–	*	*	?	*	?
AAM	?	–	–	–	*	*	?	*	?
AAS	?	–	–	–	?	?	*	?	*
ADC reg,reg	*	–	–	–	*	*	*	*	*
ADC reg,mem	*	–	–	–	*	*	*	*	*
ADC mem,reg	*	–	–	–	*	*	*	*	*
ADC reg,immed	*	–	–	–	*	*	*	*	*
ADC mem,immed	*	–	–	–	*	*	*	*	*
ADD reg,reg	*	–	–	–	*	*	*	*	*
ADD reg,mem	*	–	–	–	*	*	*	*	*
ADD mem,reg	*	–	–	–	*	*	*	*	*
ADD reg,immed	*	–	–	–	*	*	*	*	*
ADD mem,immed	*	–	–	–	*	*	*	*	*
AND reg,reg	0	–	–	–	*	*	?	*	0
AND reg,mem	0	–	–	–	*	*	?	*	0
AND mem,reg	0	–	–	–	*	*	?	*	0
AND reg,immed	0	–	–	–	*	*	?	*	0
AND mem,immed	0	–	–	–	*	*	?	*	0
BOUND reg16,mem32	–	–	–	–	–	–	–	–	–
CALL procedure-name	–	–	–	–	–	–	–	–	–
CALL memptr	–	–	–	–	–	–	–	–	–
CALL regptr16	–	–	–	–	–	–	–	–	–
CBW	–	–	–	–	–	–	–	–	–
CLC	–	–	–	–	–	–	–	–	0
CLD	–	0	–	–	–	–	–	–	–
CLI	–	–	0	–	–	–	–	–	–
CMC	–	–	–	–	–	–	–	–	*
CMP reg,reg	*	–	–	–	*	*	*	*	*
CMP reg,mem	*	–	–	–	*	*	*	*	*
CMP mem,reg	*	–	–	–	*	*	*	*	*

Assembler Format	Flags								
	OF	DF	IF	TF	SF	ZF	AF	PF	CF
CMP reg,immed	*	–	–	–	*	*	*	*	*
CMP mem,immed	*	–	–	–	*	*	*	*	*
CMPS dest$,source$	*	–	–	–	*	*	*	*	*
CMPSB	*	–	–	–	*	*	*	*	*
CMPSW	*	–	–	–	*	*	*	*	*
CWD	–	–	–	–	–	–	–	–	–
DAA	?	–	–	–	*	*	*	*	*
DAS	?	–	–	–	*	*	*	*	*
DEC reg	*	–	–	–	*	*	*	*	–
DEC mem	*	–	–	–	*	*	*	*	–
DIV reg	?	–	–	–	?	?	?	?	?
DIV mem	?	–	–	–	?	?	?	?	?
ENTER immed16,0	–	–	–	–	–	–	–	–	–
ENTER immed16,1	–	–	–	–	–	–	–	–	–
ENTER immed16,level	–	–	–	–	–	–	–	–	–
ESC immed6,mem	–	–	–	–	–	–	–	–	–
ESC immed6,reg	–	–	–	–	–	–	–	–	–
HLT	–	–	–	–	–	–	–	–	–
IDIV reg	?	–	–	–	?	?	?	?	?
IDIV mem	?	–	–	–	?	?	?	?	?
IMUL reg	*	–	–	–	?	?	?	?	*
IMUL mem	*	–	–	–	?	?	?	?	*
IMUL dest-reg,immed	*	–	–	–	?	?	?	?	*
IMUL mem16,immed	*	–	–	–	?	?	?	?	*
IMUL dest-reg,reg16,immed	*	–	–	–	?	?	?	?	*
IMUL dest-reg,mem16,immed	*	–	–	–	?	?	?	?	*
IN AL,immed8	–	–	–	–	–	–	–	–	–
IN AX,immed8	–	–	–	–	–	–	–	–	–
IN AL,DX	–	–	–	–	–	–	–	–	–
IN AX,DX	–	–	–	–	–	–	–	–	–
INC reg	*	–	–	–	*	*	*	*	–
INC mem	*	–	–	–	*	*	*	*	–

	Flags								
Assembler Format	OF	DF	IF	TF	SF	ZF	AF	PF	CF
INS dest$,DX	-	-	-	-	-	-	-	-	-
INSB	-	-	-	-	-	-	-	-	-
INSW	-	-	-	-	-	-	-	-	-
INT immed8	-	-	0	0	-	-	-	-	-
INTO	-	-	0	0	-	-	-	-	-
IRET	*	*	*	*	*	*	*	*	*
Jcc short-label	-	-	-	-	-	-	-	-	-
JMP SHORT short-label	-	-	-	-	-	-	-	-	-
JMP label	-	-	-	-	-	-	-	-	-
JMP memptr	-	-	-	-	-	-	-	-	-
JMP regptr16	-	-	-	-	-	-	-	-	-
LAHF	-	-	-	-	-	-	-	-	-
LDS reg16,mem32	-	-	-	-	-	-	-	-	-
LEA reg16,mem16	-	-	-	-	-	-	-	-	-
LEAVE	-	-	-	-	-	-	-	-	-
LES reg16,mem32	-	-	-	-	-	-	-	-	-
LOCK	-	-	-	-	-	-	-	-	-
LODS source$	-	-	-	-	-	-	-	-	-
LODSB	-	-	-	-	-	-	-	-	-
LODSW	-	-	-	-	-	-	-	-	-
LOOP short-label	-	-	-	-	-	-	-	-	-
LOOPE/LOOPZ short-label	-	-	-	-	-	-	-	-	-
LOOPNE/LOOPNZ short-label	-	-	-	-	-	-	-	-	-
MOV reg,reg	-	-	-	-	-	-	-	-	-
MOV reg,mem	-	-	-	-	-	-	-	-	-
MOV mem,reg	-	-	-	-	-	-	-	-	-
MOV reg,segreg	-	-	-	-	-	-	-	-	-
MOV segreg,reg	-	-	-	-	-	-	-	-	-
MOV segreg,mem	-	-	-	-	-	-	-	-	-
MOV mem,segreg	-	-	-	-	-	-	-	-	-
MOV reg,immed	-	-	-	-	-	-	-	-	-
MOV mem,immed	-	-	-	-	-	-	-	-	-

Assembler Format	Flags								
	OF	DF	IF	TF	SF	ZF	AF	PF	CF
MOVS dest$,source$	-	-	-	-	-	-	-	-	-
MOVSB	-	-	-	-	-	-	-	-	-
MOVSW	-	-	-	-	-	-	-	-	-
MUL reg	*	-	-	-	?	?	?	?	*
MUL mem	*	-	-	-	?	?	?	?	*
NEG reg	*	-	-	-	*	*	*	*	*
NEG mem	*	-	-	-	*	*	*	*	*
NOP	-	-	-	-	-	-	-	-	-
NOT reg	-	-	-	-	-	-	-	-	-
NOT mem	-	-	-	-	-	-	-	-	-
OR reg,reg	0	-	-	-	*	*	?	*	0
OR reg,mem	0	-	-	-	*	*	?	*	0
OR mem,reg	0	-	-	-	*	*	?	*	0
OR reg,immed	0	-	-	-	*	*	?	*	0
OR mem,immed	0	-	-	-	*	*	?	*	0
OUT immed8,AL	-	-	-	-	-	-	-	-	-
OUT immed8,AX	-	-	-	-	-	-	-	-	-
OUT DX,AL	-	-	-	-	-	-	-	-	-
OUT DX,AX	-	-	-	-	-	-	-	-	-
OUTS DX,source$	-	-	-	-	-	-	-	-	-
OUTSB	-	-	-	-	-	-	-	-	-
OUTSW	-	-	-	-	-	-	-	-	-
POP reg16	-	-	-	-	-	-	-	-	-
POP DS	-	-	-	-	-	-	-	-	-
POP ES	-	-	-	-	-	-	-	-	-
POP SS	-	-	-	-	-	-	-	-	-
POP mem16	-	-	-	-	-	-	-	-	-
POPA	-	-	-	-	-	-	-	-	-
POPF	*	*	*	*	*	*	*	*	*
PUSH reg16	-	-	-	-	-	-	-	-	-
PUSH segreg	-	-	-	-	-	-	-	-	-
PUSH mem16	-	-	-	-	-	-	-	-	-
PUSH immed16	-	-	-	-	-	-	-	-	-
PUSHA	-	-	-	-	-	-	-	-	-

Assembler Format	Flags								
	OF	DF	IF	TF	SF	ZF	AF	PF	CF
PUSHF	-	-	-	-	-	-	-	-	-
RCL/RCR reg,1	*	-	-	-	-	-	-	-	*
RCL/RCR reg,CL	?	-	-	-	-	-	-	-	*
RCL/RCR mem,1	*	-	-	-	-	-	-	-	*
RCL/RCR reg,CL	?	-	-	-	-	-	-	-	*
RCL/RCR reg,count	?	-	-	-	-	-	-	-	*
RCL/RCR mem,count	?	-	-	-	-	-	-	-	*

These three entries are prefixes, not instructions:

Assembler Format	Flags								
	OF	DF	IF	TF	SF	ZF	AF	PF	CF
REP	-	-	-	-	-	-	-	-	-
REPE/REPZ	-	-	-	-	-	-	-	-	-
REPNE/REPNZ	-	-	-	-	-	-	-	-	-
RET	-	-	-	-	-	-	-	-	-
RET pop-value	-	-	-	-	-	-	-	-	-
ROL/ROR reg,1	*	-	-	-	-	-	-	-	*
ROL/ROR reg,CL	?	-	-	-	-	-	-	-	*
ROL/ROR mem,1	*	-	-	-	-	-	-	-	*
ROL/ROR reg,CL	?	-	-	-	-	-	-	-	*
ROL/ROR reg,count	?	-	-	-	-	-	-	-	*
ROL/ROR mem,count	?	-	-	-	-	-	-	-	*
SAHF	-	-	-	-	*	*	*	*	*
SAL reg,1	*	-	-	-	*	*	?	*	*
SAL reg,CL	?	-	-	-	*	*	?	*	*
SAL mem,1	*	-	-	-	*	*	?	*	*
SAL reg,CL	?	-	-	-	*	*	?	*	*
SAL reg,count	?	-	-	-	*	*	?	*	*
SAL mem,count	?	-	-	-	*	*	?	*	*
SAR reg,1	0	-	-	-	*	*	?	*	*
SAR reg,CL	?	-	-	-	*	*	?	*	*
SAR mem,1	0	-	-	-	*	*	?	*	*
SAR reg,CL	?	-	-	-	*	*	?	*	*
SAR reg,count	?	-	-	-	*	*	?	*	*
SAR mem,count	?	-	-	-	*	*	?	*	*
SBB reg,reg	*	-	-	-	*	*	*	*	*
SBB reg,mem	*	-	-	-	*	*	*	*	*
SBB mem,reg	*	-	-	-	*	*	*	*	*
SBB reg,immed	*	-	-	-	*	*	*	*	*
SBB mem,immed	*	-	-	-	*	*	*	*	*

Instruction	OF	DF	IF	TF	SF	ZF	AF	PF	CF
SCAS dest$	*	-	-	-	*	*	*	*	*
SCASB	*	-	-	-	*	*	*	*	*
SCASW	*	-	-	-	*	*	*	*	*
SHL reg,1	*	-	-	-	*	*	?	*	*
SHL reg,CL	?	-	-	-	*	*	?	*	*
SHL mem,1	*	-	-	-	*	*	?	*	*
SHL reg,CL	?	-	-	-	*	*	?	*	*
SHL reg,count	?	-	-	-	*	*	?	*	*
SHL mem,count	?	-	-	-	*	*	?	*	*
SHR reg,1	*	-	-	-	0	*	?	*	*
SHR reg,CL	?	-	-	-	0	*	?	*	*
SHR mem,1	*	-	-	-	0	*	?	*	*
SHR reg,CL	?	-	-	-	0	*	?	*	*
SHR reg,count	?	-	-	-	0	*	?	*	*
SHR mem,count	?	-	-	-	0	*	?	*	*
STC	-	-	-	-	-	-	-	-	1
STD	-	1	-	-	-	-	-	-	-
STI	-	-	1	-	-	-	-	-	-
STOS dest$	-	-	-	-	-	-	-	-	-
STOSB	-	-	-	-	-	-	-	-	-
STOSW	-	-	-	-	-	-	-	-	-
SUB reg,reg	*	-	-	-	*	*	*	*	*
SUB reg,mem	*	-	-	-	*	*	*	*	*
SUB mem,reg	*	-	-	-	*	*	*	*	*
SUB reg,immed	*	-	-	-	*	*	*	*	*
SUB mem,immed	*	-	-	-	*	*	*	*	*
TEST reg,reg	0	-	-	-	*	*	?	*	0
TEST reg,mem	0	-	-	-	*	*	?	*	0
TEST reg,immed	0	-	-	-	*	*	?	*	0
TEST mem,immed	0	-	-	-	*	*	?	*	0
WAIT	-	-	-	-	-	-	-	-	-
XCHG mem,reg	-	-	-	-	-	-	-	-	-
XCHG reg,reg	-	-	-	-	-	-	-	-	-
XLAT mem8	-	-	-	-	-	-	-	-	-
XOR reg,reg	0	-	-	-	*	*	?	*	0
XOR reg,mem	0	-	-	-	*	*	?	*	0
XOR mem,reg	0	-	-	-	*	*	?	*	0
XOR reg,immed	0	-	-	-	*	*	?	*	0
XOR mem,immed	0	-	-	-	*	*	?	*	0

Index

Edited by Marilyn L. Johnson

Quick Index to Instructions